Why I Am Not a Roman Catholic

"The subtitle is spot on: Jerry Walls here extends the right hand of fellowship to Roman Catholics at the dinner table while he explains why he is more truly catholic than they are at the Lord's table. Anyone thinking about converting to Rome needs to grapple seriously with Walls's critiques of papal infallibility, Marian dogma, and the authority structure of the Roman church—and to do so for the sake of the greater catholic church."

—KEVIN J. VANHOOZER,
research professor of systematic theology, Trinity Evangelical Divinity School

"Jerry Walls has devoted many years to thinking about Roman Catholicism. In this well-researched and enjoyable book, he discusses a wide range of topics (e.g., apostolic succession, papal infallibility, the authentication of the canon, Mary) that inform his explanation for why he is not a Roman Catholic. There is much to learn from *Why I Am Not a Roman Catholic*, regardless of one's position about the nature of the true church."

—STEWART GOETZ,
emeritus professor of philosophy, Ursinus College

"Any Protestant who is considering converting to the Roman Catholic Church ought to read Walls's book first. Walls presents overwhelming evidence and conclusive reasons why the Catholic Church is not what it claims to be—the one true, visible, and institutional Christian church. And he demonstrates convincingly that some of its doctrines are simply false. At the same time, Walls's posture toward Catholics is irenic; he clearly does not think their church is a 'cult' as some conservative Protestants continue to claim."

—ROGER E. OLSON,
emeritus professor of Christian theology, Baylor University's George W. Truett Theological Seminary

"Jerry Walls's critical evaluation of distinctive Roman Catholic claims is ecumenical in spirit, eschews emotional appeals and character attacks, focuses on arguments, and acknowledges what evangelicals and Roman Catholics have in common. Walls makes a historical and moral case against papal primacy and infallibility, contends that the 'ordinary magisterium' is just as fallible as Protestant confessions, and deftly shows how popular Roman Catholic apologetics often 'strawmans' the Protestant conceptions of canon and sola scriptura."

—**GREG WELTY,**
professor of philosophy, Southeastern Baptist Theological Seminary, Wake Forest, North Carolina

"Wrestling with Catholicism? Jerry Walls shows from Scripture, history, and reason that key Roman Catholic claims are false or incoherent. *Why I Am Not a Roman Catholic* is a nice yet devastating critique of Catholicism. Nice because it charitably demonstrates that Protestantism is more cogent than Catholicism. Devastating because it shows that Protestants have a greater claim to catholicity than Roman Catholics. Highly recommended."

—**MATTHEW W. BATES,**
professor of New Testament, Northern Seminary

Why I Am Not a Roman Catholic

A Friendly, Ecumenical Explanation

JERRY L. WALLS

CASCADE *Books* • Eugene, Oregon

WHY I AM NOT A ROMAN CATHOLIC
A Friendly, Ecumenical Explanation

Copyright © 2025 Jerry L. Walls. All rights reserved. Except for brief quotations in critical publications or reviews, no part of this book may be reproduced in any manner without prior written permission from the publisher. Write: Permissions, Wipf and Stock Publishers, 199 W. 8th Ave., Suite 3, Eugene, OR 97401.

Cascade Books
An Imprint of Wipf and Stock Publishers
199 W. 8th Ave., Suite 3
Eugene, OR 97401

www.wipfandstock.com

PAPERBACK ISBN: 979-8-3852-2375-6
HARDCOVER ISBN: 979-8-3852-2376-3
EBOOK ISBN: 979-8-3852-2377-0

Cataloguing-in-Publication data:

Names: Walls, Jerry L. [author].

Title: Why I am not a Roman Catholic : a friendly, ecumenical explanation / Jerry L. Walls.

Description: Eugene, OR: Cascade Books, 2025 | Includes bibliographical references and index.

Identifiers: ISBN 979-8-3852-2375-6 (paperback) | ISBN 979-8-3852-2376-3 (hardcover) | ISBN 979-8-3852-2377-0 (ebook)

Subjects: LCSH: Protestant churches—Relations—Catholic Church. | Catholic Church—Relations—Protestant churches. | Papacy. | Apologetics.

Classification: BT27 W35 2025 (paperback) | BT27 (ebook)

03/24/25

To Bill and Connie Sperry
With Happy Memories
From Wilmore to Oxford

CONTENTS

Acknowledgments | ix

Introduction: Not a Roman Catholic, but a Reforming Catholic | xi

CHAPTER ONE
"If Christ Be Not Raised"; If Peter Was Not the First Pope:
    Parallel Cases of Indispensable Doctrinal Foundations | 1

CHAPTER TWO
Saving the Papal Hypothesis? | 18

CHAPTER THREE
The Problem of Bad Popes: The Argument from Conspicuous Corruption | 31

CHAPTER FOUR
Cardinal Confusions | 56

CHAPTER FIVE
Revelation, Canon, Creed: How to Affirm Catholic Faith
    while Denying the Claims of Rome | 69

CHAPTER SIX
It All Depends on Mary | 86

CHAPTER SEVEN
Catholic Conversion and Coercion | 101

CHAPTER EIGHT
"You Are Your Own Pope": The *Tu Quoque* Objection | 111

CHAPTER NINE
Protestants in the Crosshairs: Popular Roman Catholic Apologetics | 134

CHAPTER TEN
The World's Largest Pluralist Christian Denomination? | 153

Conclusion: Free to Be More Catholic Than Catholics | 173

Appendix: Matthew 16 and the Papacy | 181

Bibliography | 187

General Index | 195

ACKNOWLEDGMENTS

CHAPTERS 1 AND 2 were originally published in a slightly different form as an article entitled "'If Christ Be Not Raised': If Peter Was Not the First Pope: Parallel Cases of Indispensable Doctrinal Foundations" in *Journal of Biblical and Theological Studies* 4 (2019) 243–63.

Chapter 3 was published in an earlier version in *Perichoresis* 18 (2020) 87–104.

The Appendix is a slightly modified version of material from an article entitled "Assessing Papal Probabilities: A Reply to Joseph Blado" in *Perichoresis* 18 (2020) 105–16.

Portions of this publication were originally published in *Roman but Not Catholic* by Kenneth J. Collins and Jerry L. Walls, copyright © 2017. Used by permission of Baker Academic, a division of Baker Publishing Group.

I am grateful to all the above for permission to use that material in this volume.

Thanks to a number of people who read significant chunks of earlier versions of this material and offered insightful criticism: Brian Hall, Andrew Hronich, Alan Rhoda, Luke Van Horn, and especially Billy Abraham. Thanks to Claire Addison for encouragement and humor all along the way.

Finally, I must thank my family: Timothy and Angela Amos, Madelyn, Mackenzie and Abigail; Jonathan and Emily Walls, Simeon and Maren. As always, they provide inspiration and motivation for everything I write.

INTRODUCTION

Not a Roman Catholic, but a Reforming Catholic

BEFORE I EXPLAIN WHY I am not a Roman Catholic, let me begin by saying a bit about my own religious background and my experiences and interactions with Roman Catholics. I was born and raised in Knockemstiff, Ohio, a small and now somewhat legendary hamlet in the southern part of the state.[1] I accepted Christ when I was eleven years old in an emotional conversion experience during a revival in a small country church and was later baptized in a creek across the road from my house. I have warm memories of loving nurture from those formative years. I attended Bethel Chapel Christian Union Church, and my faith has never seriously wavered since my conversion experience.

I knew very little about Roman Catholicism growing up and don't recall having any particular opinions about it. Looking back, I have no distinct memories of interacting with Catholics until I went to Princeton Seminary from 1977–1980. No doubt I had met Catholics before then, but my world was very much a Protestant Evangelical one. At Princeton, there were several Roman Catholic students, and one of my professors was a Roman Catholic. Those were balmy post-Vatican II days (though I did not know much about the details of Vatican II at the time), and the issues that divided us from Rome were not on the front burner but rather a growing sense of unity among Christians. I do not recall any discussions or debates about the doctrines that divided us or any concern from Catholics to make an issue of them.

My first serious engagement with Roman Catholicism that I can recall came when I enrolled as a graduate student in the philosophy department at Notre Dame in the fall of 1984. My years there were some of the best of my

---

1. Knockemstiff has achieved a certain notoriety thanks to my classmate Donald Ray Pollock, who has featured it in his critically acclaimed fiction. For my review of his first novel, see Walls, Review of *The Devil All the Time*.

life, and I am not only a proud graduate of that great university, but I recall my years there with both fondness and gratitude. Notre Dame was in the process of building a great Christian philosophy department with an ecumenical composition during this period, and the excitement was palpable. In addition to a number of serious Catholics, Notre Dame had attracted some noted Protestants, including the great Alvin Plantinga and Tom Morris, who had recently completed graduate school at Yale and was already off to a roaring start in his academic career by the time I arrived.

While I was getting a great philosophical education at Notre Dame, I was also getting an informal education of another sort, namely, about Roman Catholicism, at least of the American variety. In addition to faculty members, several of my fellow graduate students were Roman Catholics and my conversations with them were the first I can recall in which I ever discussed at length the differences that divide Protestants from Catholics; they not only took those issues seriously but were eager to defend their side of the debate. Indeed, I came to realize that many conservative Roman Catholics view Evangelicals as Catholics just waiting to happen and would love to help push us over the edge. I had numerous conversations about these issues with my Catholic friends and teachers, and I distinctly recall the parting shot of one of my professors, Fred Freddoso, when I left Notre Dame: "I'm disappointed as hell you did not become a Catholic."

But I was not done with these sorts of conversations. Several years later, I had the good fortune to meet Richard John Neuhaus and to get to know him a bit. We hit it off, and he was intrigued to learn that I was a Protestant who was defending a version of the doctrine of purgatory in the book I was then writing about heaven.[2] Shortly thereafter he invited me to join the Dulles Colloquium, an ecumenical theology discussion group hosted by him and Avery Dulles, after whom it was named. The Dulles Colloquium met once or twice a year in New York, usually at the Union League Club, and the official business of the day was to discuss a paper that had been sent to us several weeks before.

My participation in this group for several years was one of the great blessings and privileges of my life, for which I remain deeply grateful. One of my lasting regrets is that personal circumstances caused me to miss the last meeting to which I was invited in the spring of 2008, not knowing it was my last chance to see both Father Neuhaus and Cardinal Dulles in this life. Through the years I was involved in the Colloquium, I got to discuss matters of vital importance with some remarkable people: Gary Anderson, Jody Bottum, Chuck Colson, Shalom Carmy, Robert George, Paul Griffiths,

---

2. Walls, *Heaven: The Logic.*

INTRODUCTION xiii

David Hart, Stanley Hauerwas, Robert Jensen, George Lindbeck, Gilbert Meilaender, Bruce Marshall, David Novak, Michael Novak, James Nuechterlein, Tom Oden, Rusty Reno, Steve Webb, George Weigel, Robert Wilken, and many others. The group was composed of persons from a number of different traditions, including Lutherans, Roman Catholics, Anglicans, Orthodox, Methodists, and Evangelicals, as well as a few Jews.

The paper topics covered a wide range of theological and moral issues, and often dealt with matters of ecumenical concern. After the formal session, conversation continued more casually over dinner. Then we usually retired to the bar to continue to talk until bedtime. Occasionally, a few of us were invited to Neuhaus's apartment for drinks and conversation. Not infrequently these more informal talks centered on issues dividing Protestants and Catholics, with Neuhaus leading the way in making the case for Rome with his characteristic wit, charm, and ecumenical sensibilities. I regularly defended the Protestant view in these discussions with Neuhaus and other members of the group.

In retrospect, I suspect that an unofficial agenda of the Dulles Colloquium—and I say this with all due affection—was to be a Catholic Conversion Club, particularly with the aim of converting Protestant intellectuals to Rome. Indeed, I cannot help but wonder if part of the reason I was invited to join the group was because Neuhaus thought I might be ripe for conversion to Rome since I was defending the doctrine of purgatory.

In any case, several of the members of the group were Evangelicals, Anglicans, Lutherans, and so on when I joined the Colloquium, and later converted to Rome. I cannot read their minds, and I cannot speak for them, so I will not presume what role, if any, their participation in the Dulles Colloquium might have played in their conversion. But I will say that in my experience, the dynamics of the group encouraged conversion to Rome. Indeed, the same might be said for the highly regarded magazine *First Things* that Neuhaus founded. Rusty Reno, a convert from the Episcopal Church and current editor of *First Things*, commented playfully on the matter in an issue of the magazine featuring two articles by Protestants.

> On the topic of Catholic triumphalism: Not a few Protestant friends complain that *First Things* is a Catholic party with a few Protestants and Jews invited. That always makes me wince, because it's not altogether false. After all, the magazine was begun by a man who had just published a book titled *The Catholic Moment*. But I hope the two forceful essays about Protestantism

in this issue convince readers that it's not altogether true. . . . There's no requirement that one kowtow to Catholicism.[3]

Reno's somewhat whimsical comment accurately conveys my experience as a participant in the Dulles Colloquium for several years. Certainly there was no requirement to "kowtow to Catholicism," but the claim of Rome to be the one true Church was promoted, sometimes in subtle ways, sometimes in humorous flourishes, but always with urbane sophistication. But then, what else should one expect in group named after, and attended by, a distinguished Roman Catholic cardinal and led by a famous Lutheran convert to Rome?

So, in one sense the experience was deeply and richly ecumenical, but it also vividly, and sometimes painfully, showed the limits of Roman Catholic ecumenism. A few times the Protestants among us attended mass with our Catholic friends, and it always struck me how odd it was that we had more genuine Christian unity and fellowship around the dinner table than we did at the table of the Lord. The welcome that was extended to those of us who did not regard Rome as the one true Church only went so far, as we watched from a distance when our Roman Catholic brothers shared the sacrament of communion.

These are the sorts of experiences that have generated my interest in the issues of this book and led me to think it needed to be written. I also share these experiences to emphasize that my experiences and interactions with Roman Catholics have been overwhelmingly positive overall. I also want to make clear, if it is not already evident, that I warmly embrace my Roman Catholic brothers and sisters as fellow Christians and followers of our Lord.

In the past several years, I have had further positive interactions with Roman Catholics, partly because of further work I have done on purgatory. (Indeed, because of this work, not infrequently it has been assumed that I *am* a Roman Catholic!) Since my earlier discussion of the doctrine in my book on heaven, I have written a whole book defending an ecumenical version of the doctrine, the first book-length defense of purgatory ever by a Protestant, so far as I know.[4] I hope this also shows that I am not automatically critical of a doctrine just because of its Roman Catholic pedigree or associations. To the contrary, it is always my aim to weigh doctrinal claims on their biblical, theological, and rational merits, regardless of their ecclesial connections.

---

3. Reno, "While We're at It," 69.
4. Walls, *Purgatory*. See also Walls, *Heaven, Hell and Purgatory*.

I should frankly say that I have never been seriously tempted to convert to Rome, although I have obviously considered it, as indicated by the experiences described above. Somewhat ironically, that is part of why I wanted to write this book. We have heard from lots of Evangelicals who have converted to Rome in recent years. (Most of them, it seems, feel they need to write a book or at least contribute an essay to one of those collections of conversion narratives that are so popular among Catholic apologists.) I thought it might be helpful to hear from one who has thought about the issues carefully but has not converted to Rome. We have heard from lots of people who have read Newman's famous essay on doctrinal development and found his arguments compelling. I thought it might be helpful to hear from one who has read Newman but found his arguments deeply confused and his conclusions badly overstated.

I also want to emphasize that this book aims to be ecumenical in the best sense of the word. Indeed, I believe that challenging the exclusive claims of Rome is essential to true ecumenism and for advancing unity in the body of Christ. While committed Roman Catholics no doubt believe that promoting their exclusive claims is necessary to their very identity, I believe there is a better way forward.

SO WHY DID I WRITE THIS BOOK AND FOR WHOM?

Given what I have written in this introduction so far, some readers may think there is something ironic, perhaps even inconsistent, in writing a book explaining why I am not a Roman Catholic. Is this book not inevitably an assault on the ecumenism I profess? In response to these questions, I want to make clear that I recognize the potential danger here. In a letter to one of his Roman Catholic correspondents, C. S. Lewis wrote:

> The question for me (naturally) is not, "Why should I not become a Roman Catholic" but "Why should I?" But I don't like discussing such matters, because it emphasizes differences and endangers charity. By the time I had really explained my objections to certain doctrines which differentiate you from us (and also in my opinion from the Apostolic and even Medieval Church), you would like me less.[5]

I have already hinted at some of the reasons why I thought this book needed to be written, despite the potential hazards Lewis noted. Perhaps the

---

5. Lewis, *Letters of C. S. Lewis*, 230. For a detailed exploration of why Lewis was not a Roman Catholic, see Goetz, *Philosophical Walking Tour*.

most basic reason is simply because many people are concerned with these issues and are struggling with them. A significant number of Evangelicals have converted to Rome, just as many Roman Catholics have converted to Evangelicalism and other Protestant traditions, including Pentecostalism.[6] Part of this is due to aggressive apologists on both sides who have taken as their mission the "conversion" of fellow Christians to their church.[7] They unsettle the faith of fellow Christians, and frankly, many people seem to be confused and are pressured to "convert" because of claims that their faith is deficient, somehow inconsistent, or lacking in full integrity unless they join a particular church or denomination. To be sure, many who have "converted" have done so only after careful study, consultation, and prayer for discernment. But many others, I suspect, have done so under the pressure of dubious reasons, spurious arguments, and misinformation.

I have written this book for persons who are grappling with these issues and want to think about them honestly and carefully, as well as for those who minister to such persons. You are my primary audience, and my concern for you is as much pastoral as it is theological. Roman Catholics who are interested in these issues may also find it helpful, but I emphasize that I have not written with the aim of converting Roman Catholics to Protestantism.

So, if you have an interest in the issues that divide Evangelicals and other orthodox Protestants from Rome, and particularly if you are struggling with whether you need to cross the Tiber to practice your faith with full integrity, I have written this book to explain why you need not do so. You are my primary audience.

Most of the chapters that follow are straightforwardly critical, sometimes pointedly so. Still, I emphasize that we are dealing with family issues. Sometimes families are divided and face unsettling conflict. I do not shy away from that reality even as I aim to speak the truth in love. As my subtitle indicates, I aim to write in a friendly, ecumenical fashion even as I write forthrightly. And ultimately, I aim to serve the cause of true Christian unity in the common faith we profess.

---

6. Indeed, Pentecostalism has grown dramatically in many traditionally Roman Catholic countries, especially in the global south.

7 To explain the convention I am using for capping c/Church: contemporary convention is only to cap church when it refers to the name of a specific church community or building (All Soul's Church in Lexington) or a denomination (the Catholic Church, the Methodist Church). Every other use is "church," including references to the universal church. Outside of quotes, I only use "the Church" when it is shorthand for The Catholic Church or The Methodist Church, etc.

REFORMED CATHOLICITY

Before concluding this introduction, I want to reiterate that rejecting Roman Catholicism does not mean rejecting catholicity. Quite to the contrary. Indeed, I very much agree with the distinguished Reformed theologian Kevin Vanhoozer that the "only good Protestant is a catholic Protestant—one that learns from, and bears fruit for, the *whole* church."[8] Vanhoozer's claim here is one that I have noticed is increasingly emphasized by Protestant leaders. I noticed this particularly while doing research for the book on Roman Catholicism I co-authored with Kenneth Collins, namely, *Roman but Not Catholic: What Remains at Stake 500 Years After the Reformation*. These Protestant leaders I was reading used different phrases, like "Reformed catholicity," "mere Protestant orthodoxy," and others as well. But the essential idea was that Protestants need to recover a deeper awareness of their own catholic heritage to be true to the legacy of the Reformers, who very much aimed to preserve and promote apostolic, catholic Christianity.[9]

I was also intrigued by this notion because I had seen from my research how often Roman Catholic apologists fasten on to the differences among Protestants and paint the Reformation as a movement that led to endless division and factions. Sola Scriptura, they claimed, inevitably results in chaos. The more I thought about this, the more I wondered whether the idea of Reformation catholicism really existed, and if so, what it would look like. Is there in fact substantial catholic unity among the diverse heirs of the Reformation, and if so, shouldn't we be able to show what this looks like in a concrete way? Or is the notion of Protestant catholicism a mere intellectual abstraction, or worse, an outright contradiction?

To make a long story short, I approached Vanhoozer several years ago with the idea that we should produce a Reforming Catholic Confession to celebrate the five-hundredth anniversary of the Reformation. The goal would be a document that would demonstrate substantial Protestant unity in a way that would honor the Reformers' catholic convictions and intentions. Kevin was intrigued, and a little surprised, that an Arminian would approach a Reformed theologian with such an idea, but after several emails and phone conversations, he agreed to co-chair the drafting committee and to author the initial draft of the Confession. Together, we assembled an international committee composed of noted systematic and historical theologians representing a wide spectrum of Protestant traditions: Anglican, Baptist, Lutheran, Pentecostal, Reformed, and Wesleyan.

8. Vanhoozer, *Biblical Authority After Babel*, 33.

9. In addition to Vanhoozer's book cited above, see Leithart, *End of Protestantism*; Allen and Swain, *Reformed Catholicity*; and Sanders, "Why the Reformation."

Working on the Drafting Committee of the Confession was one of the great ecumenical experiences of my life. Kevin's original document was subjected to extensive criticism and went through two rounds of revision at the hands of the committee. We corresponded by email, and the critical comments and constructive suggestions totaled some sixty single-spaced pages between the two rounds of revisions. The spirit of mutual respect and cooperation was remarkable throughout, especially when we dealt with difficult issues that had divided the Reformers and remained points of contention between our various traditions, such as the sacrament of the Lord's Supper. It was very gratifying to see Pentecostals and Lutherans, for instance, working together collegially to find language we could all agree upon. And Kevin, as the lead author, modelled throughout what a world-class reforming catholic theologian looks like as he graciously and expertly incorporated the many suggestions coming his way.

Of course, the final document does not fully express the views of any of the traditions represented. Still, it was very encouraging that we could find substantial common ground even on contested issues historically fraught with controversy. The issue for our document is not, "does this say everything you would prefer?" but rather, "can you agree with us thus far?" And again, the ground of common agreement is both robust and rich. The Confession makes no pretense of eliminating all our differences, nor does it aim to replace the official doctrinal confessions of our various churches. But it does show that the diverse heirs of the Reformation who follow the principle of sola Scriptura (Scripture alone is our final authority for doctrine) are deeply united on core Christian doctrine. And this was impressively confirmed by the hundreds of Protestant leaders from around the world who signed the final document.[10]

I tell this story not only to make clear where I am coming from but also to underscore that my quarrel is not with catholic faith. My critique centers on what is distinctively Roman, not what is catholic.[11] To this I now turn.

---

10. To read the Confession, to see who was involved in it and who signed it, see www.reformingcatholicconfession.com.

11. Some readers may object to the term "Roman Catholic" on the grounds that there are other Catholics in communion with the bishop of Rome besides Roman Catholics. See the discussion of this issue in McBrien, *Catholicism*, 4–5. McBrien notes: "In addition to the Latin, or Roman tradition, there are seven other non-Latin, non-Roman ecclesial traditions: Armenian, Byzantine, Coptic, Ethiopian, East Syrian (Chaldean), West Syrian, and Maronite. Each of these is a Catholic church in communion with the Bishop of Rome; none of these is a *Roman* Catholic Church" (5). My use of the term Roman Catholic does not ignore the reality that there is a small minority of Catholic churches in communion with Rome that are not Roman, strictly speaking.

CHAPTER ONE

"IF CHRIST BE NOT RAISED"; IF PETER WAS NOT THE FIRST POPE

Parallel Cases of Indispensable Doctrinal Foundations

A FEW YEARS AGO, one of the most famous Christian philosophers in the world visited Houston Christian University, where I work. At dinner with our philosophy department, we asked him several questions, and the issue of Roman Catholicism came up. I asked him if he had ever been inclined to convert to Rome, and if not, why not. His answer was as simple as it was straightforward: "I reject both papal infallibility and the Marian doctrines." By the latter, he meant both the dogmas of Mary's immaculate conception, which is the doctrine that she was born without sin and the doctrine of her bodily assumption into heaven.

This concise answer from a great Christian philosopher sums up some of the core reasons why I am not a Roman Catholic, so I shall give a fair amount of attention to these issues, especially the papacy. As we shall see, there are interesting and important logical connections between the issues of papal infallibility and the Marian dogmas. Before proceeding, it is important to clear up one source of common confusion and misunderstanding about the Roman Catholic doctrine of papal infallibility. This doctrine does not claim, as it is sometimes popularly construed, that the pope is infallible in all his teaching or proclamations. Rather, as we shall see below, it is a much more limited claim.

It is hard to overstate the importance of the doctrine of papal infallibility, and the papacy more generally, to Roman Catholicism. Rome's distinctive authority claims and ecclesial identity hinge crucially on the claims that Christ made Peter the head of the church and the bishops of Rome have succeeded him in this role. Indeed, as I shall argue below, the papacy has the same sort of importance for Roman Catholicism that the resurrection of Jesus has for orthodox creedal Christianity.[1]

THE ORDER OF KNOWING AND THE ORDER OF BEING

The fact that the resurrection of Christ is utterly foundational to classic creedal Christianity is a familiar one. One way to bring this point into sharp focus is to consider the difference between what we can call the order of being and the order of knowing. By the order of being, I simply mean there is a certain logical priority in the relationship among central creedal convictions. In the order of being, Trinity is the aboriginal fact, the most fundamental reality from which everything else originates and follows. The incarnation of the Son of God in Jesus comes later in the order of being, and his atoning death on the cross is later still in the order of events. Finally, the resurrection of Jesus comes as the climax of the story of incarnation and redemption. And shortly after the resurrection, the Holy Spirit was poured out on the church on the day of Pentecost.

In the order of knowing, however, it is exactly the opposite. The resurrection was the explosive act of God that set-in motion the definitive revelation of the extraordinary truths that followed from this singular event in human history. The resurrection was the decisive demonstration that the man Jesus was more than a mere human being. As remarkable as his miracles surely were, and as profound and authoritative as his teaching undoubtedly was, his unique identity as the Son of God was not fully disclosed until the resurrection. As Paul put it, Christ was "declared to be the Son of God with power according to the spirit of holiness by resurrection from the dead" (Rom 1:4). The realization that it was the very Son of God who died on the cross and was resurrected led to the insight that the meaning of his death was to save us from our sins. And the truth that God is a Trinity was eventually understood and formally articulated as the apostles and church fathers reflected on the revelation that Jesus was the Son of God incarnate who was distinct from the Father (and the Holy Spirit who came at Pentecost), yet in some sense one with them.

This is only a bare sketch of the unfolding revelation of the central doctrines that are most distinctive to orthodox Christianity, but the central

---

1. Of course, Roman Catholicism affirms orthodox creedal Christian faith. My point here is that their claims about the papacy are similar in interesting ways to this more general affirmation of orthodoxy.

point is clear: the essential doctrines of incarnation, atonement, and Trinity flow from the stunning event of the resurrection of Jesus. When Jesus was raised from the dead, this event demanded a profound rethinking and a startling reformulation of the non-negotiable truth that God is one, and a surprising account of how he saves us from our sins.

All of this must be taken into account when we read Paul's stark and pointed reflections on the resurrection in 1 Corinthians 15 and his insistence that it is utterly essential to the integrity of the Christian faith. In a series of counterfactual statements, Paul unflinchingly drives home the enormous consequences that would ensue if Christ were not raised. "If Christ has not been raised, your faith is futile, and you are still in your sins" (1 Cor 15:17). There is no salvation from our sins in the death of Christ if he has not been raised. If Christ is not raised, Paul's preaching has been in vain (v. 14). If Christ has not been raised, rather than being blessed with the greatest of all gifts, we are most to be pitied (v. 19). If Christ has not been raised, Christians are speaking falsely of God (v. 15). They are ascribing things to him and insisting those things are of monumental importance, but in fact, they are falsehoods.

Here it is important to emphasize that the resurrection is not only crucial for us to know and understand these vital truths but also that the resurrection itself was crucial for our salvation. In the resurrection God was not only revealing vital truths about himself but also acting decisively and definitively to achieve our salvation.

Indeed, if Christ has not been raised, Christians badly misrepresent God and what he has done to reveal himself when they proclaim incarnation, atonement, and Trinity. These truths sketched above in the order of being depend completely on the truth and reality of the resurrection of Jesus. The resurrection is the pivotal truth that generates knowledge of these distinctive, albeit difficult, doctrinal claims. To show that incarnation or Trinity is false, it is not necessary to show they are incoherent. The truth of these complex doctrines hinges essentially on the relatively straightforward claim that Christ was raised from the dead.

PARALLEL CLAIMS WITH LARGE IMPLICATIONS

Now let us turn to consider how claims about the papacy play a role in Roman Catholic theology that is analogous to the role of the resurrection of Jesus in orthodox Christianity. That is, the distinctive claims of Roman Catholicism depend on papal claims in a way that is similar to how our knowledge of the truth of core Christian doctrines such as incarnation and Trinity depend on the resurrection.[2]

Roman Catholic claims about the papacy have undeniably played a central part in the issues that divide Roman Catholics not only from Protestants but also the Eastern Orthodox. These points of contention are undoubtedly ecclesial broadly speaking and reflect different views about the nature of the church, but claims about the papacy are integral to these disputes. Rome views itself and churches in communion with it as the only ones that have full Christian integrity in terms of doctrine and ecclesial authority. Other Christians and ecclesial communities are seen (at best) as "separated brethren" who remain out of communion with the one true church. Consider, in this light, the claim that the task of interpreting the word of God is the exclusive prerogative of the teaching office of the Roman Catholic Church.

> "The task of giving an authentic interpretation of the Word of God, whether in its written form or in the form of Tradition, has been entrusted to the living teaching office of the Church alone. Its authority in this matter is exercised in the name of Jesus Christ." This means that the task of interpretation has been entrusted to the bishops in communion with the successor of Peter, the Bishop of Rome.[3]

In the same vein, consider this claim: "It is clear therefore that, in the supremely wise arrangement of God, sacred Tradition, Sacred Scripture, and the Magisterium of the Church are so connected and associated that one of them cannot stand without the others."[4] The magisterium, again, is composed of those bishops in communion with the pope, the bishop of Rome. The claim that scripture and tradition cannot stand without the magisterium obviously denies the rational viability of any church that seeks to follow the authority of scripture but rejects the distinctive claims of Roman Catholicism and the authority of the pope.

The apex of Roman Catholic claims pertaining to papal authority was articulated in the doctrine of papal infallibility, which was dogmatized at Vatican I in 1870. This dogma, which is rejected by the Orthodox as well

---

2. Of course Roman Catholics affirm these central doctrines and the resurrection as grounding them. The point I am making here is that Rome affirms other doctrines as infallible and these doctrines hinge on papal authority in much the same way those core doctrines hinge on the resurrection.

3. *Catechism*, para. 85. The quoted text in this paragraph comes from Paul VI, "*Dei Verbum*," para. 10.

4. *Catechism*, para. 95.

as Protestants, declares that when the pope speaks *ex cathedra* ("from the chair") in defining a doctrine of faith or morals "he possesses, by the divine assistance promised to him in blessed Peter, that infallibility which the divine Redeemer willed his Church to enjoy in defining doctrine concerning faith or morals. Therefore, such definitions of the Roman Pontiff are of themselves, and not by the consent of the Church, irreformable."[5]

As strong as this claim is, and as important as it is to the claims of Roman Catholicism, it may be somewhat surprising that in all the centuries since there has been a bishop of Rome, there are only two undisputed cases of the pope speaking *ex cathedra*, and both pertain to the Virgin Mary.[6] First, in 1854, Pope Pius IX definitively affirmed the doctrine of Mary's immaculate conception, which is now recognized as an infallible dogma. This doctrine is sometimes confused with the doctrine of Jesus' virginal conception, but it is a different claim altogether, namely, that Mary was herself born without sin. Second, in 1950, the doctrine of Mary's bodily assumption was declared infallible by Pope Pius XII. This is the doctrine that claims she was taken up bodily into heaven at the end of her life.

Given the fact that Rome has defined these Marian doctrines with the highest degree of dogmatic authority possible, these doctrines are also emblematic of the sharp lines of division that separate Rome from the Orthodox as well as most Protestants.[7] Readers can perhaps anticipate the logical connections between the doctrine of papal infallibility and the Marian dogmas.

ROBUST ROMAN PAPAL CLAIMS

Now let us delve into these matters more deeply by considering classic Roman Catholic claims about the grounds and nature of papal authority. In particular, I will quote at some length from the aforementioned First Vatican Council, where papal infallibility was formally defined. More specifically, I will quote from Session Four of this Council, which has the following heading: "First Dogmatic Constitution on the Church of Christ." The definitive dogmatic authority of this material is further emphasized by the fact that

---

5. "First Vatican Council" 4.4.

6. There are some who insist that there is other infallible teaching. I have asked a number of Roman Catholics about this and have gotten conflicting answers. But again, only the two dogmas pertaining to Mary are undisputed.

7. The doctrine of Mary's bodily assumption is affirmed by the Orthodox as an ecclesiastical conviction, but is not a dogma as it is in Rome. The Orthodox reject the doctrine of the immaculate conception.

each of the four chapters of Session 4 concludes with an anathema directed at those who deny the teaching that is promulgated. Examining these passages will make clear not only what Rome has traditionally claimed about the papacy, but also what is at stake in these claims.

> 1.1. We teach and declare that, according to the gospel evidence, a primacy of jurisdiction over the whole Church of God was immediately and directly promised to the blessed apostle Peter and conferred on him by Christ the lord. . . .
>
> 1.3. And it was to Peter alone that Jesus, after his resurrection, confided the jurisdiction of Supreme Pastor and ruler of his whole fold, saying: Feed my lambs, feed my sheep.
>
> 1.4. To this absolutely manifest teaching of the Sacred Scriptures, as it has always been understood by the Catholic Church, are clearly opposed the distorted opinions of those who misrepresent the form of government which Christ the lord established in his Church and deny that Peter, in preference to the rest of the apostles, taken singly or collectively, was endowed by Christ with a true and proper primacy of jurisdiction. . . .
>
> 1.6. Therefore, if anyone says that blessed Peter the apostle was not appointed by Christ the lord as prince of all the apostles and visible head of the whole Church militant; or that it was a primacy of honor only and not one of true and proper jurisdiction that he directly and immediately received from our lord Jesus Christ himself: let him be anathema.[8]
>
> 2.2. For no one can be in doubt, indeed it was known in every age that the holy and most blessed Peter, prince and head of the apostles, the pillar of faith and the foundation of the Catholic Church, received the keys of the kingdom from our lord Jesus Christ, the savior and redeemer of the human race, and that to this day and forever he lives and presides and exercises judgment in his successors the bishops of the Holy Roman See, which he founded and consecrated with his blood. . . .
>
> 2.5. Therefore, if anyone says that it is not by the institution of Christ the lord himself (that is to say, by divine law) that blessed Peter should have perpetual successors in the primacy over the whole Church; or that the Roman Pontiff is not the successor of blessed Peter in this primacy: let him be anathema.[9]

---

8. "First Vatican Council" 4.1.
9. "First Vatican Council" 4.2.

> 3.2. Wherefore we teach and declare that, by divine ordinance, the Roman Church possesses a pre-eminence of ordinary power over every other Church, and that this jurisdictional power of the Roman Pontiff is both episcopal and immediate....
>
> 3.3. In this way, by unity with the Roman Pontiff in communion and in profession of the same faith, the Church of Christ becomes one flock under one Supreme Shepherd.
>
> 3.4. This is the teaching of the Catholic truth, and no one can depart from it without endangering his faith and salvation.[10]

This is only a small selection from similar passages in the preface and first three chapters of session four of the First Vatican Council leading up to the climactic chapter 4, which affirms and defines the doctrine of papal infallibility.

It is worth noting that the Second Vatican Council, in its document "*Lumen Gentium*," reiterated the doctrine of infallibility for the "successor of Peter" and "the supreme shepherd and teacher of all the faithful."[11] This council also attempted to balance the claims of Vatican I by giving a stronger emphasis to collegial leadership for the whole council of bishops. But this effort was resisted by Pope Paul VI, who thought the document had compromised papal authority, and he made an unusual move to rectify the matter. After the document had already passed the Council, he inserted a "Note of Explanation" that asserted a stronger view of his own authority than the document seemed to affirm. Part of the Note reads as follows.

> It is up to the judgment of the Supreme Pontiff, to whose care Christ's whole flock has been entrusted, to determine, according to the needs of the Church as they change over the course of centuries, the way in which this care may be best exercised—whether in a personal or a collegial way. The Roman Pontiff, taking account of the Church's welfare, proceeds according to his own discretion in arranging, promoting, and approving the exercise of collegial activity.
>
> As Supreme Pastor of the Church, the Supreme Pontiff can always exercise his power at will, as his very office demands.[12]

I have quoted at length here to show both the substance of the classic Roman Catholic claims about the papacy and, moreover, how strong these claims are. Both the substance and the strength of these claims show how

---

10. "First Vatican Council" 4.3.
11. *Documents of Vatican II*, 39–40.
12. "*Lumen Gentium*" Appendix 3.4, in *Documents of Vatican II*, 76.

much is riding on them for the distinctive claims of Roman Catholicism. These passages also enable us to see how Roman claims about the papacy are analogous to the role of the resurrection of Jesus in classic creedal orthodoxy. If these papal claims are not true, Rome's distinctive claims founder and fail. So let us spell out some of the ways Roman Catholic claims about the papacy are analogous to the resurrection.

First, both claim that God has acted in certain definitive ways to reveal his truth to us for our salvation. God the Father acted in the resurrection by raising Jesus from the dead to vindicate him and demonstrate that Christ is his divine Son. In a similar fashion, the Roman Catholic claim is that God the Son acted to found the papacy by appointing Peter prince of the apostles and visible head of the whole church militant, immediately and directly promising him, and thereby conferring upon him, a primacy of jurisdiction over the whole church (1:1.6). Moreover, he instituted the papacy as a permanent office so that Peter should have perpetual successors with jurisdiction over the whole church (2:5; 3:2). Notice also that Rome claims that its understanding of Christ's words to Peter in this regard represents the "absolutely manifest teaching of the Sacred Scriptures" (1:4).

Second, in both cases it is claimed that these acts of God were performed in the context of human history and the effects were observable by human witnesses. God the Father did not raise Jesus in such a fashion that it was a closely guarded secret that no one knew or witnessed. It is noteworthy that Paul begins his discussion of the resurrection by citing the various appearances of the risen Jesus (1 Cor 15:3–8). His confidence that the risen Christ truly appeared to various witnesses, including himself, matches his insistence that our faith is not in vain. Similarly, the claim that Christ instituted the papacy in the fashion Roman Catholicism teaches also strongly implies that it would be clearly known by Peter, and presumably his successors, especially if the Roman interpretation represents "the absolutely manifest teaching of the Sacred Scriptures." Peter would presumably hand on to his successors what he had "immediately and directly" received so clearly from Christ, just as Paul carefully handed on what he had received (cf. 1 Cor 15:3). Moreover, the claims of Rome entail that Peter had immediate and ongoing successors, men who existed in history and were known as the bishop of Rome by their contemporaries. Indeed, notice that the First Vatican Council insists that it "was known in every age" and cannot be doubted that Peter received the keys of the kingdom from Christ, and "that to this day and forever he lives and presides and exercises judgment in his successors the bishops of the Holy Roman See, which he founded and consecrated with his blood" (2:2).

It is important to emphasize that the claim that this "was known in every age" makes best sense if it is taken to refer to the Roman interpretation of Jesus' words about the keys of the kingdom and not the mere fact that Jesus spoke these words to Peter. For it is hardly a matter of controversy between Roman Catholicism and other Christian traditions that Jesus spoke these words. On that we all agree, so there is no reason to insist upon it. The issue is the correct *interpretation* of those words.[13]

Third, given the claims made about both the resurrection and the papacy, our salvation is at stake in accepting or denying these claims. Faith in Christ for salvation essentially involves the belief that God raised him from the dead. Faith that he died for our sin hinges on the belief that he rose from the dead, and confessing that he is Lord hinges on believing that God raised him from the dead (Rom 10:9–10). Similarly, the document cited above repeatedly anathematizes those who deny its claims and warns that no one can depart from its teaching about the status and authority of the pope "without endangering his faith and salvation" (3:4). In both cases, very strong claims are made about the vital importance of accepting the truth of what is proclaimed and the clear implications that follow.

A MAJOR EVIDENTIAL DIVIDE

Now then, with these similarities and analogies in mind, let us turn to consider a way in which the case of the resurrection and that of the papacy sharply diverge. In short, there is impressive historical evidence for the resurrection, but there is not such evidence for Roman Catholic papal claims. My point here is a simple one, but one with far-reaching implications. If the

---

13. Suan Sonna has argued against me that the only thing Vatican I claims "was known in every age" was that Peter received the keys of the kingdom from Christ. He cites Denzinger's translation of 2.2 which has a semi-colon after the line which claims that Peter "received the keys of the kingdom from our Lord Jesus Christ, the Savior and Redeemer of the human race." This implies, he suggests, "a stronger distinction" between the clause pertaining to the keys and the claim that follows, namely, that Peter "up to this time and always lives and presides and exercises judgment in his successors, the bishops of the holy see of Rome, which was founded by him and consecrated by his blood." I find this to be a rather frail objection. Even with the semi-colon, it seems doubtful to suggest that the passage is claiming merely that the only thing known in every age was the simple fact that in some sense Peter had the keys of the kingdom. For again, that is a straightforward claim of Scripture. What is at stake is the correct *interpretation* of the text. It is also worth noting that this is the only historical passage Sonna cites. Passages 1.1, 1.4, and 1.6 assert that it is utterly clear that Peter was "endowed by Christ with a true and proper primacy of jurisdiction." See Sonna, "Roman *and* Catholic," 120–34.

historical evidence is at odds with Roman papal claims, then Rome's distinctive claims for itself are undermined and lose credibility.

Of course, how one assesses the relevance of historical evidence depends on how much credence one gives evidence in general when assessing theological truth claims. Those who for various reasons place little stock in purported objective evidence may dismiss this negative historical evidence as utterly irrelevant. But for those with evidentialist inclinations, historical facts and considerations can hardly be waved off in this fashion.

So let us consider the issues before us in the light of a very modest evidentialist standard, namely, one suggested by Pascal. But first, consider this couplet in which Pascal indicates that revelation from God imposes obligations on us, but also that God has certain obligations to us not to mislead us in his revelation. "Men owe it to God to accept the religion he sends them. God owes it to men not to lead them into error."[14] The claims involved in the Christian revelation are so monumentally important that Pascal repeatedly stresses that all rational persons must earnestly seek the truth until they find it. While he is under no illusion that reason is the ultimate source or measure of truth, he is also confident that reason is an essential guide that we must trust so far as it goes. While the truths of faith surpass reason and empirical evidence, God never requires us to go against clear deliverances of reason or empirical evidence in our quest for truth. He writes: "Faith certainly tells us what the senses do not, but not the contrary of what they see; it is above, not against them."[15]

More generally, Pascal proposes the following modest standard as what we should expect as we consider the relevant evidence for Christianity: "But the evidence is such as to exceed, or at least equal, the evidence to the contrary, so that it cannot be reason that decides us against following it, and can therefore only be concupiscence and wickedness of heart."[16] Keep this especially in mind in what follows.

Returning to our two cases, it is a happy fact for orthodox Christian belief that there is substantial evidence for the resurrection of Jesus. A robust belief in his bodily resurrection can be defended by rigorous critical scholarship. Indeed, the evidence arguably far surpasses Pascal's minimal standard. Numerous first rank biblical scholars, theologians, and philosophers have defended this claim, and there is no need to belabor this point. Of course, I do not mean to deny that there are numerous scholars on the other side who are more skeptical or who strongly deny the resurrection.

---

14. Pascal, *Pensees*, no. 840.
15. Pascal, *Pensees*, no. 185.
16. Pascal, *Pensees*, no. 835.

These issues are deeply contested to be sure. But the fact remains that there are many outstanding scholars who have brilliantly defended traditional claims about the resurrection and have argued that there is ample reason for doing so. Here I will simply cite a couple of interesting examples to illustrate the point.

Several years ago, Richard Swinburne employed probability theory to defend the resurrection. Taking all of what he took to be the relevant factors into account, Swinburne argued that the balance of probability heavily favored the resurrection. In fact, in a formalization of the argument, Swinburne contended that the resurrection had a probability of 0.97.[17] More recently, Michael Licona has defended the resurrection by employing rigorous standards of evidence as employed by historians. Relying only on what he calls "historical bedrock" composed of facts that are a matter of consensus among almost all scholars, he concluded that "Jesus' resurrection is 'very certain,' a rendering higher on the spectrum of historical certainty than I had expected."[18]

THE PAPACY IS ANOTHER MATTER

When we turn to the Roman claims about the papacy, however, matters are altogether different. In brief, there is a strong scholarly consensus that the classic belief that Peter was the first pope is a pious myth, and indeed, there was not even a monarchical bishop in Rome—let alone anyone who was recognized as having jurisdiction over the entire church—until sometime in the latter half of the second century, if not later. It must be stressed that this is not merely a consensus among Protestant and Eastern Orthodox scholars, but Roman Catholics as well. Given the importance of this claim, let us take a few minutes to document it.

A good place to begin is with the distinguished Roman Catholic papal historian Eamon Duffy (who served on the Pontifical Historical Commission) and his observation that "all modern discussion of the issues must now start from the exhaustive and persuasive analysis by Peter Lampe, *From Paul to Valentinus: Christians at Rome in the First Two Centuries*, London 2003. This is a difficult read for the non-specialist, but it conveys as no other work does the extraordinary ferment of early Roman Christianity."[19] Lampe's work is exhaustive in the sense that he studied every scrap of archaeological

---

17. Swinburne, *Resurrection of God Incarnate*, 204–16.
18. Licona, *Resurrection of Jesus*, 619.
19. Duffy, *Saints and Sinners*, 469. Lampe is a Protestant scholar.

evidence as well as pertinent literary sources in his account of early Roman Christianity.

We can hardly go into the details of this technical work here, but it is important to note Lampe's "fractionation" thesis, in which he shows that the early Roman church was composed of house churches in various districts that matched the layout of the city. "The fractionation in Rome favored a collegial presbyterial system of government and prevented for a long time, until the second half of the second century, the development of a monarchical episcopacy in the city."[20] Lampe documents the significant fact that early Christian writers living in Rome or familiar with church life in Rome in the late first and early second century consistently describe the leadership there in terms of plural leaders, with no indication that there was a single leader who exercised the sort of authority claimed by later monarchical bishops.

Another facet of Lampe's work worth noting is his historical analysis of Irenaeus's famous list of Roman bishops,[21] a passage popular apologists use to support Roman Catholic papal claims. This list begins with Linus, the alleged successor of Peter as bishop of Rome, and concludes with Eleutherius, the bishop of Rome when Irenaeus wrote. Irenaeus is concerned to refute gnostic heretics, and he is arguing that orthodox Christianity, as represented by the church at Rome, is the authentic faith that goes back to the apostles.

This passage may be quite impressive taken in isolation. However, it provides little weight for supporting Roman Catholic papal claims in the world of serious historians. Irenaeus's list, when taken as support for a Roman bishop in the first or early second century, is not supported by the bedrock historical evidence from earlier witnesses and accounts of church life in Rome at that time. Lampe has subjected Irenaeus's list to a careful historical and grammatical analysis and has argued that this list "is with highest probability a historical construction from the 180s, when the monarchical episcopacy developed in Rome."[22] In other words, it anachronistically imports into earlier decades what was emerging in the 180s. If Lampe's historical and grammatical analysis of this list is correct, it has little value as a historical source for the contested issues about the papacy.[23]

20. Lampe, *From Paul to Valentinus*, 397.

21. Irenaeus, *Against Heresies* 3.3.3.

22. Lampe, *From Paul to Valentinus*, 406. See the whole of Lampe's chapter 41 for his analysis of this passage. For an excellent account of Lampe's argument, and a discussion of the larger issues, see Addison, "Quest."

23. In *An Oxford Dictionary*, Kelly and Walsh take a conservative view of the bishops lists in affirming that the men listed were historical figures, including Linus. It acknowledges, however, that the idea of a monarchical bishop only "finally emerged in Rome in the mid to late second century" (2). Speaking of Linus, it says: "While his

In view of this evidence, it is hardly surprising that right at the outset of his authoritative book on the history of the papacy, Duffy begins by sorting out the crucial distinction between legend and reliable history. After noting that legend filled in the details of Peter's later life where the New Testament is silent, Duffy went on as follows:

> Neither Peter nor Paul founded the Church at Rome, for there were Christians in the city before either of the Apostles set foot there. Nor can we assume, as Irenaeus did, that the Apostles established there a succession of bishops to carry on the work in the city, for all the indications are that there was no single bishop of Rome for almost a century after the deaths of the Apostles. In fact, wherever we turn, the solid outlines of the Petrine succession at Rome seem to blur and dissolve.[24]

These are stark observations indeed in view of the strong claims of traditional papal theology and all that rides on those claims.

Duffy, however, is not an exception in this regard, but again, his claims here represent the consensus of critical historians.[25] Consider now these words of Roman Catholic historian Klaus Shatz critiquing traditional papal historical assertions.

> If one had asked a Christian in the year 100, 200, or even 300 whether the bishop of Rome was the head of all Christians, or whether there was a supreme bishop over all the other bishops and having the last word in questions affecting the whole Church, he or she would certainly have said no.[26]

For one more example, consider the Roman Catholic papal historian Robert Eno, who sizes up the evidence as follows.

> But the evidence available seems to point predominantly if not decisively in the direction of a collective leadership [in Rome]. Dogmatic a priori theses should not force us into presuming or requiring something that the evidence leans against. . . . This evidence (Clement, Hermas, Ignatius) points us in the direction

---

existence and leading position in the Roman church need not be doubted, it is impossible, in view of the late development of the monarchical episcopate at Rome, to form any clear idea of his role and functions" (3).

24. Duffy, *Saints and Sinners*, 2.

25. See Brent, "How Irenaeus Has Misled," 35–52. For a notable example of an Eastern Orthodox scholar, see Behr, *Irenaeus of Lyons*. For an example of a Roman Catholic who challenges the consensus, see Jones, "Was There a Bishop," 128–43. For a critique of Jones, see Duffy, "Was There a Bishop," 301–8.

26. Shatz, *Papal Primacy*, 3. See 1–40 for Shatz's account of the origins of the papacy.

of assuming that in the first century and into the second, there was no bishop of Rome in the usual sense given to that title.[27]

The three names mentioned by Eno represent bedrock historical evidence because all of them lived in Rome or were familiar with the church in Rome and wrote about it. But as Eno observes, none of them give any indication that there was a bishop in Rome or any single leader who had anything like the authority popes were supposed to have. We do not have space to look in detail at any of the three figures Eno mentions, but let us take a brief look at them, beginning with Ignatius.

Ignatius is particularly interesting because the theme of episcopal leadership was such a prominent theme in his letters to various churches. In the seven letters we have, he made frequent mention of the bishop, and his authority, mentioning him by name in some cases. Consider, for instance, these typical lines from his letter to the Magnesians.

> Inasmuch as I was found worthy to see you in the persons of Damas, your godly bishop, and your worthy presbyters Bassus and Apollonius, and my fellow servant, the deacon Zotion—may I enjoy his company, because he is subject to the bishop as to the grace of God, and to the council of the presbyters as to the law of Jesus Christ.... Be eager to do everything in godly harmony, the bishop presiding in the place of God and the presbyters in the place of the apostles and the deacons, who are especially dear to me, since they have been entrusted with the ministry of Jesus Christ.[28]

So prevalent is the theme of the importance of the episcopacy and the authority of the bishop and so often does he reiterate these points that it is no exaggeration to say he almost seems obsessed with these issues. There are over forty such passages referring to bishops scattered throughout these letters.

But here is what is interesting and telling for our concerns: all these references occur in just six of his seven letters. Such passages fail to appear in only one of his letters, namely, his letter to the Romans. Remarkably, in his letter to the church—where the bishop of bishops, the visible head of the whole church, is supposed to reside, according to Roman Catholicism—there is *no mention* of the bishop. Eno is not alone in finding it strange that there are no comparable passages in his letter to the Romans if Rome had

---

27. Eno, *Rise of the Papacy*, 26, 29. For a concise discussion of this evidence, see Duffy, "Was There a Bishop," 303–8.

28. See "Letter of Ignatius to the Magnesians" 2.1, 6.1, in Holmes, *Apostolic Fathers*, 202–13.

a bishop. "But we have only silence, which leads many to conclude that Ignatius did not address such a person because the Roman community of the time had no such leader."[29] Indeed, this silence speaks volumes, especially when combined with the similar silence of other early Christian writers who were situated to comment on the presence of a bishop in Rome had there been one, but did not.[30]

Now let us more briefly consider Clement and Hermas. Clement, who lived in Rome and was active in the church there, wrote a letter to Corinth around the year 90. He speaks of bishops and deacons in the plural, but gives no indication of a single bishop, either in Rome or in Corinth. This is all the more telling since Roman Catholics actually claim Clement was the pope at this time. Hermas wrote in about 120, and in his text he gives instructions for a copy of his document to be given to Clement so that Clement can send it to other cities and they can read it as well. Some think this is the same Clement who wrote the letter to Corinth, but that is not certain. In any case, the fact remains that in describing leadership in the church of Rome Hermas refers to presbyters who are over the church but gives no suggestion of a single bishop having unique authority. Duffy comments as follows on the significance of this evidence.

> Even if we accept that the man who wrote I Clement was the same Clement (not a rare name) referred to thirty years later by Hermas, neither of these, the earliest and most important non-biblical texts to emanate from the Church of Rome, contains so much as a hint that Clement was the presiding bishop of Rome, or indeed that there existed at that stage any such creature. In referring to Church order, and in marked contrast to Ignatius, they always speak of bishops, presbyters, and deacons in the plural. . . . And in this context, Ignatius's otherwise puzzling silence about the role of the Roman bishop begins to seem more intelligible.[31]

---

29. Eno, *Rise of the Papacy*, 27.

30. For a formalized version of an argument from silence that takes into account Clement, Hermas, Ignatius, and Justin Martyr, see Collins and Walls, *Roman but Not Catholic*, 244–51.

31. Duffy, "Was There a Bishop," 304–5.

POPULAR APOLOGETICS AND YOUNG EARTH CREATIONISM

Now given the fact there has been a consensus along these lines among historians, including Roman Catholic historians, for some time now, it is somewhat surprising that popular Roman Catholic apologetics often proceeds as if the claims of the First Vatican Council remain altogether intact. These apologists are either unaware of the state of scholarship in their own church or they blithely ignore it and assure their readers that traditional papal claims are the uncontroverted truth. In so doing, they mimic what Roman Catholic historian John W. O'Malley calls the "historical naivete" of Vatican I. He writes: "The most basic problem with *Pastor Aeternus* was its historical naivete. It took the present situation as the norm for interpreting the past and projected present practice and understanding onto it."[32]

For an example of the claims of popular apologetics, consider these lines from Devin Rose: "The Church had a pope, a visible head, from the beginning. In fact, we know the names and approximate dates of all the popes, all the way back to the first century: Peter first, then Linus, Anacletus, and Clement I."[33] It is hard to overstate the profound difference between the lines from Duffy, quoted above, and those of Rose. Indeed, the difference is quite striking. What a serious historian acknowledges to be simply false is trotted out as the simple uncontroversial truth by a popular apologist.

It is also worth noting here that popular Roman Catholic apologists are reminiscent of young earth creationists who continue to assert that the earth is only ten thousand years old in the face of the massive scientific evidence that it is much older, evidence which is acknowledged by leading Christian physicists and cosmologists as well as other scientists. Popular apologists who continue to assert traditional papal history in the face of the best scholarship of their own church are doing the same sort of thing.

But perhaps there is more going on than simple disregard for serious scholarship in such popular apologetics. Perhaps what we see reflected in Rose's breezy reiteration of traditional papal claims is a stark recognition of what is at stake in those traditional claims and the implications that follow if those claims are given up.[34] If Rome's distinctive claims to be the one true church do indeed hinge essentially upon the truth of its traditional papal

---

32. O'Malley, *Vatican I*, 197.

33. Rose, *Protestant's Dilemma*, 35.

34. Cf. Duffy's comment on David Albert Jones and his attempt to defend the traditional view (cited in note 25): "I suspect that he feels that Catholic orthodoxy and church order will be compromised if it turns out that after all there was not a pope in first-century Rome" (Duffy, "Was There a Bishop," 308).

theology and the related historical claims, then to give up that theology and history is to give up those distinctive claims to be the one true church. And if those claims are given up, the motivation and mission for popular Roman Catholic apologetics is lost.

In any case, the main point here is that whereas there is arguably excellent historical evidence in favor of the resurrection of Jesus that far surpasses Pascal's modest evidentialist standards, the historical evidence in favor of traditional papal claims falls far short of Pascal's standards. Indeed, it is worse, for the historical evidence, starting with the "historical bedrock" excavated by Lampe, counts strongly against Rome's claims. And for those committed to Rome's distinctive claims to ecclesial authority, poses a serious difficulty.[35]

Indeed, the strong historical consensus against Rome's traditional papal claims is a major reason not to be a Roman Catholic. However, before concluding this point, we should consider some moves Roman Catholics might make to defend their traditional papal claims. So let us turn to examine these in the next chapter.

---

35. For more on these issues, see chapters 6 and 11 in Collins and Walls, *Roman but Not Catholic*.

CHAPTER TWO

SAVING THE PAPAL HYPOTHESIS?

In the last chapter, we saw that bedrock historical evidence poses a serious challenge to traditional Roman claims about the origins and early history of the papacy. And this is a powerful challenge to the normative claims of Rome. Now then, what sort of moves are available to Roman Catholics who are apprised of the consensus of historians within their own church but want to maintain Rome's distinctive ecclesial claims, and the papal theology that underwrites those claims? I will mention four.

OBJECTIVE EVIDENCE IS OVERRATED

One obvious move to make is to simply insist that the consensus of critical historians is irrelevant. Even Pascal's modest evidentialist principles should be rejected. The essential claim is that Christ "immediately and directly" conferred on Peter and his successors jurisdiction over the whole church, and that this "was known in every age," not that there is objective historical evidence for these claims. There was a visible head of the church from the beginning even if he was invisible to history for some time. Indeed, the truth of these claims is perfectly compatible with the historical evidence pointing "predominantly if not decisively" (as Eno put it) in another direction altogether. There are possible scenarios we can imagine in which these claims are true, even if this requires us to construe the available evidence in a way that is at odds with the conclusions historians think most probable. Perhaps among the multiple bishops in early Rome, one always had preeminence, and it was he who was Peter's successor even if he is never identified as such by writers such as Ignatius, Clement, and Hermas.

Duffy addresses this sort of appeal in his response to Fr. David Albert Jones, who acknowledges that Clement says nothing to indicate that there was a monoepiscopate in Rome, but insists that this possibility is not excluded and, strictly speaking, is compatible with the evidence. In reply, Duffy observes that "Fr Jones's valiant insistence that nevertheless, Clement *might* have been the presiding bishop of Rome, which he then modulates into the claim that it is just as likely as not that he was, looks like historical fideism, assertion unencumbered by the need for evidence."[1]

The view Duffy is criticizing here represents a classic dogmatic approach to the matter, one that requires no solid evidence. Consider this description of such an approach.

> In dealing with these claims we are passing along the border line between history and dogmatic theology. The primacy of Peter and his appointment by Christ to succeed Him as head of the Church are accepted by the Catholic Church as the indubitable word of inspired Gospel, in its only possible meaning. That Peter went to Rome and founded there his See is just as definitively what is termed in Catholic theology a dogmatic fact. This has been defined by an eminent Catholic theologian as "historical fact so intimately connected with some great Catholic truths that it would be believed even if time and accident had destroyed *all* of the original evidence therefor."[2]

Notice: these claims would be believed as "dogmatic facts" even if all the original evidence for them had been destroyed and is no longer accessible to us.

So long as the standard is possibility, or an appeal to what *might be true,* or to a "dogmatic fact" lacking any sort of evidence to which we have access, this sort of move can provide an ever more elusive sort of option. It does come with certain costs, however. First, it appears to be an *ad hoc* appeal that one would not otherwise rely on. It will be awkward, to say the least, for those who make this move to appeal to objective historical evidence when it supports their beliefs (as in say, the resurrection), unless they have some principled reason why they trust history in some cases but not others. Second, and far more serious, it is deeply counterintuitive that truths as important as traditional papal claims with so much riding on them must be believed in the face of considerable counterevidence. Recall that those who reject these claims are anathematized and their salvation is said to be in jeopardy. This is a rather jarring conclusion to swallow, to put it mildly.

1. Duffy, "Was There a Bishop," 305.
2. Thompson and Loomis, *See of Peter*, xxiii–xxiv.

Would a good God, let alone a perfectly loving God, require us to believe something on pain of damnation that even the best Christian historians, including Roman Catholic historians, judge to be highly improbable? But again, for those not troubled by these implications, this remains an option.

PAPAL DOCTRINE NEEDED TIME TO DEVELOP

Next, it is often argued that papal doctrine required time to develop in a fashion similar to the way the doctrines of incarnation and the Trinity developed over time. It was present in seed form all along but required centuries to mature. In view of this, it should not be surprising that there was not a monarchical bishop in Rome until the late second century and that papal doctrine took even longer to emerge.

While the appeal to doctrinal development is a natural one for Roman Catholics who must defend infallible dogmas first given formal definition in the nineteenth and twentieth centuries, it is doubtful that the appeal can be made for its traditional papal claims. First, what is at stake here are purported factual claims about history which underwrite the distinctive Roman papal and ecclesial claims, namely that Peter was "immediately and directly" given universal jurisdiction over the church by promise from Christ and that his successors also had this role. It was allegedly to "Peter alone" that Jesus "confided the jurisdiction," saying, "Feed my lambs, feed my sheep."[3]

For traditional papal theology to be underwritten, it must have a secure foundation in these claims about Peter and his successors. If the claims just cited are true, we have very strong reason to think Peter and his successors (and probably the other apostles as well) understood these essential claims from the outset, and that it did not take several decades to develop this understanding. This is all the more likely if it is true that the Roman Catholic Petrine doctrine is the "absolutely manifest teaching of the Sacred Scriptures, as it has always been understood by the Catholic Church"[4] and that "it was known in every age that the holy and most blessed Peter . . . received the keys of the kingdom from our lord Jesus Christ . . . and that to this day and forever he lives and presides and exercises judgment in his successors the bishops of the Holy Roman See." In short, these claims seem clearly to insist that the fundamental elements of papal doctrine were clear from the outset rather than only emerging or developing gradually over time. The

---

3. This is, of course, a reference to John 21:15–17.
4. Of course scripture had not yet been canonized at this point but the events recorded in scripture would have been known by the apostles even before the Gospels were written.

classic papal theology of Vatican I rests on robust historical claims, not on the far more modest notion of more recent vintage that the papacy of the first several decades was present only in "embryonic" form.

Now it is worth noting that the claim that the Roman Petrine doctrine is the "absolutely manifest teaching of Sacred Scriptures" is, of course, a hermeneutical claim, not a historical one. However, the claim that "it was known in every age" that Peter and his successors had the distinct role and authority that Rome claims they had is very much a historical claim, and one that it is reasonable to think would be confirmed by the historical record.

Here is a preliminary question worth pondering in the light of this claim: Why is there no affirmation or even reference to Peter's extraordinary authority in the Epistles of Peter?[5] If he received directly and immediately from Christ the sort of authority Rome claims, why does Peter not invoke, or at least mention, his unique role? He merely identifies himself as an apostle of Jesus Christ, or an apostle and a servant of Christ, and he goes on in his first epistle to address the elders as a fellow elder (1 Pet 1:1; 5:1; 2 Pet 1:1).

The fact that he does not invoke any special kind of authority is all the more noteworthy when we consider that Paul, by contrast, repeatedly underscores his distinctive commission from Christ to be the apostle to the gentiles, and the authority that entailed (Acts 9:15; Rom 11:13-14; 15:15-16; Gal 1:15-17; 2:6-10; Eph 3:7-9). Surely it is surprising that Peter, who allegedly had a far more important commission, with far more authority, never records that fact.[6]

It is in Galatians, incidentally, where Paul informs us that he withstood Peter when Peter was acting in a way that was contrary to the gospel (Gal 2:11-14). A few verses previous to this report, Paul notes that "he who worked through Peter making him an apostle to the circumcised worked through me in sending me to the Gentiles" (Gal 2:8). Paul's understanding of Peter's role as apostle to the circumcised parallel to his role as apostle to the gentiles hardly suggests that he thinks Peter was given jurisdiction over the whole church. He does point out that James, Peter, and John (in that order) are acknowledged as pillars, but again, he does not single out Peter in any way (Gal 2:9).[7]

---

5. The authorship of the Epistles of Peter is, of course, controversial, especially 2 Peter.

6. It might be suggested that Peter never invoked his special authority due to his humility. But this objection is based on a misunderstanding of humility. True humility owns God's calling and aspires to live up to it and to fulfill it, not to hide it or downplay it.

7. It is worth noting that Peter drops out of the narrative of Acts after chapter 15 and Paul is the dominant character throughout the rest of the book. Peter's primary bases

Here is another historical fact that must be noted, and one that is hard to square with the traditional claims of Rome. The first known appeal to the classic texts in Matthew by a bishop of the Roman Catholic Church to support his unique authority was not until the middle of the third century by Bishop Stephen. He invoked this text in a dispute over rebaptism with Cyprian, an African bishop, and Firmilian, a Greek bishop. But what is even more telling is that these bishops neither yielded to his claim to authority, nor did they accept his appeal to the authority of Peter. Indeed, according to Eno, "We must note as well that Firmilian not only does not accept the claim, he seems never to have heard of it before."[8] This is rather surprising if the claims of the First Vatican Council that we have been examining are true. One would have expected that the fundamental claims of the Petrine theory would have been reasonably well known, at least among bishops, and not disputed as a novel claim.[9]

Doctrinal development as represented in the classic creeds was a matter of giving a more exact definition to beliefs that had been very much in evidence for centuries. Long before Nicea and Chalcedon, Christians had already been affirming their belief that Jesus was raised from the dead and ascended into heaven, that he was Lord, that he was the Son of God, and so on. The extraordinary substance of classic Christology, the "raw material," was already heartily affirmed and its meaning was discussed and debated long before Nicaea and Chalcedon provided philosophically precise language to express these convictions.

The papacy emerging in later centuries was not a similar case of doctrinal development because there was no similar affirmation all along of the substance of the classical Petrine theology as traditional Roman papal theology claims. It is not the case that all along reasonably informed Christians believed that Peter and his successors had been given authority over the whole church directly and immediately from Christ, even if the precise details of what that meant still needed to be worked out. In short, we do not have the same sort of robust body of raw material supporting the papacy that would be necessary to make the case that it is a doctrinal development that parallels classic Christology.

---

of ministry were Jerusalem and Antioch. Late in his life, he likely went to Rome, where he was martyred. There is no indication of his being there earlier. In Paul's Epistle to the Romans, for instance, he greets numerous persons in chapter 16, but Peter is not among them. See Collins and Walls, *Roman but Not Catholic*, 216–20.

8. Eno, *Rise of the Papacy*, 64.

9. Likewise, early patristic interpretation of John 21 does not support the Roman claim that their interpretation of this text is the "absolutely manifest teaching of Sacred Scripture." See Bradshaw, "Giving Honor," 239–50.

There is another reason why the late second-century emergence of the episcopacy in Rome is not a case of doctrinal development analogous to Christology. And that is the simple fact that traditional papal theology is not conceptually challenging and difficult in anything remotely like the way Trinity and incarnation are. Indeed, these doctrines are extremely difficult and have proved challenging to some of the greatest minds in human history down to the present day. It is hardly surprising that it would take some time reflecting on the fundamental data of biblical revelation to articulate these doctrines with some degree of precision. By contrast, there is nothing particularly difficult in traditional papal theology. If the traditional claims of Roman Catholicism are true, there is no reason the fundamental elements of papal theory should not have been understood and affirmed all along, at least in Rome and among bishops and other leaders.

Finally, it is important to note another sense in which papal doctrine is not analogous to the development of orthodox Christology, namely, papal doctrine has never come close to attaining the sort of ecumenical consensus that the classic creeds enjoy. It is sometimes pointed out that creedal doctrine was only developed when formal challenges were raised, as Arius did in the case of Christology and the Nicene Creed. Similarly, it is argued that papal doctrine only required explicit formulation when it was challenged. The problem, however, is that papal doctrine never achieved the sort of consensus the classic creeds have enjoyed. To the contrary, rather than being a matter of ecumenical agreement, papal doctrine has instead been an ongoing source of division and conflict, not only with Protestantism but with Eastern Orthodoxy as well. This fact undermines the claim that papal doctrine is a natural development of the teaching of scripture that only required time and challenge to be made more precise, analogous to classic Christology.

OKAY, LET'S REBUILD WITH DIFFERENT MATERIAL

A third suggestion, similar to the idea of development, is that perhaps papal theology can be justified on other grounds than a literal claim that Christ instituted the papacy immediately and directly by conferring authority on Peter and his immediate successors. Even if history undermines these traditional claims and warrants for papal authority, perhaps the actual history of how the papacy emerged can provide suitable material to justify it. In the conclusion of Eno's book, he writes as follows:

> The history of the Papacy in antiquity can be divided into two periods. The first is that before the time of Damasus, the period in which the documentary evidence, especially that concerning Roman sources, is very sketchy and episodic. The texts and historical cases surveyed and evaluated are subject to a variety of interpretations, some of which, to be sure, are more likely than others. Yet there is enough evidence of a Roman consciousness of its authority to show that the later firm and steady claims did not arise *ex nihilo* after 366. Non-Roman attitudes are another matter.[10]

In view of this, one might appeal to "a Roman consciousness of its authority," even as one recognizes that the texts and cases to support this are "subject to a variety of interpretations." Eventually, Rome came to make unequivocal claims for its unique authority and to justify those claims by insisting that Christ bestowed upon Peter and his successors authority over the whole church, even if the historical evidence is at odds with those claims. Is this enough to underwrite and sustain traditional Roman Catholic papal authority?

Well, the mere fact that Rome had a certain "consciousness of its authority" is hardly enough to warrant that authority or to legitimize it. The question remains: What is the source and warrant for this sense of authority?

These questions are particularly pertinent when we consider the "non-Roman attitudes" that Eno mentions. Roman claims to authority have not in fact been a source of unity in the church as they are supposed to be, but quite the opposite. Indeed, the claims of Rome to have authority over the whole church have been a point of contention with the Orthodox for centuries before it was an issue for Protestants, and the papacy remains a point of contention to this day. While the Orthodox have acknowledged a "primacy of honor" to the Roman See, they reject the Roman claims to papal authority. (Recall that the First Vatican Council anathematized those who hold the Orthodox view of Roman primacy; 1.6.)

A notable emblem of the historic conflict between Rome and the Orthodox is the famous Canon 28 of the Council of Chalcedon, which acknowledged Constantinople as the New Rome when it became the capital of the empire. The rationale for this is particularly interesting.

> For the Fathers rightly granted privileges to the throne of old Rome, because it was the imperial city. And the One Hundred and Fifty most religious Bishops, actuated by the same consideration, gave equal privileges to the most holy throne of New

---

10. Eno, *Rise of the Papacy*, 147.

> Rome, judging justly that the city which is honored with the Sovereignty and the Senate, and enjoys equal privileges with old imperial Rome should in ecclesiastical matters also be magnified as she is, and rank next after her.[11]

This canon was rejected by Rome, but the point remains that it shows that the fathers of Chalcedon judged that Roman authority rested in no small part on the fact that it had been the capital city, not on an irrevocable conferral of authority by Christ. To what extent these political realities shaped Rome's "consciousness of its authority" is debatable, but for these early fathers, Rome's authority was in no small part due to political factors.

When we consider the larger history of the papacy, with its ever growing bid for secular power and the moral and spiritual corruption that often attended those bids for power, it is even more difficult to sanctify Rome's "consciousness of its authority" as warranted by God.[12] Indeed, it appears to be very much an unholy grasping for power and political control, as both Orthodox and Protestant critics have argued.

The deeper problem with trying to vindicate papal claims in this fashion, however, is that it is a rather radical break with the traditional claims of the First Vatican Council. Consider again the analogy with the resurrection. In particular, consider how liberal theologians explain how faith in Jesus's resurrection actually emerged. Here, for instance is how Roman Catholic theologian Edward Schillebeeckx thinks this happened.

> May it not be that Simon Peter—and indeed the Twelve—arrived via their concrete experience of forgiveness after Jesus' death, encountered as grace and discussed among themselves (as they remembered Jesus' sayings about, among other things, the gracious God) at the "evidence for belief": the Lord is alive? He renews for them the offer of salvation; this they experience in their own conversion; he must therefore be alive.[13]

According to Schillebeeckx, faith in the resurrection was not generated by actual appearances of Jesus after his death, nor by an empty tomb, as traditional biblical scholars contend. Rather, it was produced by a conversion experience in which the disciples were gathered together and felt that they were forgiven by Jesus for their cowardice when he was crucified. If they were forgiven by Christ, they inferred that he must therefore be alive. The stories about the appearances and the empty tomb only came later.

---

11. Cited by Carlton, *Truth*, 117.
12. See Collins and Walls, *Roman but Not Catholic*, 220–43.
13. Schillebeeckx, *Jesus*, 391.

It is important to stress how much of a radical reversal this sort of approach represents. In short, it is not the case that actual appearances of a bodily resurrected Jesus, along with an empty tomb, are what actually generated belief in his resurrection. Rather, experiences of forgiveness generated the belief that he was alive, and later, the stories of the appearances and the empty tomb.

Now Schillebeeckx's views are hardly the consensus of critical scholars. But now let us suppose they were. Let us suppose that there was a strong consensus among scholars of all stripes that Jesus did not in fact appear to the disciples after his death, nor did they actually witness an empty tomb. Rather, belief in the resurrection was entirely generated, as Schillebeeckx suggests, by a conversion experience in which the disciples felt themselves forgiven. Moreover, let us suppose that only late in the second century did anyone claim that Jesus had actually appeared bodily to the disciples and that the tomb was empty.[14] And only centuries later was there any sort of clear theology of resurrection based on appearances of Jesus and an empty tomb. Given this sort of scenario, would it not undermine rational confidence that the resurrection as traditionally understood really did happen? And would it not make it highly doubtful that this rather amorphous account of resurrection could provide warrant for the traditional doctrines, such as incarnation and Trinity, that are premised upon it?

Likewise, it is dubious that historically "sketchy" accounts of how papal theology arose out of Rome's sense of its own authority can support the strong claims that have traditionally been made for papal authority. If the robust historical claims that have traditionally supported papal theology emerged out of that theology rather than producing it, we have a radical reversal similar to that represented in Schillebeckx's account of the resurrection.

In the same vein, consider the views of the distinguished Roman Catholic New Testament scholar Raymond Brown, who agrees with the consensus of scholars that Peter was not the first pope, that the episcopacy in Rome did not emerge until the second century, and indeed that the episcopacy in general was not founded by the historical Christ.[15] Brown defends the episcopacy (including presumably the papacy), however, as established by Christ "in the nuanced sense that the episcopate gradually emerged in a Church that stemmed from Christ and that this emergence was (in the eyes of faith) guided by the Holy Spirit." Brown insists that it does not detract

---

14. Schillebeeckx, of course, does not claim that these reports were that late.

15. Brown, *Priest and Bishop*, 51–54, 72–73. For a concise account of the gradual emergence of the papacy, see Wilken, *First Thousand Years*, 163–73.

from the dignity of bishops to trace the "appearance of the episcopate more directly to the Holy Spirit than to the historical Jesus."[16]

Again, robust claims about objective events that are visible to the "eyes of history" are replaced by a much more subjective gradual emergence ascribed to the guidance of the Holy Spirit visible only to "the eyes of faith."

SKIRTING HISTORY WITH A BRILLIANT EPISTEMOLOGY

The fourth and final strategy for saving the papal hypothesis that I will mention here is one that might be inspired by Alvin Plantinga's justly celebrated account of warranted Christian belief. Plantinga famously defends the rationality of Christian belief by arguing for an account of faith that is "a belief-producing process or activity, like perception or memory."[17] As such, when faith is produced in the right way, it leads to knowledge just as our other faculties do when functioning properly. For instance, when my faith in the divinity of Jesus is produced in the right way by the faculty of faith, I am warranted in this belief in the same way I am warranted in believing I had scrambled eggs for breakfast when my faculty of memory is functioning properly.

The aim of faith is to allow us to know a particularly important set of truths, namely, what God has graciously done to provide for our salvation. In order to do this, Plantinga contends that God first arranged for the production of scripture, the inspired set of books of which he is the primary author. But our knowledge of the truth of scripture does not depend on us and our critical reading skills. Rather, this knowledge is ultimately due to the presence and activity of the Holy Spirit, who witnesses to our hearts and minds to convince us of the truth of the gospel.

> We read Scripture, or something presenting scriptural teaching, or hear the gospel preached. . . . What is said simply seems right; it seems compelling; one finds oneself saying, "Yes, that's right, that's the truth of the matter; this is indeed the word of the Lord." I read, "God was in Christ, reconciling the world to himself"; I think: "Right; that's true; God really was in Christ, reconciling the world to himself!"[18]

---

16. Brown, *Priest and Bishop*, 73.
17. Plantinga, *Warranted Christian Belief*, 256.
18. Plantinga, *Warranted Christian Belief*, 250.

When we find ourselves believing the gospel in response to the witness of the Holy Spirit in this fashion, this counts as knowledge just as much as our memory and perceptual beliefs do when these faculties are functioning properly. Indeed, Plantinga emphasizes that faith produced in this way is warranted "even if I don't know of and cannot make a good historical case for the reliability of the biblical writers or for what they teach. I don't *need* a good historical case for the truth of the central teachings of the gospel to be warranted in accepting them."[19]

Here the defender of traditional Roman papal theology may appeal to Plantinga's model of warranted Christian belief to support his convictions. He may say that when he reads Matthew 16, he finds himself believing traditional Roman claims about Peter and his successors. Maybe he even finds those claims compelling. He admits he has no good historical case for these views, but insists he does not need such a case. He believes the Holy Spirit has witnessed to him that traditional Roman papal claims are true, and he is altogether warranted in holding that belief and even insisting he knows it is true.[20]

Now the first thing to notice here is that Plantinga's "extended" model of warranted Christian belief is only extended to "the central teachings of the gospel," the beliefs that are "common to the great creeds of the main branches of the Christian church."[21] It makes no claims about controversial doctrines that divide the various Christian denominations and traditions. So it is doubtful that Plantinga would endorse stretching it to form an "extra-extended Plantinga/Papal" model for settling denominational disputes.

But setting this worry aside, there is a deeper problem for such an attempt to employ Plantinga's model to this issue. Here it is. While Plantinga insists that belief in the central truths of the gospel can be warranted

---

19. Plantinga, *Warranted Christian Belief*, 259.

20. A similar move to defend papal doctrine was made several years ago by Cardinal Alfons Stickler, in response to Brian Tierney's erudite historical argument that the doctrine of papal infallibility was invented in the thirteenth century during a debate on the place of poverty in the Franciscan tradition. Stickler responded to Tierney as follows: "Theology deals with revealed data, and all scholarly research in *theology*, therefore, must begin with the acceptance of a valid revelation even when it exceeds rational verifications, and it must accept as its own scientific criteria not only the written revealed truths but also their cognitive development and their binding definitions through the living magisterium supported by a tradition which is likewise under the guidance of a higher revealed light. If, therefore, a historian sets up criteria of research, with the results derived therefrom, of a purely rational nature, he is not a historian of theology" (Stickler cited in Abraham, *Canon and Criterion*, 79). The similarity here is that Stickler appeals to the authority of the magisterium, "under the guidance of higher revealed light" to warrant papal doctrine.

21. Plantinga, *Warranted Christian Belief*, vii.

even if there is no good historical case for the reliability of the Gospels, this does not mean that there can be warrant in the face of any and all sorts of historical evidence. Warrant does not require a positive historical case, but a sufficiently strong negative case has the potential to undermine warrant.

> Isn't it clearly *possible* that historians should discover facts that put Christian belief into serious question, count heavily against it? Well, maybe so. . . . The Christian faith is a *historical* faith, in the sense that it essentially depends on what in fact did happen: "And if Christ has not been raised, your faith is futile" (1 Cor 15:17). And it could certainly happen that by the exercise of reason we come up with powerful evidence against something we take or took to be a deliverance of the faith. . . . Then Christians would have a problem, a sort of conflict between faith and reason.[22]

And this would be a serious problem indeed if we assume that our divinely given belief-forming faculties, functioning properly and at their best, should deliver beliefs that are mutually incompatible. If our reasoning faculty when properly functioning led us to believe that a historical claim was very probably or almost certainly false, it would be quite a conundrum if that claim was a foundational belief of the deliverances of faith.

Plantinga concludes his discussion of this matter in a rather open-ended way as he ponders what the appropriate response would be if he were actually faced with such powerful negative evidence. After mentioning several possibilities, he acknowledges that does not know which, if any, of those possibilities he should choose. But what is clear is that he does not think such evidence could simply be waved off or defeated by taking the deliverances of faith as properly basic beliefs.

What Plantinga raises as a mere hypothetical possibility for Christian faith appears to be an actual dilemma for conservative Roman Catholics who affirm traditional papal doctrine. The bottom line here is that the strong claims that Rome makes for herself require sufficient warrant if those claims are to be taken as true. The robust claims of traditional papal doctrine have purported to provide that warrant. The dilemma is posed by the fact that there is a very strong consensus that the historical claims that have traditionally underwritten papal theology and Rome's distinctive claims to authority are simply false, a consensus that includes leading papal historians.

It is worth emphasizing again before I conclude this chapter that the papacy is an essential mark of identity for the Roman Catholic Church that sets it apart from both Eastern Orthodoxy and the churches of the

---

22. Plantinga, *Warranted Christian Belief*, 420–21.

Reformation. It is no small matter that leading papal historians in the Roman Catholic Church are now frankly dubious of its historical claims. This raises a serious question: Would God allow such an important claim as the papacy to rest on such flimsy grounds?

Indeed, the situation here is analogous to the one all Christians would face if a scholarly consensus emerged that Christ was not in fact raised from the dead. In that case the best we could have would be something like Schillebeeckx's scenario in which the disciples had some sort of experience that eventually generated belief in the resurrection and the empty tomb. But it is clear I think that Christianity simply could not survive if its faith in the resurrection were undermined in this sort of fashion. Likewise, it is hard to see how traditional Roman Catholicism can survive, given that the historical foundations of papal doctrine have been discredited by the consensus of scholarship, including Rome's own leading papal historians. All in all, this is a powerful reason not to be a Roman Catholic.

CHAPTER THREE

THE PROBLEM OF BAD POPES

The Argument from Conspicuous Corruption

IT MIGHT BE SHOCKING to people who know little about church history, but for anyone with even a casual knowledge of that history, it is well known that there have been a number of remarkably bad popes. I do not mean merely that they did a bad job in their role as pope, or that they were incompetent, but that they were very bad men. One of the most notorious of these is Pope Alexander VI, who was pope when Martin Luther was a teenager. Eric Metaxas provides a colorful account of this infamous pope as follows.

> When his predecessor Innocent VIII died, Alexander declined to lobby for the golden throne, which was the accepted corrupt practice at that time, but simply leaped ahead of his competitors by purchasing it outright with cash. As the story goes, four muscular mules bore the extraordinary weight of reinforced panniers laden with silver. They staggered from Rodrigo Borgia's [his name before becoming pope] spectacular palace to the palace of his chief rival, Asconio Sforza, to deliver the gleaming argentine load. In his years as a cardinal, the virile pope-to-be fathered seven children, all of whom were considered illegitimate. But now, armed with the great powers of the papacy, he was able to "legitimize" whom he pleased. . . . Just prior to purchasing the papacy, Alexander at the age of fifty-nine ambitiously took as his mistress one Giulia Farnese, forty-three years his junior, who already at the age of sixteen was a celebrated beauty, most renowned for her cataract of golden tresses that tumbled to the

marble floors of the Vatican. Some called her "the pope's whore," while cleverer detractors referred to her as "the bride of Christ."[1]

For those who have never encountered these colorful popes, it might be helpful to compare them to some of our contemporary TV evangelists, who seem to be clever charlatans who exploit religion for their own power, pleasure, and privilege. Pope Alexander makes these TV preachers look like choirboys.

Of course, there have been many good popes as well as some truly outstanding ones. Gregory the Great was not called that for no reason, and more recently Pope John Paul II was widely and deservedly admired and loved by Christians all over the world, Protestants as well as Roman Catholics. This is as it should be. Given the critical role the pope serves in the Roman Catholic Church, one would expect that popes would not only be persons of exemplary Christian character and reputation but also men gifted with theological understanding, spiritual maturity, and practical leadership skill. This is the sort of profile for any bishop/presbyter in the New Testament (1 Tim 3:1–7; Titus 1:5–9), so anyone chosen to be the bishop of bishops, the vicar of Christ, the supreme pastor, and the chief shepherd of the church should certainly be expected to fit this profile. It is precisely because of these expectations that bad popes can be so disconcerting.

While these bad popes are an embarrassment to Roman Catholics, they are often dismissed as irrelevant to the claims of Rome. They have no evidential significance when assessing the claims of Rome, we are told, and they are dismissed with a wave of the hand. I want to argue otherwise.

To get a preliminary idea of what I have in mind, consider a similar argument from the opposite direction, namely, the classic argument from "conspicuous sanctity." This is an interesting and attractive argument for Christianity that appeals to the notable saints Christianity has produced. The fact that persons who have embraced Christ and his gospel have often been morally transformed is suggestive evidence for the power and truth of Christ and the gospel. Indeed, if Christianity is true, we should expect such sanctity to be exhibited. Of course, such evidence is hardly sufficient to establish the truth of Christianity by itself, but the fact that conspicuous sanctity is exhibited is one piece of evidence for Christianity.[2] In a parallel way, I want to suggest that bad popes provide material to construct an argument from "conspicuous corruption" against the claims of Roman Catholicism.

---

1. Metaxas, *Martin Luther*, 22–23.

2. For a recent discussion, see Abraham, *Soundings*, 55–58; *Systematic Theology*, 231–45.

Before honing in on the argument, however, I want to lay some more groundwork by considering several more concrete cases of papal mischief. I want to make clear that Pope Alexander, while one of the most corrupt popes ever, is far from an anomaly. To the contrary, he represents a pattern that has recurred all too often. To get a sense of this, let us consider several snapshots from the annals of papal history of popes behaving badly. I reiterate that this material is common knowledge among historians, but these particular snapshots are drawn from Eamon Duffy's authoritative work tellingly entitled *Saints and Sinners: A History of the Popes*.[3]

As we examine these snapshots, it is important to emphasize that many of these stories cannot be fully understood without taking into account the broader historical and political factors influencing the papacy at the time. Indeed, the context of many of these cases is a power struggle between popes and emperors and kings over whose authority was greatest. Readers who want the larger story are encouraged to read Duffy's book.

After our quick stroll through the gallery of bad popes, I shall state more precisely just what is the problem raised by these notorious bishops of Rome. Then I shall consider and assess two different strategies to account for bad popes and argue that both of them face serious difficulties.

A GALLERY OF IMPIOUS POPES AND PERVERSE POLITICS

Snapshot One: A Son of a Pope Versus Another Pope

Let us begin with Vigilius (537–555), a classic case of a pope whose unbridled ambition drove him to seek the papacy, and whose story is filled with characteristic political intrigue. Our story takes off with the death of Pope Agapitus, whose papacy lasted only one year (535–536). Vigilius immediately set to work to get himself appointed pope by currying the favor of the wife of the emperor of Constantinople, a sexually-adventurous woman who wielded considerable power. At this time orthodox Chalcedonian Christology was controversial in the east, and was not favored by the emperor's wife, so Vigilius assured her that he would repudiate Chalcedonian Christology. Taking bags of money for a bribe, he rushed to Rome with the dead body of Pope Agapitus, anxious to claim the papacy for himself. But, alas, he was too late, for when he got to Rome, a king, who was a rival to the emperor, had

---

3. Duffy, *Saints and Sinners*. It is worth noting that Duffy is a distinguished Roman Catholic historian, and was a member of the Pontifical Historical Commission. See also Rosa, *Vicars of Christ*.

already appointed a new pope, namely Silverius (536–537), who was the son of another previous pope, Hormisdas (514–523). Undeterred, however, and determined to achieve his goal, he managed to trump up false charges against Silverius, resulting in Silverius's demotion and banishment. With his rival out of the picture, Vigilius was finally elected pope. But the power struggle was not over. A bishop in the town where Silverius was banished took up his defense and persuaded the emperor to bring him back for a fair trial. But, again, Vigilius triumphed, and once more had Silverius arrested and banished, this time to an island, where he died of malnutrition. Summing up this rather convoluted tale, Duffy writes: "To all intents and purposes, one pope, and he the son of a pope, had been deposed and murdered by another."[4]

Snapshot Two: Matronly Mafioso Maneuvers

For hundreds of years, the pope had not only vied for power with the Roman emperor but also had formed an uneasy alliance with him and been protected by him. When the Roman Empire was dissolved, the papacy was left vulnerable. It was not a pretty picture, as Duffy explains.

> Deprived of the support of the empire, the papacy became the possession of the great Roman families, a ticket to local dominance for which men were prepared to rape, murder, and steal. A third of the popes elected between 872 and 1012 died in suspicious circumstances—John VIII (872–82) bludgeoned to death by his own entourage, Stephen VI (896–7) strangled, Leo V (903) murdered by his successor Sergius III (904–11), John X (914–28) suffocated, Stephan VIII (939–42) horribly mutilated.[5]

John X was one of the few popes who tried to resist aristocratic domination, but he was murdered by the Theophylacts, the powerful family who had been his patrons in getting him appointed pope. Duffy fills in the details as follows.

> The key figure in both John X's appointment and his deposition was the notorious Theophylact matron, Marozia. She also appointed Leo VI (928) and Stephen VII (928–31), and she had been the mistress of Pope Sergius III, by whom she bore an

---

4. Duffy, *Saints and Sinners*, 55.
5. Duffy, *Saints and Sinners*, 103–4.

illegitimate son whom she eventually appointed as Pope John XI (931–36).⁶

Snapshot Three: Is This Kid Old Enough to be Pope?

Marozia's son, Alberic II, was the secular ruler of Rome and appointed a number of popes, some of whom were at least decent. His legacy as pope-maker is mixed however, as Duffy explains, because he persuaded the clergy and nobility to make his own son Octavian pope when Agapitus II (946–955) died. "Octavian was duly elected Pope John XII (955–64) at the ripe old age of eighteen. He was to die at the age of twenty-seven, allegedly from a stroke while in bed with a married woman."⁷

Snapshot Four: A Meteoric Rise

Pope John XIX (1024–1032) perhaps wins the prize for the most rapid rise to the top. "He was a typical representative of his age. He had bribed his way to the papacy, and had been elevated from the status of layman to pope in a single day."⁸

Snapshot Five: A Bewildering Number of Ways to Become Pope

The current practice of electing a new pope by the College of Cardinals goes back to the year 1059 when it was decreed that the seven cardinal bishops should choose the pope. This was controversial at first, and the rules remained murky for some time. The number of cardinals who elect the pope has increased over the years. "Popes in the past had been appointed in a bewildering variety of ways—elected by assemblies of clergy and people, hailed by acclamation at the funerals of their predecessors, nominated by local gang-bosses, appointed by emperors."⁹

---

6. Duffy, *Saints and Sinners*, 104.
7. Duffy, *Saints and Sinners*, 105.
8. Duffy, *Saints and Sinners*, 108.
9. Duffy, *Saints and Sinners*, 118.

Snapshot Six: Spiritual Weapons for Political Ends

> From Innocent IV onwards many of the popes forfeited moral credibility by using some of the most solemn spiritual weapons of the reform papacy for purposes which were blatantly political. Innocent, for example, preached "crusade" against Frederick and his successors, and Martin IV (1281–5) and Honorius IV (1285–7) supported as a "crusade" what was blatantly a dynastic war waged by France against the kingdom of Aragon. . . . In the hands of these lesser men the lofty spiritual claims of Gregory VII and Innocent III came increasingly to look like a cloak for cynical political manipulation.[10]

Snapshot Seven: A Pope in Hell

Boniface VIII (1294–1303) achieved a certain literary distinction by being one of the popes that Dante consigned to hell in his monumental poem, *The Divine Comedy*. Boniface was a complex figure who was accused by his critics not only of sodomy but also of being a rank unbeliever who even denied the resurrection. With more than a little irony, Duffy observes: "But whatever Boniface did or did not believe about God, sex, or the afterlife, he believed passionately in the papacy."[11] Believing in the papacy meant believing in supreme papal power, which included power over kings and earthly rulers. King Philip of France was not willing to accede to these claims and had plans of his own to extend the range of his empire. "Boniface was having none of this, and in 1302 he issued the bull Unum Sanctam, the culminating blow in a propaganda war against the French crown. In it the pope notoriously claimed that 'it is altogether necessary for salvation for every human creature to be subject to the Roman pontiff.'"[12]

Snapshot Eight: How Many Popes? One, Two, or Three?

It is a complicated story, but one of the most infamous episodes in the history of the papacy is what is called "the great schism." We can begin the story with the fact that for several reasons, mostly political, the papacy was located for seventy years in Avignon, France. As yet another example

---

10. Duffy, *Saints and Sinners*, 156.
11. Duffy, *Saints and Sinners*, 161.
12. Duffy, *Saints and Sinners*, 162.

of the fact that the popes very much reflected regional interests, all the popes during this period were French. The last of these, Pope Gregory XI (1370–1378), returned to Rome, the historic seat of the papacy. When he died, there was fear that the cardinals, many of whom were now French, would elect another French pope. The citizens in Rome loudly protested this idea, and the cardinals, fearing their wrath, elected an Italian, Pope Urban VI (1378–1389). Unfortunately, he turned out to be violent, domineering, and paranoid. In less than six months, the cardinals who had elected him declared his election invalid, fled Rome, and elected another pope, namely, Clement VII. Clement then returned to Avignon with the cardinals who had elected him, while Urban appointed twenty-nine new cardinals, from all across Europe. "There were now two popes, two papal administrations, two self-contained legal systems. The countries of Europe would have to choose which Pope they would obey."[13]

Cardinals from both sides recognized this to be a problem, and in 1409, a council at Pisa attempted to resolve the matter. They deposed both the Roman pope and the Avignon pope, and they elected a new pope, Alexander V (1409–1410). The two popes who were deposed rejected the authority of the council, so there were now three men who claimed to be pope. The matter was finally resolved later by the Council of Constance. So who was really pope during the great schism?

> Even saints were confused about the rights and wrongs of the situation. St Catherine of Siena supported Urban. St Vincent Ferrar supported Clement. Nations tended to choose their allegiance along dynastic and political lines.... The popes excommunicated each other and placed their rivals' supporters under interdict.
>
> In the long perspective of history, the Roman Catholic Church has accepted that the "real" popes were Urban and his successors elected by his cardinals and their successors. At the time, however, and throughout the thirty-nine years during which the schism persisted, this sort of clarity was hard to come by. Certainly there is no getting around Urban's near insanity, and his brutal treatment of opponents—at one point he had six cardinals under torture, five of whom eventually simply disappeared.[14]

---

13. Duffy, *Saints and Sinners*, 168.
14. Duffy, *Saints and Sinners*, 168–69.

Snapshot Nine: Renaissance Rakes

Renaissance popes are among the most colorful and infamous. Patrons of the arts, they typically lived lavish and extravagant lifestyles. Pope Sixtus IV (1471–1484), for instance, spent 100,000 ducats on his coronation tiara, "more than a third of the papacy's annual income."[15] The most notorious of these Renaissance popes was Roderigo Borgia, who became Alexander VI (1492–1503), as we saw at the beginning of the chapter. It is worth noting that one of his illegitimate children, Cesare Borgia, was the inspiration for Machiavelli's classic book, *The Prince*, in which the author commended various forms of deceit, manipulation, and other immoral means in order to achieve political ends.

Snapshot Ten: A Barely Teenage Cardinal Grows Up to Be Pope

Innocent VIII (1484–92), "having married his son into the Medici family, obligingly made Lorenzo the Magnificent's son Giovanni a cardinal—at the age of thirteen . . . this Cardinal Medici would be elected Pope Leo X. . . . When in 1517 Leo X discovered a plot against him among the cardinals, he executed the ringleader and swamped the Sacred College by creating thirty-one new cardinals in a single day."[16]

HONING IN ON THE PROBLEM

This gallery could be extended considerably, but these ten snapshots are enough to raise the issue I want to discuss.[17] In short, how do we explain the actual history of the papacy with all of its raw ambition, scandal, and sordid corruption? Were all these men chosen by God to occupy the office of pope? What, if anything, does providence have to do with choosing the popes? One might think a great deal, given the singular importance of the papacy according to Rome. Consider these lines from Vatican I, from the First Dogmatic Constitution on the Church of Christ. It was this document that formally defined and affirmed the doctrine of papal infallibility in 1870, as we saw in chapter 1. After stating that the papacy was founded by Christ for the permanent benefit of the church, the document goes on to make the following claims.

---

15. Duffy, *Saints and Sinners*, 185.
16. Duffy, *Saints and Sinners*, 191–92.
17. For more, see Collins and Walls, *Roman but Not Catholic*, 221–43. See also Rosa, cited in note 3 of this chapter.

> Therefore, whoever succeeds to the chair of Peter obtains by the institution of Christ himself, the primacy of Peter over the whole Church. So what the truth has ordained stands firm, and blessed Peter perseveres in the rock-like strength he was granted, and does not abandon that guidance of the Church which he once received.
>
> For this reason it has always been necessary for every Church—that is to say the faithful throughout the world—to be in agreement with the Roman Church because of its more effective leadership.[18]

Notice, Peter's "rock-like strength" is said to reside in his successors and to empower succeeding popes to guide the church. And this is why all faithful Christians should be in agreement with Rome, "because of its more effective leadership."

Now then, consider this conditional statement. Given the strong claims Roman Catholicism makes about the pope, one might find it to be very probable.

> (P): If (A) Peter was indeed given authority over the whole church; if his successors, the bishops of Rome, have the same authority; if God has providentially preserved an unbroken succession from Peter to the present; if the pope is the supreme pastor of the church, the vicar of Christ, and he has the singular role of preserving the church from error and preserving unity; then (B) it is reasonable to expect that all popes would meet the basic New Testament standard for bishops, or at the very least be persons of sincere faith in Christ, and basic moral integrity.

I emphasize that this is a very minimal standard. If the New Testament criteria for bishops is too high a standard for the bishop who has jurisdiction over all bishops, then perhaps the slightly less stringent standards for deacons might be expected (1 Tim 3:8–13). The standard is not perfection. These men might have various flaws, blind spots, and weaknesses. They might have some embarrassing sins in their past. But still, a sincere faith in Christ and the gospel and some discernible evidence of sanctification should be expected.

The sad truth, of course, is that several of the popes have not lived up to even these modest expectations. And this poses a problem for anyone who is inclined to judge this conditional statement to be true. That is, if one is inclined to think (B) is to be expected given (A), then the fact that (B) is

---

18. "First Vatican Council" 4.2.

not true makes (A) highly improbable. Roman Catholics have little option but to deny (P). That is, since (A) is essential to their faith, they will want to deny that (B) is to be expected, given (A).[19]

A COUPLE OR SO OBJECTIONS

It might be objected that even such modest standards should not be expected if we consider a biblical example, namely the actual history of the kings of Israel and Judah. While some of those kings were godly men who led with integrity, many others fell far short of this ideal. Moreover, consider that some of the authors of the Bible, such as Moses and David, committed some egregious sins, including adultery and even murder. In the light of this history, we should hardly be surprised at the unsavory history of the papacy.

While this objection might have a certain initial plausibility, it is not convincing for at least three reasons. First, the Old Testament monarchy was instituted at least partly due to a rejection of God as King, a concession to Israel's preference for an earthly king, so they could be like other nations. A major lesson to be learned from the story is the inevitable failure that results when God's leadership is rejected. The bigger lesson yet is our need for Christ, David's greater Son.

Second, the Old Testament monarchy was a genetic dynasty, in contrast to the papacy, which is a charismatically chosen succession of bishops. Again, the Roman Catholic claim is that God has providentially assured an unbroken succession, beginning with Peter, to the present. God, through the Holy Spirit, provided guidance in the choice of the popes. So, the better comparison is not between the Old Testament kings and the papacy, but between the Old Testament prophets and the papacy. When we consider the Old Testament prophets, all of them who are recognized as true prophets were indeed men of basic moral integrity and genuine love for God, even prophets like Jonah, who were less than perfect in reflecting God's love and grace. If all the prophets that God called were men of integrity and true faith, it hardly seems too much to think all of the "chief shepherds" of the church would meet the modest standards of our conditional statement. The papacy, after all, has the advantage not only of the coming of Christ but also the resources of Pentecost. So much more should be expected of the papacy than Old Testament kings, whose history is marked by greed, treachery, political intrigue, and lust for power.

---

19. For a more formal version of this argument, see Collins and Walls, *Roman but Not Catholic*, 251–55.

Third, as for the fact that some of the authors of the Bible committed serious sins, including murder, we should note that they repented of those sins. There is all the difference in the world between sinners who are sincere lovers of God and who repent of their sins and charlatans who show no evidence of genuine faith and love of God. Moses and David were both lovers of God whose sins should be viewed in light of the larger story of their lives.

Another objection might come from a different direction. It might be suggested that this argument proves too much. Given this argument, perhaps we should expect *all* clergymen to be persons of basic moral integrity and a sincere faith in Christ. While initially plausible, this is unrealistic, and indeed the New Testament contains warnings that would hardly lead us to expect this. When Paul spoke to the Ephesian elders, he emphasized that part of their role as overseers and shepherds of the church was to guard against false teachers. "I know that after I leave, savage wolves will come in among you and will not spare the flock. Even from your own number men will arise and distort the truth in order to draw disciples after them" (Acts 20:29–30).

Given the reality of sin and imperfect human discernment, it is not surprising that ambitious and dubiously motivated persons should sometimes enter the ranks of the clergy or that some would be corrupted. But it is another matter to think that the "chief shepherd" who is uniquely chosen to lead the church, who represents a providentially guaranteed succession beginning with Peter, should be as vulnerable and given to corruption as the history of the papacy shows it has been.

A third objection I have heard is that we should not be surprised by bad popes since one of the apostles Jesus chose ended up betraying him. If Jesus chose Judas, bad popes are only par for the course. I find this a curious argument. Judas played a unique role in the narrative of Jesus' crucifixion and the sense in which that was providential is something of a mystery. But in any case, the pope is supposed to be the successor of Peter, not just any of the apostles, and certainly not Judas. It is Peter's "rock-like strength" that is supposed to be embodied in subsequent bishops of Rome, not the treachery of Judas.

Finally, another sort of objection has been offered by Tyler McNabb. He points out that the larger church has its own share of failings and argues that we should be no more surprised at the moral failures of the papacy than we are at the failures of the church at large. In particular, he points to the sad phenomenon of anti-Semitism that we have seen all too often in the history of the church. He suggests that if what he calls the "Pestilence of Popes Problem" is a major concern for Catholics, then there is an equally big problem for orthodox Christians in general in this history of anti-Semitism, which he calls the "Church Pestilence Problem." There is, he notes, a parallel between these problems.

> Both arguments are motivated by the intuition that if the hypothesis in question were true, there would be better moral behavior from the relevant religious practitioners. In the case of Catholicism, we would expect the Vicar of Christ to be a morally decent human being. And in the case of the hypothesis that Jesus is the Jewish messiah, we would expect the advent of Jesus to lead to an end of anti-Semitism, not a great expansion of it by Jesus' own followers.[20]

As McNabb sees it then, the ugly history of anti-Semitism in the church is just as surprising as the history of corruption in the papacy. So, we should not appeal to the corruption in the papacy as an argument against the claims of Rome unless we are prepared to grant that the history of anti-Semitism counts equally against the claims of the church.

McNabb's argument is clever but not convincing. First, it is worth noting that the advent of Jesus has in fact led to a repudiation of anti-Semitism by the church. To be sure, this did not happen immediately, and there are shameful instances of anti-Semitism in the history of the church. But the Holocaust was the pivotal event that clarified this once and for all, and in its aftermath the church has been firmly united in rejecting it.

But here is where I think McNabb's response is most mistaken. There is a radical difference between being sincerely Christian, but flawed at various points, and being an out and out charlatan. The church has been, and still is, an imperfect witness to Christ and the gospel. Many of the figures in church history, from Bernard of Clairvaux to Martin Luther, had blind spots in their reprehensible attitude toward the Jews. But it is possible to have various blind spots and still be a sincere believer in Christ who is on the way to sanctification. By contrast, a number of popes have been charlatans who showed no evidence whatever of sincere faith or sanctification. It is the reality of such charlatans in the history of the papacy that undermines the claims Rome wants to advance for the papacy.

I maintain, then, that the conditional statement above is highly probable. At the same time, I readily grant that those who disagree, untroubled by the history of papal corruption, will likely be unmoved by my argument. So let's proceed.

---

20. McNabb, "Pestilent Popes," 4.

A MORE RECENT EXAMPLE THAT POSES THE PROBLEM

Recall Duffy's observation above that popes have been "appointed in a bewildering variety of ways." Still, if all of these popes have been successors of Peter, if they are part of the unbroken chain of succession from Peter to the present, it is natural to assume they were all providentially chosen in some sense. Here it is worth emphasizing that more recently popes have been chosen in a more orderly fashion. Here is Duffy's account of some of the procedures in the election of popes.

> In preparation for the enclave the cardinals are addressed by two preachers, chosen for their orthodoxy and wisdom, who reflect on the church's needs and the considerations which the cardinals should bear in mind in making their choice. The conclave begins with a solemn mass invoking the aid of the Holy Spirit in St Peters, and takes place within the Sistine Chapel within the Vatican palace itself, into which the cardinals process while a hymn to the Holy Spirit is sung.[21]

Duffy goes on to observe that for over eight hundred years, the normal method of choosing a pope has been by secret ballot. The following is a description of a particularly significant part of the voting process.

> Taking the folded form [the voting ballot] between thumb and index finger of the right hand, the cardinals then approach the altar of the Sistine Chapel in order of seniority, each one announcing in a clear voice "I call as my witness Christ the Lord who will be my judge, that my vote is given to the one whom, before God, I think ought to be elected."[22]

Given that the men who make this declaration are indeed outstanding men of God and given their sincerity in their invocation of the aid of the Holy Spirit in the whole process, one should be inclined to have great confidence in the outcome and its providential direction.

Now let us consider a much more recent example that illustrates the problem I have been focusing on in this section. I refer to the pope who is in office as I write, namely, Pope Francis. The current pope has many admirers, to be sure, but he has also come increasingly under fire the past several years, especially from conservatives. The following lines come from

---

21. Duffy, *Saints and Sinners*, 452.
22. Duffy, *Saints and Sinners*, 453.

an article by R. R. Reno, the editor of the conservative journal *First Things*. The article is tellingly entitled "A Failing Papacy."

> The current regime in Rome will damage the Catholic Church. Pope Francis combines laxity and ruthlessness. His style is casual and approachable; his church politics are cold and cunning. There are leading themes in this pontificate—mercy, accompaniment, peripheries, and so forth—but no theological framework.... This has created a confusing, even dysfunctional atmosphere that will become intolerable, if it hasn't already....
>
> The tendency of this pope is to undermine the Church's most loyal servants. This is surely galling. His lack of interest in theology—in ideas generally—reduces his pontificate to the raw exercise of ecclesiastical power....
>
> Pope Francis seems to regard the uncertainty and instability as desirable....
>
> I have the impression that the majority of the cardinals and other churchmen in positions of responsibility are increasingly aware the Francis pontificate is a failure.[23]

As scathing as this criticism is, it is not only fairly typical of the sort of criticism leveled against Francis, in some ways it is even mild, comparatively speaking.

In particular, Francis has been criticized for undermining traditional Roman Catholic theology in the controversial encyclical *Amoris Laetitia*, among other things. Many see that document as compromising Roman Catholic theology on divorce and remarriage, homosexuality, and other moral issues in a way that threatens to completely unravel traditional Catholic moral teaching.[24] He has been sharply attacked for covering up the extensive sexual abuse in the ranks of the clergy, including bishops and cardinals. Among his critics on this matter is Archbishop Vigano, who has accused the pope of lying and has even called for his resignation.[25] Indeed, some theologians and clergy more recently have gone so far as to accuse him of heresy.[26] And recently, his predecessor, Pope Benedict XVI issued a letter on sexual abuse that was perceived as a corrective to Francis.[27] All of

---

23. Reno, "Failing Papacy."
24. Last, "Catholic Church Is Breaking Apart."
25. Harlan and Pitrelli, "He Called on the Pope."
26. Weinandy, "Is Pope Francis."
27. Harlan and Pitrelli, "Ex-Pope Benedict."

this has contributed to the "confusing, even dysfunctional atmosphere" that Reno laments in his article.[28]

More recently controversy has surrounded the Vatican declaration *Fiducia Supplicans*, which also deals with issues of sexuality.[29] In particular, the document has come under fire because it affirms that priestly blessings can be extended not only to same-sex couples but also to those who are in "irregular relationships" because they are divorced and remarried and thus, according to Rome, living in adultery. The document states that "one who asks for a blessing show [sic] himself to be in need of God's saving presence in his life and one who asks for a blessing from the Church recognizes the latter as a sacrament of the salvation that God offers."[30] It goes on to urge a "more pastoral approach to blessings" as has been exemplified by Pope Francis. Such an approach is one "considered outside of a liturgical framework" where "these expressions of faith are found in a realm of greater spontaneity and freedom."[31]

It is important to emphasize that the document clearly insists on a traditional view of marriage. However, given this "greater spontaneity and freedom," it also offers the following rationale for blessing those engaged in homosexual relationships as well as "irregular" heterosexual relationships.

> Within the horizon outlined here appears the possibility of blessings for couples in irregular situations and for couples of the same sex. . . . In such cases, a blessing may be imparted that not only has an ascending value but also involves the invocation of a blessing that descends from God upon those who—recognizing themselves to be destitute and in need of his help—do not claim a legitimation of their own status, but who beg that all that is true, good, and humanly valid in their lives and their relationships be enriched, healed, and elevated by the presence of the Holy Spirit.[32]

The controversy pertains to what is implicit in the document and where it will almost certainly lead. In particular, Catholics on both the right and the left agree that it will influence their church to become more tolerant and accepting of homosexual practice. The noted gay activist Fr. James

---

28. I also discuss this encyclical below in chapter 10.

29. "Declarations" are more substantial and therefore more authoritative than more narrowly focused documents such as a "responsum," which responds to a specific question.

30. Francis, "*Fiducia Supplicans*" 2.20.

31. Francis, "*Fiducia Supplicans*" 2.23.

32. Francis, "*Fiducia Supplicans*" 3.31.

Martin, for instance, has observed that some will try to pretend that nothing significant has really happened in the release of this document. But the day after the declaration, Martin underscored the nature of the shift that had just occurred. "The change here is that these blessings are now officially sanctioned by the Vatican. Today with some limitations, I can perform a public blessing of a same-sex couple. Yesterday, I could not."[33]

On the other end of the spectrum, *First Things* is again a good representative. In an interview with Fr. Gerald E. Murray, he excoriated the document throughout. He then bluntly concluded that *Fiducia Supplicans* "is a manifest disaster that should be revoked and withdrawn by the Holy See. Until that happens, it should be ignored by all bishops, priests, and deacons."[34]

All of this poses an acute problem not only for "cradle Catholics," but perhaps especially for Roman Catholic converts. Indeed, many converts have gone to Roman Catholicism thinking that the Roman authority structure, headed by the pope, would provide security against the confusing conflict and divisions they encountered in Protestantism. And now the controversy and division surrounding Pope Francis may seem as bad, or even worse, than what they experienced as Protestants. Leonardo De Chirico puts the quandary raised by Reno's article as follows.

> In reading this trenchant critique, one cannot help but think: How can a Catholic author write this and still affirm Francis as the Pope? How can a conservative Catholic who has said for decades that Roman Catholicism is unique and necessary because of the authoritative voice of the Pope now criticize what the Pope is teaching and doing? Isn't there a contradiction?[35]

All this criticism of Pope Francis raises another puzzle, as Jeff Mirus frankly observes: "A common question among Catholics today is: 'What was the Holy Spirit doing during the enclave that elected Jorge Bergoglio as Pope Francis?'"[36] Conservative Catholics cannot help but wonder.

Mirus has an answer to that question as we shall see. In the next two sections we shall examine his answer as well as another option Roman Catholics might embrace in response to this troubling question.

---

33. Martin, "Pope Francis' Same-Sex."
34. Murray and Montagna, "*Fiducia Supplicans* Should Be Revoked."
35. Chirico, "'Confusion' and 'Failure.'"
36. Mirus, "On the Role."

THE WEAKER PROVIDENCE VIEW

I call this view the weaker providence view because it makes very few guarantees and emphasizes the limits of God's control over papal selection. Mirus offers this response to the question he says many Catholics today are asking:

> The answer, of course, is that the Holy Spirit was doing what He is always doing, prompting all involved to cast their votes for the good of the Church, just as He has prompted all involved to form a proper understanding of the good of the Church. But the Holy Spirit does not choose the pope; that is left to the vagaries of men, and the vagaries of their response to grace.
>
> In other words, the Holy Spirit does not arrange the votes so that the best possible candidate is elected.... To put the matter succinctly, the promptings of the Holy Spirit are as certainly real as they are frequently resisted.[37]

In a nod to the obvious corruption that has frequently marred the history of the papacy, Mirus acknowledges that the Holy Spirit does not prevent the electors of the pope "from succumbing to other influences: Ignorance, falsehood, personal partiality, ill-conceived goals, and temptations of every kind, including those that are political and financial."

Mirus does not cite any official documents in support of this view, so I don't know whether it is official Roman Catholic orthodoxy, but at the least it is a popular view. Indeed, Pope Benedict affirmed a similar view when he was Cardinal Ratzinger. He said the following in 1997 when he was asked by a Bavarian television station whether the Holy Spirit chooses the pope.

> I would not say so, in the sense that the Holy Spirit picks out the pope.... I would say that the Spirit does not exactly take control of the affair, but rather, like a good educator, as it were, leaves us much space, much freedom, without entirely abandoning us. Thus, the Spirit's role should be understood in a much more elastic sense, not that he dictates the candidate for whom one must vote. Probably the only assurance he offers is that the thing cannot be totally ruined.... There are too many contrary instances of popes the Holy Spirit obviously would not have picked![38]

---

37. Mirus, "On the Role."
38. Ratzinger quoted in Martin, "Does the Holy Spirit," para. 3.

Ratzinger's final line here is telling. Any account of the how the Holy Spirit is involved in papal elections must come to terms with the *actual history* of the papacy, and the many bad actors who have occupied the office of the pope.

The main strength of the weaker providence view is that it can more plausibly explain the many "instances of popes the Holy Spirit obviously would not have chosen." So long as the Holy Spirit does nothing more definitive than acting like a good educator who leaves much room for freedom; who prompts, but finally leaves, the choice to the "vagaries of men, and the vagaries of their response to grace," we should not be surprised if "the best possible candidate" is not elected. Indeed, we may wonder if he is ever elected!

In short, we have here a sort of "freewill theodicy" for the papacy. In other words, Roman Catholics have a distinctive variation of the classic problem of evil due to bad popes, and to solve this problem they appeal to human free will. Bad popes and failing papacies are entirely due to the fact that papal elections are done by free agents, and they may follow the promptings of ignorance, partiality, and other temptations rather than the prompting of the Holy Spirit.

While this appeal to free will may easily explain why the "best possible candidate" is not always, if ever, chosen, it does not so easily explain why so many "obviously" bad candidates have been chosen. Not a few of the popes have been so egregiously bad that it is hard to see how they could have been chosen without altogether discrediting the larger system that elected them. It would not take much spiritual discernment or even sincere faith in Christ and love for the church to see that openly immoral, transparently greedy, and unscrupulous men should not have any sort of position of church leadership, let alone that of supreme pastor and vicar of Christ. Blatantly bad popes, then, are an indictment of any church that would choose them for such a position of leadership. Any church that would choose Roderigo Borgia to lead it would have to be either utterly lacking in discernment or thoroughly corrupt.

The larger problem here is that it creates confusion and uncertainty about which popes should be trusted and followed. If there is no guarantee that the Holy Spirit providentially guides the selection of popes, at least in the minimal sense that a qualified man is chosen, how are faithful Roman Catholics to know whom to believe? Some popes have been clearly good and some have been notoriously bad, but other cases are much more ambiguous. Is there a clear criterion for sorting out the good and the bad popes? If there is, what is it? What is the advantage of having a supreme pastor if he may not be God's choice, may set a grievously bad example by his own conduct, may seriously damage the church, and may turn out to have led a failed papacy?

Consider again Pope Francis. Whom should the faithful believe? The pope and his supporters or *First Things* magazine, Archbishop Vigano, and others who have labeled him a heretic? Should they look to Francis for guidance or to the cardinals who have openly criticized him? Or should they look to his predecessor? Consider Roman Catholic theologian Bryan Flanagan's observation about Pope Benedict's letter addressing sexual abuse: "It's not good for the church to have two voices. If this is seen as Benedict attempting to give more context for his decisions, maybe this can be a helpful way to understand his mind-set. But this raises the specter of his voice being seen as an alternative to the papacy of Pope Francis. And that is bad for the unity of the church."[39]

When these sorts of questions are raised, Roman Catholics often respond by retreating to making very modest claims about the papacy. By sharp contrast, when they are making claims for the authority of the pope, the vital nature of his office, and how his authority underwrites the claims of Rome to be the one true church, they make very exalted claims. Consider the following.

> The *Pope*, Bishop of Rome and Peter's successor, "is the perpetual and visible source and foundation of the unity both of the bishops and the whole company of the faithful." "For the Roman Pontiff, by reason of his office as Vicar of Christ, and as pastor of the entire Church, has full, supreme, and universal power over the whole Church, a power which he can always exercise unhindered."[40]

But again, when we talk about historical reality and the numerous holders of the office who have made a mockery of these exalted claims, Roman Catholics remind us that there are actually very few guarantees with the papacy. Recall Pope Benedict's claim when he was still Cardinal Ratzinger: "Probably the only assurance he offers is that the thing cannot be totally ruined." To put it mildly, there is quite a step down from the exalted claims to the actual assurances. But notice also that Ratzinger's claim is quite general. He does not define more specifically what would count as the papacy being "totally ruined." Having scoundrels appointed pope who make a mockery of the office apparently does not totally ruin it. Having two or even three competing popes and generating enormous controversy and confusion all across the church over who is the actual pope does not totally ruin it. So, what would totally ruin it?

---

39. Harlan and Pitrelli, "Ex-Pope Benedict."
40. *Catechism*, para. 882. The quotation is from *Lumen Gentium* 23, 22.

Indeed, when we press for specifics, perhaps the only guarantee is that the pope will not err when he speaks *ex cathedra* about morals or doctrine. Consider this official account of infallibility in the light of our previous discussion. After stating that infallibility extends only as far as divine revelation, we read the following.

> This is the infallibility which the Roman Pontiff, the head of the college of bishops, enjoys in virtue of his office, when, as the supreme shepherd and teacher of the faithful, who confirms his brethren in their faith (cf. Luke 22:32), he proclaims by a definitive act some doctrine of faith or morals. Therefore, his definitions, of themselves, and not from the consent of the Church, are justly styled irreformable, for they are pronounced with the assistance of the Holy Spirit, an assistance promised to him in blessed Peter.[41]

Now this raises obvious questions. How is this "assistance of the Holy Spirit" different from the assistance of the Holy Spirit in papal elections? If the promptings of the Holy Spirit may be ignored and resisted in favor of more carnal consideration in papal elections, then why cannot the assistance of the Holy Spirit be ignored or resisted in *ex cathedra* proclamations? Does God override freedom to preserve infallibility if necessary? If so, then why not do so in the case of disastrous papal elections? After all, cannot bad popes lead their followers into serious error and moral confusion even if they are preserved from error in *ex cathedra* pronouncements? Is God primarily concerned with official doctrinal proclamations but less so with moral integrity?

THE STRONGER PROVIDENCE VIEW

These questions, at least some of them, have been given an ingenious answer by Thomas Flint, who appeals to Molinism to resolve them. In short, Flint's aim is to explain how papal infallibility is perfectly compatible with papal freedom.

Molinism, of course, is named after the sixteenth-century philosopher Luis de Molina, whose famous theory of providence hinges crucially on the idea of "middle knowledge." Middle knowledge, roughly speaking, is God's knowledge of what all possible persons would freely do in all possible circumstances and states of affair. The knowledge applies not only to actual persons but also to persons who will never exist and to circumstances and

---

41. Cited by Flint, *Divine Providence*, 181–82.

states of affairs that will never actually exist. For instance, suppose I had followed Alexander VI's example and had numerous children by numerous women. God knows, say, what my sixth son would have chosen for dinner for his eighteenth birthday. More interestingly, he also knows what he would have done with respect to all the morally significant choices he would have made. Molina's basic theory is that God providentially governs the world by drawing on his middle knowledge and creating people in circumstances in which they will freely choose as he prefers.

Before giving us his Molinist solution, it is worth noting that Flint acknowledges another way to maintain both papal freedom and infallibility, namely, by affirming the compatibilist account of human freedom, according to which freedom and determinism are compatible. If one affirms compatibilism, one can preserve infallibility by saying God determines and completely controls what the pope will pronounce *ex cathedra* and thereby preserves it from error.

Flint wants to preserve a stronger, libertarian account of freedom, however, and he thinks Molinism points the way. The essence of his proposal is captured in the following lengthy quote:

> It is here the concept of middle knowledge seems to come to the rescue. For if God has middle knowledge, why can't he arrange things in such a way that the pope always freely follows his guidance? How, one might ask, can he do so? By seeing to it that the *right* person *becomes* pope. If God has middle knowledge, then he knows how any candidate for the office would act—would *freely* act—if elected pope. Using this knowledge, God would then direct the cardinals to select as pope one of those men who God knows would freely cooperate with his guidance and thereby safeguard the church from error; he would also lead them away from selecting any of those men who he knows would not freely cooperate with his guidance and consequently lead the church into error. By then guiding the man selected in the ways that, as his middle knowledge tells him, will elicit a free but positive response from him, God can insure that the pope is infallible even though he respects his freedom. This respect for human freedom would presumably extend to the cardinals as well. God's direction of them toward certain candidates and away from others would most likely be accomplished, not by God's determining their actions, but by his arrangement of circumstances which he knows via middle knowledge will lead to the result he desires.[42]

---

42. Flint, *Divine Providence*, 184–85.

Flint gives us a concrete example to make all this more clear. Suppose, he says, that the two leading papal candidates are Cardinal Elfreth and Cardinal Filbert. Moreover, suppose the vote will be heavily influenced by the support of the elderly and highly respected Cardinal Rotundo. Finally, suppose that God knows by way of middle knowledge the following two propositions.

- A. If Elfreth were elected pope at time t in a world with history h, he would freely follow divine guidance and keep the Church safe from error.
- B. If Filbert were elected pope at time t in a world with history h, he would freely reject divine guidance and proclaim *ex cathedra* a falsehood.[43]

The story proceeds as follows. While Rotundo is praying and seeking the guidance of the Holy Spirit, God causes him to dwell on the many virtues of Elfreth. This causes him, as God knew by middle knowledge would surely happen, to come freely to the settled conclusion that Elfreth would make the better pope. "Acting on this conviction, Rotundo enthusiastically throws his considerable weight behind Elfreth. As a result, Elfreth is indeed elected and the Church is saved from the errors that Filbert would have proclaimed."[44]

The whole idea of middle knowledge is deeply controversial, of course, but has been ably defended by Flint and other proponents of Molinism. For our purposes, let us assume middle knowledge is possible and Molinism is a coherent account of providence. My concern is to assess whether Molinism provides help with the problem of bad popes.

In the first place, I am inclined to think Molinism does indeed provide a persuasive account of how popes could be fully free in the libertarian sense, and yet infallible in the restricted way Roman Catholic theology teaches. The scenario Flint describes for us clearly shows how this could happen. Matters are perhaps simplified by the fact that clear and uncontroversial examples of the pope speaking *ex cathedra* are relatively rare. The only such cases are the two dogmas of Mary's immaculate conception and bodily assumption.

Of course, the doctrine of infallibility assumes these doctrines are true, a claim that is itself controversial. Most Protestants reject these dogmas, and the Orthodox Church denies the immaculate conception, at least as Rome teaches it. So for many Christians, the doctrine of papal infallibility has in fact been shown to be false by these two times the pope has spoken *ex cathedra*. But leaving that aside, Flint's Molinist scenario shows how, in

---

43. Flint, *Divine Providence*, 185.
44. Flint, *Divine Providence*, 185.

principle, infallibility is compatible with libertarian freedom, and the one clear guarantee of papal theology could be true.

However, while Molinism shows, in principle, how infallibility is compatible with libertarian freedom, it may raise more questions than it answers. In particular, we might be more than a little curious to know how the Molinist accounts for the bad popes. Recall the heart of Flint's answer to the question of how God can use his middle knowledge to arrange things so the pope always freely follows his guidance and avoids error: "By seeing to it that the *right* person *becomes* pope." Moreover, he applies the same essential claims to the cardinals who select the pope. "God's direction of them toward certain candidates and away from others would most likely be accomplished, not by God's determining their actions, but by his arrangement of circumstances which he knows via middle knowledge will lead to the result he desires."[45]

So here is the question clamoring for an answer: Are we to believe that all the popes, including the notoriously bad ones, were the right person to become pope? Did God arrange things through his middle knowledge and providential direction so that each of these men would be appointed pope through the free choices of those who chose them? Is Ratzinger mistaken in thinking it obvious that the Holy Spirit would not have chosen some of the popes who have been picked? Or have all the popes in fact been picked by the Holy Spirit, in something like the way Elfreth was picked in Flint's scenario, contrary to what we might think?

An ingenious Molinist is not without possible replies. One possible move he might make is to suggest that, unfortunately, there were no better candidates available to be selected pope when the various bad popes were chosen. Perhaps the harsh reality is that God was faced with a situation in which all the viable candidates for pope were depraved, and the one chosen was actually the best one available at the time.[46] So when Octavian was made Pope John XII at the age of eighteen, for instance, there was simply no better choice at the time for the papal office. I must say I find this suggestion wildly implausible. Surely out of all possible candidates there were better choices to be made. However, we must concede to the determined Molinist that it is at least possible that no better choice was to be had, however improbable that may be.

Another variation on this suggestion, inspired once again by the theodicy literature, is to suggest that we are simply not in any position to

---

45. Flint, *Divine Providence*, 185.

46. Those familiar with theodicy literature will recognize a parallel with the idea of "transworld depravity." We might call this "trans-papal depravity."

judge what providential reasons God may have for picking some of the popes he has. The theodicy parallel is "skeptical theism," the view that finite human beings cannot possibly understand the reasons God may have for permitting the terrible evils that he does. There may be goods we cannot conceive and connections between terrible evils and these goods that we cannot begin to fathom. Similarly, the "skeptical papist" may say that there may be providential purposes for choosing the bad popes that we cannot begin to imagine or understand. While there may have been any number of papal candidates who were spiritually and morally much more suited to the papacy than Roderigo Borgia was, God may have had reasons entirely beyond our comprehension for arranging things so that he was elected Pope Alexander VI.

Once again, I find this suggestion highly implausible, even though it may still be possible in the strict sense of the word. It is worth noting, however, that Protestants might find it plausible for their own reasons. More specifically, Protestants might think the bad popes play the providential role of exposing the falsity of Roman Catholic papal theology. The numerous bad popes are a vivid demonstration that the pope is not the vicar of Christ or the supreme pastor of the church. These popes demonstrate just how hollow are the claims of Vatican I, such as this one, cited above: "For this reason it has always been necessary for every Church—that is to say the faithful throughout the world—to be in agreement with the Roman Church because of its more effective leadership."

It is very much worth remembering that when Roderigo Borgia was chosen to be Pope Alexander VI that Martin Luther was a teenager. In view of this we might suggest that the providential purpose of the bad popes was to inspire the Protestant Reformation.

SUMMING UP THE PAPAL PROBLEMS

I conclude that the argument from "conspicuous corruption" has considerable force, and the problem of bad popes is a serious one for Roman Catholicism. While there are possible moves to make to mitigate the problem, I find them highly implausible, whether of the weaker or stronger providence view.

Indeed, I judge the reality of bad popes and the numerous instances of conspicuous corruption to be much better explained on the assumption that the Roman Catholic view of the papacy is merely human, all too human, in its ultimate origins. The papacy, marred as it has often been by greed, violence, and the quest for power and pleasure is perfectly explicable in terms of merely human, even sinful, desires and aspirations. Given this reality, the actual history of the papacy is only to be expected.

But these conspicuously corrupt popes provide a very good reason to doubt the Roman claims about the papacy, and indeed, another good reason not to be a Roman Catholic. It is worth noting here that the argument of this chapter complements the argument of the previous two and compounds the problems for Roman Catholicism. Here is the connection. Roman apologists often dismiss the problem of bad popes by insisting that the authority of the pope resides solely in his role as the latest successor in the unbroken line of bishops of Rome that goes back to the apostle Peter. As we have seen, that claim lacks historical credibility and is therefore a frail reed indeed to ward off the problems posed by bad popes. Taken together, these chapters provide powerful reasons not to be a Roman Catholic.

CHAPTER FOUR

CARDINAL CONFUSIONS

Here is an interesting and telling irony that exposes some of the deepest rifts that divide Protestants and Roman Catholics. On the one side, Protestants often argue, from their Protestant assumptions, that many of the claims of Roman Catholicism are false because they lack sufficient scriptural support. Scripture is the ultimate source for doctrine, and no doctrine is required to be believed if it lacks adequate biblical warrant. On the other side, Roman Catholics often argue from their basic assumptions that Protestants have no rational grounds to appeal to the authority of scripture if they reject the claims of the Roman Catholic Church.

Indeed, it is even worse for Protestants, the argument goes, for their position is hopelessly inconsistent, because their view lacks objective authority and reduces to subjective individualism. For the church, it is contended, gave us the Bible, so Protestants cannot consistently appeal to the authority of scripture without acknowledging the prior authority of the church. Consider these lines from Peter Kreeft, a former Evangelical, who is now a Roman Catholic:

> If Scripture is infallible, as traditional Protestants believe, then the Church must be infallible too, for a fallible cause cannot produce an infallible effect, and the Church produced the Bible. The Church (apostles and saints) wrote the New Testament, and the Church (subsequent bishops) defined its canon.[1]

This argument is confused at a number of levels, but for now, I simply want to highlight the claim that "a fallible cause cannot produce an infallible effect." Suppose this is true. Does it follow that an infallible cause cannot employ a fallible instrument to produce an infallible effect? Cannot God, as an

---

1. Kreeft cited by Allison, *Roman Catholic Theology*, 95n62.

infallible cause, inspire and direct fallible human beings to infallibly convey his truth? Does Paul need to be infallible for God to use him to write, say, epistles that have infallible authority to teach doctrinal and moral truth? It seems clear that Paul need not be infallible for an infallible God to inspire him in this fashion.[2]

Similar claims to those made about the Bible are made about the classic creeds. Protestants who reject the claims of the Roman Catholic Church, it may be argued, have no principled reason to insist the Nicene Creed is correct or to appeal to its authority to fend off heretical claims about Christ.

This basic line of argument is often employed to unsettle Evangelicals and other Protestants and to pressure them to convert to Rome. On one level, it is not surprising that these lines of argument are so effective with many such believers. After all, Evangelicals love scripture and their faith in Christ is the very heart of what gives meaning and direction to their lives. If they become convinced that the only way they can preserve their faith in Christ and the authority of the Bible is by going to Rome, well, they will go to Rome.

But while the appeal of this line of argument, not least its emotional appeal, is undeniable in a number of ways, its rational credentials are another matter altogether. In this chapter and the next, I want to argue that Reformation Christians can heartily affirm the authority of the Bible and the classic creeds with full intellectual integrity while rejecting the claims of the Roman magisterium.

ALL OR NOTHING?

So let us begin to explore the grounds of the Roman Catholic position by looking again at this passage (cited in an earlier chapter) from the *Catechism of the Catholic Church*, which spells out the Roman Catholic claims about the magisterium and its teaching authority.

> "The task of giving an authentic interpretation of the Word of God, whether in its written form or in the form of Tradition, has been entrusted to the living teaching office of the Church alone. Its authority in this matter is exercised in the name of Jesus Christ." This means that the task of interpretation has been entrusted to the bishops in communion with the successor of Peter, the Bishop of Rome.[3]

---

2. As Allison notes, no one ever claimed that Israel had to be infallible to produce the Old Testament scriptures. See Allison, *Roman Catholic Theology*, 95n62.

3. *Catechism*, para. 85. The sentences quoted in this paragraph come from Paul VI, "*Dei Verbum*," para. 10.

The first thing I particularly want to underscore at this point is that the magisterium is identified with "bishops in communion with the successor of Peter, the Bishop of Rome." So this clearly gives distinctive, if not exclusive, interpretive authority to the pope and those bishops in communion with him. The magisterium *alone* has the task of "giving authentic interpretation of the Word of God."

Consider now this passage, also cited in an earlier chapter. This passage is particularly significant for our concerns as it encapsulates the issues we shall consider in this chapter and the next:

> It is clear therefore that, in the supremely wise arrangement of God, sacred Tradition, Sacred Scripture, and the Magisterium of the Church are so connected and associated that one of them cannot stand without the others. Working together, each in its own way, under the action of the one Holy Spirit, they all contribute effectively to the salvation of souls.[4]

A few things are worth noting here. First, notice the claim that one of these three factors—namely, sacred tradition, sacred scripture, and the magisterium—"cannot stand without the others." Now it is worth asking whether this also means that no two of them can stand without the third. That is not explicitly stated, but it appears to be the claim.

Second, note the claim that these three factors, working under the direction of the Holy Spirit, "all contribute effectively to the salvation of souls." So the ultimate aim is eternal salvation, not merely intellectual curiosity. However, we should not in any way draw a contrast between justified dogmatic belief and the salvation of our souls. Indeed, dogmatic belief is essential to our spiritual formation and final salvation.

> There is an organic connection between our spiritual life and the dogmas. Dogmas are lights along the path of faith; they illuminate it and make it secure. Conversely, if our life is upright, our intellect and heart will be open to welcome the light shed by the dogmas of faith.[5]

Clearly, then, there is a lot at stake in the matter of discerning "authentic interpretation of the Word of God" and the dogmas that should bind our minds and hearts.

So here is the important claim we want to examine, namely, that there is some sort of necessary connection or linkage between scripture, tradition, and the Roman Catholic magisterium. Consequently, anyone who wants to

---

4. *Catechism*, para. 95.
5. *Catechism*, para. 89.

affirm any one of them must also affirm the other two, or anyone who affirms any two must also affirm the third. Let's call this "the all or nothing argument." That is, if you don't affirm all three, you get none. Clearly, this claim is a frontal challenge to Christians in other traditions who do not acknowledge the authority of the Roman magisterium and the claims of papal authority. To consider and assess this claim, we need to get clear on just what is meant by the claim that no one or two of these factors can "stand without the others."

Just what is involved in failing to stand? Are these three factors like the legs of a three-legged stool, so that if any one of them is removed, the stool cannot stand even for a moment, let alone bear any weight?[6] Is the claim that anyone who attempts to maintain or rationally accept the authority of scripture and traditional creedal orthodoxy while rejecting the claims of the Roman magisterium will inevitably fail? Does it mean that all such efforts will suffer from inconsistency or other rational defects? Is it actually a weaker claim to the effect that any one or two of the factors is less effective without the others? Is it a prediction or a claim about historical inevitability? Does it mean that any effort to maintain the authority of one or two of these factors without the magisterium will fizzle out and eventually come to nothing? Are such efforts inherently unstable and bound to disintegrate?

Exactly what the claim is here is not altogether clear. I shall not attempt to settle which one of these options is the correct interpretation of this claim, as that is up to Rome. But perhaps we can make headway in assessing the "all or nothing" argument by considering a famous version of the argument that has been very influential in Roman Catholicism, namely that of John Henry Newman. Cardinal Newman developed his "all or nothing" argument in his celebrated book *An Essay on the Development of Christian Doctrine*. Newman is quite popular among Roman Catholic apologists, but he is no mere popularizer or blogger. To the contrary, he is a major intellectual whose work on the nature of rationality and argument is admired not only by Roman Catholics but by Protestants as well. So his account of this argument is well worth our attention.

DOCTRINAL DEVELOPMENT TAKES TIME

Newman is particularly interesting for our concerns because his book aims to answer the Protestant challenge we noted at the beginning of this chapter, namely, that many of Rome's essential doctrinal claims have scant support at

---

6. Allison uses this image to explain the claim of the *Catechism*. See Allison, *Roman Catholic Theology*, 80.

best in the explicit teaching of scripture. Indeed, they also find little support in the earliest patristic sources. To the contrary, they were articulated much later, often after centuries of development from many historical factors and influences. It is important to be clear that Newman's whole theory is premised on the reality of this problem. If it were not recognized as a serious problem, there would be no need for his famous theory.

Newman's ingenious solution, in short, is to argue that these doctrinal developments of later centuries were in fact present from the beginning, albeit in embryonic form. The later development simply brought to maturity the various seeds that were planted in the original revelation given to the apostles. The very heart of Christian orthodoxy, after all, was not formulated in dogmatic terms until the Nicene Creed in 325/381. In a parallel way, Newman argues, later Roman Catholic doctrinal developments were simply making explicit and filling in the details of what was there all along in Christian revelation.

The claim that these developments are parallel is not only at the heart of Newman's overall argument but also crucial to his version of what I shall call the "all or nothing" argument, one that has convinced a number of Protestants to migrate to Rome. So let's take a careful look at Newman's rather ambitious argument.

After making his case for development, Newman proceeds to the heart of his argument for the rational necessity to accept the authority of Rome.

> If the Christian doctrine, as originally taught, admits of true and important developments, as was argued in the foregoing Section, this is a strong antecedent argument in favor of a provision in the Dispensation for putting a seal of authority upon those developments. The probability of their being known to be true varies with that of their truth. The ideas indeed are quite distinct, I grant, of revealing and of guaranteeing a truth, and they are quite often distinct in fact.... If then there are certain great truths, or duties, or observances, naturally and legitimately resulting from the doctrines originally professed, it is but reasonable to include these true results in the idea of the revelation itself, to consider them parts of it, and if the revelation be not only true, but guaranteed as true, to anticipate that they too will come under the privileges of that guarantee.[7]

Notice a few things about this passage. First, he distinguishes *revealing* a truth from *guaranteeing* it. It is one thing for God to reveal a truth, but

---

7. Newman, *Essay*, 79–80.

something else is required to guarantee it. What exactly is involved in this guarantee that goes beyond revelation itself?

Second, he describes "certain great truths" that "naturally and legitimately" result from the original revelation, claiming that these are part of the revelation and consequently share in whatever guarantees pertain to that revelation itself. Now the question that is crucial here is how we shall identify natural and legitimate development, and whether everything that might be called natural can be guaranteed to be true. Just what qualifies a development as a legitimate one? We shall come back to these questions, which we now raise in a preliminary way.

Next, it is important to emphasize that Newman advances his argument for an infallible guarantor of revelation in terms of what seems probable or reasonable. Indeed, he appeals to judgments of antecedent probability, of what seems likely, dozens of times throughout his book. Here is how he casts his argument for an infallible guarantor of revelation: "A probable infallibility is a probable gift of never erring; a reception of the doctrine of probable infallibility is faith and obedience towards a person founded on the probability of his never erring in his declaration or commands."[8]

He also takes care to point out that infallibility is often confused with certitude, and insists that the argument for probable infallibility is not an attempt to achieve certitude.[9] Probabilities remain just that: probabilities. Technically, probabilities range anywhere from 0 to 1, and impossibilities have a probability of 0, while necessary truths have a probability of 1. Newman appears to think his argument for the probability of an infallible guarantor of revelation lies somewhere between 0 and 1, but much closer to 1 than to 0.

Now, with this in mind, we can turn to Newman's "all or nothing" argument. He proceeds toward this argument by reiterating that the intellectual content of the Christian faith inevitably grew and developed as it was reflected on by many generations of people, and its implications were applied to various matters and situations. He then writes as follows:

> If development must be, then, whereas Revelation is a heavenly gift, He who gave it virtually has not given it, unless He has also secured it from perversion and corruption, in all such developments as come upon it by the necessity of its nature, or, in other words, that the intellectual action through successive generations, which is the organ of development, must so far as it

---

8. Newman, *Essay*, 81.
9. Newman, *Essay*, 81–82.

can claim to have been put in charge of the Revelation, be in its determinations infallible.[10]

A number of things are worth highlighting here. First, he reiterates the point that revelation has virtually not been given unless it is secured from perversion and corruption. For revelation to successfully occur, God must oversee the revelation and make sure it is properly received and preserved. Any developments of this revelation must be developments that God intends to occur.

But notice here the specific sort of developments to which this pertains, namely, "such developments as come upon it by the necessity of its nature." Now the language of necessity is interesting and considerably stronger than his earlier language about developments that "naturally and legitimately" result from Christian revelation. Indeed, necessity is typically understood along the lines of logical necessity of some sort. So is Newman here limiting his claim to developments that follow with logical necessity from the original revelation?

CARDINAL CONFUSION

While the answer to this is not entirely clear, Newman goes on in the second part of this passage apparently to restate "in other words" what he claimed in the first part of it. But notice what he is saying in the second part. For one thing, he identifies the "organ of development" as "the intellectual action through successive generations." Again, development occurs through reflection on revelation over the course of many generations and even centuries. Presumably, this includes not only the church fathers but also the great medieval and modern thinkers as well. So here are two accounts of development that Newman takes to be equivalent, and to have the stamp of infallibility:

D1) All such development as comes upon the original revelation by the necessity of its nature

D2) All development that occurs as the product of intellectual action upon revelation through successive generations.

Now the notion that these two accounts of development are equivalent is a very important one. But another more significant point here is that Newman claims that the development in D2 is infallible in its determinations "so far as it can claim to have been put in charge of the Revelation."

10. Newman, *Essay*, 92.

Now this claim, too, raises a number of questions. What is entailed in being "put in charge of the Revelation"? Is there a clear answer to who can *rightfully claim* to be in charge of revelation, as opposed to who *merely claims* to be? And does the responsibility of being put in charge of the revelation really warrant anything more than faithfully preserving and passing it on?

Most fundamentally, here is the question that must be pressed: Is it really the case that D1 is essentially the same as D2? Newman, of course, is arguing that the Roman Catholic Church, particularly the Roman magisterium, rightfully claims to be in charge of the revelation; thus, the deliberations resulting from its intellectual action are infallible. So we can rephrase the question as follows: Can the claim plausibly be made that all the official deliberations of the Roman Catholic magisterium represent developments of revelation that are due to the "necessity of its nature"?

Consider now this passage, which comes shortly after the one above. Newman reiterates his argument, in slightly different language.

> And if again, Christianity being from heaven, all that is necessarily involved in it, and is evolved from it, is from heaven, and if, on the other hand, large accretions actually do exist, professing to be its true and legitimate results, our first impression naturally is, that these must be the very developments which they profess to be.[11]

Notice again the language of necessity, but here the claim pertains to "all that is necessarily involved in" the revelation as well as what is "evolved from it." Once more, it is far from clear what this means. Is Newman claiming that all that is necessarily involved in revelation will necessarily evolve from it?

The notion of evolution period, let alone evolution in terms of ideas and religious practices, is not one easily stated in terms of *necessity*, for things evolve over a long process, typically involving countless subtle changes caused by numerous historical and other causal factors.[12] Moreover, beliefs and practices that evolve this way can result in changes that are so dramatic that the product that is evolved in later stages is altogether unrecognizable in comparison to earlier ones. In any case, Newman contends that if Christianity is from heaven, all that is necessarily involved in it, and evolved from it, is also from heaven.

---

11. Newman, *Essay*, 93.

12. Physical evolution could be thought necessary on the assumption of all-encompassing physical determinism. That is, it could be claimed that all physical events and states of affairs are determined by laws of nature and previous states of the universe.

The results of this evolution, Newman seems to be saying, are as much guaranteed as the original revelation. This is what he appears to be claiming when he says that "large accretions" that profess to be true and legitimate development are likely what they claim to be. So again, we have two accounts of development that Newman takes to be equivalent.

D3) All that is necessarily involved in Christian revelation or evolved from it.

D4) Large accretions on the Christian revelation that profess to be its true and legitimate developments.

Now the assumption that all the "large accretions" to the Christian revelation in Roman Catholic theology are likely to be true developments is a rather generous one, to put it mildly, but let us continue to examine how Newman expands his argument. Several lines later in the same paragraph, he writes as follows:

> These doctrines are members of one family, and suggestive or correlative, or confirmatory, or illustrative of each other. One furnishes evidence to another, and all to each of them; if this is proved, that becomes probable; and if this and that are both probable, but for different reasons, each adds to the other its own probability.[13]

This passage is an interesting one because of the various ways Newman thinks the doctrinal developments can gain rational support and credence. His claims here range from metaphorical suggestions, as when he says the doctrines are "members of a family," to modest claims that some doctrines illustrate others or correlate with them, to rather general claims about how one or more doctrinal claims may render others more probable.

ALL OR NOTHING?

But then Newman immediately continues as follows. I quote him at length here to show how strong and wide ranging are his claims about doctrinal development.

> The Incarnation is the antecedent of the doctrine of Mediation, and the archetype both of the Sacramental principle and the merits of the Saints. From the doctrine of Mediation follow the Atonement, the Mass, the merits of Martyrs and Saints, their

13. Newman, *Essay*, 93.

invocation and *cultus*. From the Sacramental principle come the Sacraments properly so called; the unity of the Church, and Holy See as its type and centre; the authority of Councils; the sanctity of rites; the veneration of holy places, shrines, images, vessels, furniture and vestments. Of the Sacraments, Baptism is developed into Confirmation on the one hand; into Penance, Purgatory and Indulgences on the other; and the Eucharist into the Real Presence, adoration of the Host, Resurrection of the body and the virtue of the relics. Again, the doctrine of the Sacraments leads to the doctrine of Justification; Justification to that of Original Sin; Original Sin to the merit of Celibacy.[14]

This is an extraordinary passage, and any moderately attentive reader can hardly help but notice how extravagant the claims are that it advances. While Newman does not even begin to explain, let alone demonstrate, how all these doctrines "follow" or "come" from the doctrines they allegedly do, he proclaims that they do with a sense bordering on infallible authority.

The number and range of complex issues that Newman pronounces on is nothing short of stunning. To take just one example, how does baptism develop into penance, purgatory, and indulgences? While there may be some loose connections between these doctrines, it is far from clear how this "development" is supposed to have occurred or why we should affirm it.

But as extraordinary as this passage is, Newman's conclusion to this paragraph is even more so:

> You must accept the whole or reject the whole; attenuation does but enfeeble, and amputation mutate. It is trifling to receive all but something which is as integral as any other portion; and on the other hand, it is a solemn thing to accept any part, for, before you know where you are, you may be carried on by a stern logical necessity to accept the whole.[15]

Recall that earlier in this very paragraph, Newman mentioned a number of relatively modest support relations that may obtain between various doctrinal claims, ranging from suggestion and illustration to one or more claims making others more probable. Here, all those modest claims are left behind and Newman insists that one must accept all of these claims or none of them, that they are connected by nothing less than "stern logical necessity." If one accepts any part, he must beware, for before he realizes what is happening, he may be led inexorably to accept the whole. Probability has miraculously been transformed into logical necessity, though to

14. Newman, *Essay*, 93–94.
15. Newman, *Essay*, 94.

all appearances, his actual argument rests entirely on various probability judgements and alleged connections between different doctrines, many of which are highly contestable.

It will not help Newman to defend him against his extraordinary exaggeration to note that he says only that one "may" be carried on in this fashion. For it would not even be possible that one could be carried on by stern logical necessity to accept the whole unless such logical necessities actually held among these various claims. If Newman is right, then, one apparently cannot coherently accept the Nicene Creed while rejecting the Roman view of the Mass, the See of Rome as the center of the church, the merits of the saints, indulgences, and so on. It's all or nothing. And thus, by a sort of magisterial wave of the wand, all Protestants who want to be coherent are transformed into Roman Catholics.

CHARMING CONFUSION, CONFLATION, AND CARICATURE

This long paragraph we have examined in some detail encapsulates in many ways both the charm and the deep flaws of Newman's classic book. On the one hand, he appeals to a number of plausible principles and mounts an argument that, at best, gives us a result with some degree of rational probability. On the other hand, he not infrequently gets carried away with his own rhetoric and makes claims that far outstrip his evidence and arguments. Moreover, he conflates and equates his more plausible claims with his more ambitious ones, as noted in some of the examples above, and the former lend a false and confusing sense of credibility to the latter.

We see him doing the same sort of thing at the beginning of his next chapter, after the one we have just considered. After reiterating the notion that the entirety of Roman Catholic dogma and practice goes back to the apostles, at least in nascent form, he writes as follows about that body of doctrine:

> They are confessed to form one body one with another, so that to reject one is to disparage the rest; and they include within the range of their system even those primary articles of faith, as the Incarnation, which many an impugner of the said doctrinal system, as a system, professes to accept, and which, do what he will, he cannot intelligibly separate, whether in point of evidence or of internal character, from others which he disavows.[16]

---

16. Newman, *Essay*, 99–100.

Notice again how the "all or nothing" claim is articulated. If one accepts the incarnation one must also accept the whole Roman panoply of dogmas and practices, and it is impossible for "impugners" of Roman theology to "intelligibly separate" the incarnation from that larger body of claims. As Newman puts it a few lines later, "we have to choose between this theology and none at all."

Before concluding this section, it is worth noting that Newman attempts to bolster his claim by suggesting that Protestantism will inevitably end in some sort of heresy.[17] The essence of Protestantism, he seems to think, is private judgment, so it is doomed to come to a bad end. For instance, here is his take on Calvinism: "Calvinism has changed into Unitarianism; yet this need not be called a corruption, even if it is not, strictly speaking, a development; for Harding, in controversy with Jewell, surmised the coming change three centuries since, and it has occurred not in one country, but many."[18] Newman, likely, would be surprised to see the resurgence of Calvinism in the contemporary church and the vitality it enjoys not only in America but other parts of the world as well.

For another instance of his treatment of Protestants, consider his comments on John Wesley.

> One of the chief points of discipline to which Wesley attached most importance was that of preaching early in the morning. That was his principle. In Georgia, he began preaching at five o'clock every day, winter and summer. "Early preaching," he said, "is the glory of the Methodists; whenever this is dropt, they will dwindle away into nothing, they have lost their first love, they are a fallen people."[19]

One would never guess that Wesley was an Oxford don whose works fill over thirty large volumes, or that he was one of the great preachers and practitioners of scriptural holiness, or indeed that he had any other principle besides preaching early in the morning. No, Wesley is reduced here to a cartoon figure to advance Newman's narrative that Protestant Christianity is destined to "dwindle away into nothing." Newman would likely be surprised to see Pentecostal Christianity, which has deep roots in Wesleyan theology, flourishing worldwide, especially in South America, which has historically been dominated by Roman Catholicism.

---

17. Recall that one proposed interpretation of the claim that scripture, tradition, and the magisterium stand or fall together was a claim about this sort of historical inevitability.

18. Newman, *Essay*, 175.

19. Newman, *Essay* 184–85.

In any case, there are numerous similarly tendentious accounts as well as utter caricatures of other Christian traditions, including the Eastern Church, throughout his book.[20] To be sure, Newman could be more ecumenical in other contexts, but not in this book. His accounts of other Christian traditions here are designed to discredit them and to serve his larger contention that Rome alone can coherently maintain orthodoxy, so we must embrace Rome or be left with no viable place to stand.

If these really are our only options, it is altogether understandable why many lovers of Jesus, the Son of God incarnate, will choose to go to Rome. But this claim that we cannot have Jesus without Rome is a classic case of rhetorical overreach as well as deeply confused thinking, and Newman's argument does not even come close to demonstrating it.

So far then, the "all or nothing" argument appears to be a dubious one, despite its popularity and the fact that it has been supported by serious intellectuals. We shall come back to this in a later chapter, but next we need to consider how Protestants might affirm scripture and tradition while rejecting the authority of the Roman Catholic magisterium.

---

20. See Newman, *Essay*, 54, 96, 181, 192–93, 198, 205, 306, 353–54.

CHAPTER FIVE

REVELATION, CANON, CREED

How to Affirm Catholic Faith While Denying the Claims of Rome

IN THE PREVIOUS CHAPTER, we examined various "all or nothing" arguments that try to support the conclusion that scripture, tradition, and the Roman magisterium stand or fall together. In other words, there are no principled grounds for accepting the authority of scripture and traditional creedal Christianity for those who reject the claims of Rome. In this chapter, I want to show that there are perfectly good Protestant reasons to accept the authority of the Creed, and indeed, that biblical and creedal authority stand together but do not require us to accept the claim that the Roman Catholic magisterium is the exclusively authorized interpreter of scripture. Before making the case for creedal authority, I want to sketch my reasons for accepting the New Testament canon as scripture and to point out the basic rationale that is common for accepting both scriptural and creedal authority.

REVELATION AND THE NEW TESTAMENT CANON

What is fundamentally at stake here is what is involved in the basic concept of a divine revelation. In short, a divine revelation is by definition a *successful* undertaking on the part of God to reveal himself, his truth, his intentions, his purposes, and so on. Or to put it another way, "reveal" is an achievement verb. It only applies in the case that revelation is actually achieved or accomplished.[1]

---

1. For more on the notion of "reveal" as an achievement verb, see Abraham, *Divine Revelation*, 11–12.

Consider another example, namely, the verb "communicate." Suppose Calvin said that Hobbes was a great communicator, but upon being asked to identify the main points of Hobbes's speech, Calvin could not do so. Would that not undercut the claim that Hobbes was a great communicator? Assuming Calvin is a competent recipient for the message of Hobbes's speech, we could conclude that Hobbes did not in fact communicate his key points. He perhaps attempted to communicate, but failed to do so.

"Reveal" is an achievement verb in the same sort of way. William Abraham sums the matter up concisely when he writes: "Divine speaking and human sensitivity together bring about divine revelation."[2] Human sensitivity is itself a gift of God. It is not only due to the fact that apostles are made in God's image as knowers but also to the fact that the Holy Spirit illumines their hearts and minds to faithfully understand and record God's revelation.

So then, if the Christian revelation is in fact from God, we have every reason to think the recipients of that revelation understood what God intended to reveal. For a paradigmatic instance of this, consider Paul's words defending his apostleship to the Galatians: "For I want you to know, brothers, that the gospel I preached is not something that man made up. I did not receive it from any man, nor was I taught it; rather I received it by revelation from Jesus Christ" (Gal 1:11–12). To receive a revelation from Christ is to receive a communication from a supreme authority that warrants the claim that Paul, as the recipient, knows what he is talking about. Or consider Luke's account of Jesus appearing to the disciples after he was raised from the dead to explain to them from the Old Testament scriptures the meaning of his death and resurrection (Luke 24:25–49). Given the risen Jesus as the source of this revelation, we have reason to believe the disciples correctly understood the meaning and significance of Jesus' death and resurrection. Finally, consider Jesus' promise to the disciples in the Gospel of John that the Holy Spirit would speak to them and guide them into truth (John 14:26; 15:26; 16:12–14). The point is the same. Given the guidance of the Holy Spirit upon the apostles, we have every reason to believe they would accurately communicate what God intended.

Thus far, Protestants and Roman Catholics can agree. But how, it will be asked, can we know which books are in fact those books that contain authoritative revelation for the church? The answer to this question is a major point of contention between Roman Catholics and Protestants. Well, I think the notion of revelation itself provides us resources to answer this question.

---

2. Abraham, *Divine Inspiration*, 89.

So let us turn now to consider the New Testament canon in light of these observations about the nature of revelation.

DISCERNING THE CANON

The whole notion of canon is, of course, a very controversial and deeply contested notion, and we can hardly delve into the details of that debate here. But for our purposes, I want to sketch some of the central insights of an account of canon that I think has considerable promise, and one that is most pertinent to our concerns in this chapter, namely, that of Michael J. Kruger.

Kruger's project is to develop an epistemological account of how Christians can be rationally justified in believing the twenty-seven books in the New Testament are indeed the only ones that belong there. His project is modeled after Alvin Plantinga's account of Christian knowledge in his landmark book, *Warranted Christian Belief*. One of the most impressive aspects of Kruger's account is that he incorporates into his view the strengths of a number of competing accounts of canon, while taking pains to steer clear of their weaknesses.

His model is a classically Protestant one since it rests on the claim that scripture is ultimately self-authenticating. However, he understands this claim more broadly than is often the case in Protestant theology. The essence of what he means by this claim is that one cannot authenticate the canon without appealing to the canon itself and allowing it to set the terms by which it will be validated. "A self-authenticating canon is not just a canon that claims to have authority, nor is it simply a canon that bears internal evidence of authority, but one that guides and determines how that authority is to be established."[3]

To understand what is meant by the self-authenticating authority of scripture, compare some of our basic sources of belief such as reason, sense experience, and memory. How, for instance, do we know that reason is reliable, that we can trust the basic laws of logic? The answer is that we just "see" them to be true. For instance, one cannot argue for reason without assuming its basic reliability, because the very act of arguing consists of giving reasons for a conclusion.[4] To defend reason we must use reason! In a similar way, to account for the authority of scripture, we have to appeal to scripture itself.

---

3. Kruger, *Canon Revisited*, 91.

4. For the similarity between the self-authentication of scripture and basic sources of belief, see Plantinga, *Warranted Christian Belief*, 260–62.

Kruger offers an illuminating angle on the self-authenticating nature of scripture by reflecting on the question of how we can recognize God himself. He writes:

> After all, how does a person know when he has encountered God? Does God need some external authority to confirm his identity? When men encounter God, they are vividly aware of his beauty, majesty, and perfection and need no further "evidence" that he is God (Pss 27:4; 50:2; 96:6; Isa 6:1–7; Rev 1:12–17; 4:3). In addition, Scripture itself is described over and over again throughout the Bible as bearing these very same attributes.[5]

When God is encountered, the evidence for this is in himself, so to speak, and scripture, as the word of God, is self-authenticating in a similar way.

At first glance, it might be objected that Kruger is begging the question against potential critics, but in fact he is not. To see why this is not begging the question, it is important to be clear what Kruger is and is not attempting to do. He is *not* trying to give an account of why anyone comes to believe the gospel or accepts the authority of scripture in the first place. Nor is he presenting an argument to skeptics to try to convince them that the twenty-seven books of the New Testament are canonical. If he were arguing with such persons, his case might be question begging. "Instead, the issue that concerns us here is not about our having knowledge of the canon (or proving the truth of the canon) but *accounting* for our knowledge of the canon. It is about whether the Christian religion provides sufficient grounds for thinking that Christians can know which books belong in the canon and which do not."[6]

In terms of the concerns of this book, the issue can be put as follows: Can Protestants deploy these grounds and resources to account for the authority of the canon without appeal to the Roman Catholic magisterium? Indeed, do they have an account of the authority of the canon that is a satisfactory, indeed preferable, alternative to that of Rome?

Kruger answers the question he has raised by pointing to three crucial components that ground and provide adequate warrant for Christians to be justified in believing they know the twenty-seven books of the New Testament are the books God intended for the canon.[7] Let us look at each of these to see how they bear on our concerns.

---

5. Kruger, *Canon Revisited*, 127. Kruger goes on to cite Pss 19:7–8; 119:103, 129.

6. Kruger, *Canon Revisited*, 21; cf. 91–92.

7. Kruger puts this claim in terms similar to Plantinga's account of warranted Christian belief when he writes that "God has created the proper epistemic environment wherein belief in the New Testament canon can be reliably formed" (Kruger, *Canon Revisited*, 94).

THREE CRUCIAL COMPONENTS IN A CASE FOR THE CANON

The first of these is "providential exposure." The idea here is fairly straightforward. If God intends for the church to recognize certain books as canonical, then God would preserve those books and make sure they were exposed to the larger church, not merely the body of believers who originally received them. For instance, if God intended, say, Paul's letter to the Galatians to be in the canon, it is reasonable to think he would preserve that letter and expose it to the larger church for their discernment.

The second of these components that warrant our knowledge of the canon consists of three "attributes of canonicity" that distinguish canonical books from all other books. The first of these attributes are the divine qualities of canonical books, such as their beauty, their spiritual power, and their harmony. By exhibiting such marks, the canonical books bear the imprint of the Holy Spirit. Next, there is the attribute of apostolicity, a traditional condition that a canonical book must be the result of the redemptive activity of the apostles. The third attribute is corporate reception, which means that a canonical book must be accepted by the church as a whole, not merely a segment of it.[8]

Now this third attribute is of particular interest for our concerns in this chapter and it points up a matter of conflict that often divides Roman Catholics from Protestants. On the one hand, Roman Catholics have often emphasized the authority of the church as either the primary or the sole factor to determine the canon. Recall the quote from Kreeft at the beginning of the preceding chapter, in which he contends that accepting the authority of scripture requires a prior commitment to the infallibility of the church, since the church defined the canon. On the other hand, Protestants have sometimes downplayed or denied the role of the church in determining the canon in their concern to defend the self-authenticating authority of scripture.

One of the strengths of Kruger's account is that he offers a distinctively Protestant view of the canon that strongly emphasizes the essential role of the corporate reception of canonical books. "The books received by the church inform our understanding of which books are canonical not because the church is infallible or because it created or constituted the canon, but because *the church's reception of these books is a natural and inevitable outworking of the self-authenticating nature of Scripture.*"[9] He continues a

---

8. I have reversed the second and third attributes. Kruger has apostolic origins as the third attribute.

9. Kruger, *Canon Revisited*, 106 (original emphasis).

few lines later, further distinguishing his view of corporate reception from the Roman Catholic account of this matter.

> In the self-authenticating model, however, the church's reception of these books proves not to be evidence of the church's authority to create the canon, but evidence of the *opposite*, namely, the authority, power and impact of the self-authenticating Scriptures to elicit a corporate response from the church. Jesus' statement that "my sheep hear my voice . . . and they follow me" (John 10:27) is not evidence for the authority of the sheep's decision to follow, but evidence for the authority and efficacy of the Shepherd's voice to call. After all, the act of hearing is, by definition, derivative not constitutive. Thus, when the canon is understood as self-authenticating, it is clear that the church did not choose the canon, but the canon, in a sense, chose itself. . . . In this way then, the role of the church is like a thermometer, not a thermostat. Both instruments provide information about the temperature in the room—but one determines it and the other reflects it.[10]

Now, having considered the three attributes of canonicity (which together comprise the *second* of Kruger's components that warrant rational belief in the canon), we come to the third crucial component in his account, which is the illumination and witness of the Holy Spirit. This component is not only involved with the first component of providential exposure but the second as well, for it is the work of the Holy Spirit that leads the church to discern the divine attributes of scripture. Moreover, the three attributes of canonicity mutually support and imply each other. Divine qualities can be expected to exist if a book is the product of an inspired apostolic author. "In addition, any book with divine qualities (and apostolic origins) will impose itself on the church and, via the work of the *testimonium*, be corporately received."[11]

It is important to understand the role of the illumination and witness of the Holy Spirit in this larger context to avoid subjectivism and individualism. Indeed, it is the work of the Holy Spirit in the corporate church, the discernment of the church at large that gives us reason to believe the twenty-seven books of the New Testament do indeed comprise the canon God intended us to receive.

---

10. Kruger, *Canon Revisited*, 106 (original emphasis).
11. Kruger, *Canon Revisited*, 115.

NO SIMPLE ANSWER TO DATE THE ORIGIN OF THE CANON

Moreover, this account of why we are justified in accepting the New Testament canon does not give us Cartesian certainty, nor does it give us a simple answer to the question, "what is the correct date for the origin of the canon?" Indeed, this account of canon recognizes that there was a historical process involved in the formation and recognition of the canon. How we define the canon will determine how we date its origin. If we define the canon *ontologically*, we can say the canon existed in its entirety the minute after the final book of the New Testament was written, likely sometime in the first century. If we define the canon *functionally*, we could date it sometime in the mid second century, if not before, when most of the books were being used as scripture in the early church. If we define it *exclusively*, we would date it in the third or fourth century, when a consensus was reached about the twenty-seven books of the canon.[12] Kruger sums this up as follows.

> When these three dates are viewed as a whole, they nicely capture the entire flow of canonical history: (1) God gives his books through the apostles; (2) the books are recognized and used as Scripture by early Christians; (3) the corporate church achieves a consensus around these books. The fact that these three dates are linked in such a natural chronological order reminds us that the story of the canon is indeed a *process*, and therefore it should not be artificially restricted to one moment in time. Put differently, the story of the canon is less like a dot and more like a line.[13]

The fact that the church reached this consensus on the canon in the way it did in the fourth century undermines the Roman claim that the church created the canon. As Kruger observes, "It was not until the Council of Trent in 1546 that the Roman Catholic Church ever made a formal and official declaration on the canon of the Bible, particularly the Apocrypha."[14]

---

12. Kruger writes: "There are numerous examples of this consensus, most notably The Festal Letter of Athanasius of 367, where he affirms the precise twenty-seven books of our current New Testament. In agreement are also Eusebius, Codex Claromontanus, Rufinus, Jerome, Augustine, the African Canons, and the Synods of Hippo and Carthage. Although there was not absolute uniformity (which is still true today), after this period the church coalesced around these books with remarkable unity" (Kruger, *Canon Revisited*, 286–87).

13. Kruger, *Canon Revisited*, 119.

14. Kruger, *Canon Revisited*, 45.

Surely the church was not without a canon those fifteen centuries before the formal definition at Trent.

Now, let us bring this discussion of the canon back to the larger issue we raised at the beginning of this section, namely, what is involved in the very idea of revelation. Recall that revelation is an achievement verb, and that it implies something about the recipients of revelation as well about the one who gives the revelation. For revelation actually to be achieved, those who receive it must grasp or understand what the revealer intended to be revealed. But where Protestants will disagree with Roman Catholics is what this implies about the authority of the church, particularly the Roman magisterium.

Recall again Kruger's point that for the self-authenticating model "the church's reception of these books proves not to be evidence of the church's authority to create the canon, but evidence of the *opposite*, namely, the authority, power, and impact of the self-authenticating scriptures to elicit a corporate response from the church." It is important to see here that both views agree that there is an essential role to be played by the corporate church, but they disagree in how they understand the relationship between the authority of scripture and the authority of the church. Again, to cite that earlier passage from Kruger: "After all, the act of hearing is, by definition, derivative not constitutive." So we have good reason to believe the church correctly heard and got the canon right, but that is primarily a statement about the authority and power of the one who gave the canon, not about those who received it.[15]

BIBLICAL AUTHORITY IMPLIES CREEDAL AUTHORITY

Now I want to argue that the same basic points I made about the nature of revelation lead us to the conclusion that the classic creeds are faithful summaries of biblical revelation, particularly the most ecumenical of these, the Nicene Creed.[16] But, it may be objected, it is one thing to believe the apostles faithfully wrote and recorded what God intended to reveal, and that a self-authenticating canon was correctly discerned by the corporate church, but it is another matter to take post-apostolic creeds as authoritative. At this point, many Protestants may instinctively appeal to the slogan "no creed but the Bible," and even pit the authority of scripture against the authority of the

---

15. For more on these issues, see Collins and Walls, *Roman but Not Catholic*, 11–45.

16. Here I revisit issues I discussed in my first book several years ago. See Walls, *Problem of Pluralism* [1986], 87–98.

classic creeds. Indeed, they may even think that the Protestant principle of *sola scriptura* requires them to do so.

But this is a profound distortion of that principle, and indeed one that actually undermines biblical authority. As Michael Allen and Scott R. Swain have argued, the Reformers themselves insisted that scripture could not be read alone but rather must be read in the larger Christian community, particularly in light of Christian tradition. "The Bible itself calls for the exercise of pastoral authority, confessional authority, and what we could call ecumenical authority. . . . *To be more biblical, then, one cannot be biblistic. To be more biblical, one must also be engaged in the process of traditioning.*"[17] This will entail, they recognize, a certain fixed content to the Christian faith.

> God has spoken in Holy Scripture, and the church by God's grace has made a faithful confession. In this regard, "dogmas"—the church's public and binding summaries of scriptural truth—stand as "irreversible" expressions of the rule of faith, expressions with which all later summaries of the rule of faith must cohere and which all further summaries of the rule of faith must exhibit.[18]

I very much agree with these sentiments and concur with the judgment that a proper understanding of *sola scriptura* will make one *more* catholic, not less so. Indeed, I want to argue that a sound understanding of biblical authority implies the dogmatic authority of the Nicene Creed, the very heart of catholic orthodoxy.

The *Catholic Catechism* underscores the significance of this classic statement of faith as follows: "The *Niceno-Constantinopolitan* or *Nicene Creed* draws its great authority from the fact that it stems from the first two ecumenical Councils (in 325 and 381). It remains common to all the great Churches of both East and West to this day."[19] As such, the Nicene Creed represents something as close to a doctrinal consensus among all Christians as anything. While I agree that this creed has "great authority," I think the reason this is so is slightly different than the *Catechism* claims. It is precisely the authority of scripture as the definitive written revelation of God that leads us to this conclusion.

The basic thrust of my argument is very similar to some of Newman's claims, particularly his more modest claims noted in the previous chapter.

---

17. Allen and Swain, *Reformed Catholicity*, 84–85 (original emphasis). For more on this, see especially chapters 2–3.

18. Allen and Swain, *Reformed Catholicity*, 112. The word "irreversible" in the quote comes from Robert Jenson.

19. *Catechism of the Catholic Church*, para. 195.

Recall, for instance, his claim that "whereas Revelation is a heavenly gift, He who gave it virtually has not given it, unless He has also secured it from perversion and corruption, in all such developments that come upon it by the necessity of its nature."[20] What I particularly want to underscore here is his notion of "developments that come upon it by the necessity of its nature."

Consider now his similar claim that "there is a high antecedent probability that Providence would watch over His own work, and would direct and ratify those developments of doctrine which were inevitable."[21] Now a development that is inevitable is perhaps not as strongly implied or required by the original revelation as one that follows by the necessity of its nature, but it is still a rather strong one. The main point I am driving at is that these forms of development are indeed ones that it seems likely would be true ones if the original revelation is one that was given by God.

This is not to say that everything in that revelation will be clear or immediately apparent. God may have reasons for some of his revelation to be difficult to understand, or even to remain debatable in terms of its intended meaning. But if something follows from that revelation by some sort of necessity, or inevitability, it is reasonable to think the recipients of the revelation would correctly discern it if it concerns something that is essential or central to the revelation.[22]

Now let us consider the Nicene Creed and its famous affirmation that Jesus Christ is "begotten, not made, being of one substance with the Father, through whom all things were made." This is the very heart of the Christian faith, this conviction that Jesus is nothing less than the fully divine Son of God who became incarnate and died to save us. Is it possible that the church could have gotten this wrong? Does a Protestant have a principled reason for insisting that the Nicene Creed got this matter definitively right?

WHY THE NICENE FATHERS GOT IT RIGHT

As we reflect on this question, notice also that this issue that was raised by Arius is just the sort of question inevitably raised by the Christian revelation. Given the nature of that revelation, and the extraordinary things

---

20. Newman, *Essay*, 92.
21. Newman, *Essay*, 100.
22. This qualification is worth noting for the simple reason that countless things follow from the Christian revelation that are not theologically significant. For instance, from the simple claim "God has revealed himself," a number of things immediately follow, such as: there is a word "revealed"; it has eight letters in English; there is more than one word; and so on.

it teaches us about Christ, this is a query that "necessarily" demands an answer. Christ is clearly the central character of the New Testament, and he inescapably requires us to respond to his question, "Who do you say that I am?" (Matt 16:15).

It must be acknowledged that Arius gave at least one plausible reply, one that was held by a number of Christians of his time. We have the benefit of hundreds of years of hindsight, but at the time Arius gave his answer to Jesus' question, consensus had yet to be achieved. We should not be too hard on Arius and those who followed him during this period.

But while his answer was plausible, the Nicene Fathers insisted that it did not accurately reflect what the New Testament teaches about Christ. We need to be clear that what was at stake here was the whole Christian doctrine of God. Indeed, the affirmation of the full divinity of Christ is a statement not only about the Son of God but also about the Trinitarian nature of the entire Godhead. The Nicene Creed is a landmark in affirming the Trinitarian nature of God by its confession of the divinity not only of the Father and the Son but also the Holy Spirit, "who together with the Father and the Son is worshiped and glorified."[23]

Why should we think the Nicene fathers got it right? I am arguing that an essential part of the answer hinges on the very idea that God has definitively revealed himself in Christ. It is precisely insofar as we affirm the authority of the biblical revelation that we have reason to hold that the Nicene fathers correctly and truly defined these fundamental Christian doctrines. Indeed, the Protestant principle of the clarity and perspicuity of scripture is also at stake here.

For if the Nicene fathers were competent readers of scripture, if they were making their best effort to correctly interpret what it teaches about matters that are utterly central to the faith, we have every reason to believe they got it right. To suggest they may have gotten it wrong not only undermines any substantive claim about the clarity of scripture, but even worse, it discredits the very claim that scripture is inspired revelation from God.

The claim here is not simply about the grammatical clarity of scripture and the linguistic competence of the fathers. Far more important is the activity of the Holy Spirit, who Jesus promised would lead us into all truth (John 16:13). The same Holy Spirit who inspired scripture in the first place can be counted on to illumine and guide the church in discerning a doctrinal matter so clearly central to scripture. Moreover, the fact that the views of Nicaea prevailed and have been defended over and over by great

23. For an excellent, concise account of the doctrine of Trinity and its significance, see Abraham, *Systematic Theology*, 39–53. Another excellent source is Sanders, *Deep Things of God*.

theologians and biblical scholars down the centuries only confirms the conclusion that the Nicene fathers correctly discerned the meaning of scripture on the vital issue of the nature of Christ.

In short, the *a priori* judgment that the early church would correctly interpret the meaning of scripture when formally defining its most fundamental doctrines, confirmed by the *a posteriori* fact that Nicaea has achieved a "truly catholic consensus," gives us ample warrant on Protestant principles to affirm the Nicene Creed as authentically binding doctrinal development. So anyone who wants to make strong claims about the authority and clarity of scripture should have a firm commitment to catholic Christianity as represented in the Nicene Creed.

Before moving on, let us recall the significance of this argument as it relates to the larger purposes of this chapter and the previous one, in particular the various "all or nothing" sort of arguments Roman Catholics often press on Protestants to try to convert them to Rome. I have argued that Protestants have perfectly good reasons on their own principles to accept the authority of scripture and the doctrines of catholic Christianity. This does not in any way commit us to accept the whole panoply of claims Newman says we must.

DEEP DISAGREEMENT DESPITE DEEPER AGREEMENT

As we draw this chapter to a close, let us consider some comments on the nature of revelation from contemporary Roman Catholic theologian Matthew Levering. His recent book on revelation is deeply informed not only by biblical exegesis but also by broad ecumenical sympathies. I find myself in the interesting position that I largely agree with Levering's account of revelation, even as I profoundly disagree with him about a number of particular doctrinal claims. Near the end of his book he writes as follows.

> Against all ecclesiastical fall narratives, I have argued in this book that the Church truthfully mediates God's revelation to us, due to the efficacious missions of the Son and the Holy Spirit. ... The Holy Spirit's inspiration of Scripture and the Holy Spirit's guidance of the people of God are inextricably bound together.[24]

By ecclesiastical fall narratives, Levering means those accounts of the history of the church that view it as the story of one long departure from the purity of the apostolic age. By contrast, Levering insists on the continuing

---

24. Levering, *Engaging the Doctrine of Revelation*, 286.

guidance of the Holy Spirit in the church. Now, what he means by the church here is a bit ambiguous. Does he mean the Church of Rome or the larger church, as composed of all those who have faith in Christ and have been baptized into his body? In any case, I agree with Levering that the very claim that God has revealed himself in the Christian revelation entails that the church has faithfully mediated that revelation and indeed, that has been one of the central convictions driving this chapter. But what one means by "the church" will determine what one means by the claim that "the church" truthfully mediates God's revelation.

Several pages later, Levering reiterates this crucial claim about revelation and elaborates on it as follows.

> In my view, however, Christians should be loath to grant that the Holy Spirit has not ensured the fidelity of the Church's doctrinal development. Indeed, Christians are generally agreed about the truthfulness of the doctrinal developments of the first few centuries. For persons who deny that the Holy Spirit has ever guided the Church (or, for that matter, that the Holy Spirit has ever existed), it makes sense to reject a consistent Tradition or doctrinal development. But it does not make sense for the Christian to do so, especially once one recognizes that doctrine develops in ways that reflect historical vitality rather than a strict logical unfolding.[25]

This passage is reminiscent of some of those passages from Newman that we analyzed earlier. It begins with a claim that is not only highly plausible, but one that most orthodox Christians should readily accept (again, depending on what one means by "the church"). But it concludes with one that is much more dubious, one that the author seems to think should follow for anyone who accepts the earlier claim about the work of the Holy Spirit in ensuring the fidelity of doctrinal development. Notice the claim that "doctrine develops in ways that reflect historical vitality rather than strict logical unfolding."

And here is where fundamental differences once again emerge between Reformation Christians and our Roman brothers and sisters. As Levering notes, we can agree with the "truthfulness of the doctrinal developments of the first few centuries," and we have good reason to believe the same Holy Spirit who inspired scripture gave discernment and insight to the church as they gave formal definition to those central doctrines revealed in scripture. But it is another matter altogether to suggest that later Roman Catholic claims are equally warranted by the observation that "doctrine develops

---

25. Levering, *Engaging the Doctrine of Revelation*, 296.

in ways that reflect historical vitality." Despite the positive, dynamic connotations of this phrase, it is far too vague and open ended to provide a satisfactory criterion for legitimate doctrinal development. Indeed, it is quite reminiscent of Newman's appeal to the "intellectual action through successive generations, which is the organ of development."

BACK TO NEWMAN

Recall from the previous chapter that Newman not only conflated this view of doctrinal development with more restrained and modest ones, but that he also used this more expansive view to defend the whole Roman panoply of doctrinal claims and to argue that consistency requires accepting all or accepting none. But what Reformation Christians will insist is that there are principled reasons for accepting those earlier doctrinal developments, while rejecting those that appeal to "intellectual action through successive generations" or "historical vitality" to warrant them.

Those principled reasons stem from the Reformation principle of *sola scriptura*, rightly understood. Unfortunately, this principle is not only misrepresented by its critics but sometimes by its advocates as well. Michael Allen and Scott R. Swain provide a timely caution against contemporary distortions of this principle.

> Indeed, *sola Scriptura* has served for some moderns as a banner for private judgment and against catholicity. In so doing, however, churches and Christians have turned from *sola Scriptura* to *solo Scriptura*, a bastard child nursed at the breast of modern rationalism and individualism. Even the Reformational doctrine of perspicuity has been transformed in much popular Christianity and some scholarly reflection as well to function as the theological equivalent of philosophical objectivity, namely, the belief that any objective observer can, by the use of appropriate measures, always gain the appropriate interpretation of a biblical text.[26]

Again, insofar as we truly have reason to believe in biblical authority, we have reason to believe the doctrines of catholic Christianity. But it is the principle of *sola scriptura* that provides the proper constraints and limits on any theological developments resulting from "intellectual action through successive generations" or "historical vitality" that can rightly demand our assent.

---

26. Allen and Swain, *Reformed Catholicity*, 85.

This not to say, as Levering suggests it might, that the only legitimate doctrinal development is development that occurs by "strict logical unfolding." But it is to say that any dogma that can claim to bind the Christian conscience must have substantial support from clear biblical teaching. It is significant in this connection, and quite telling, that Newman insistently rejected this sort of scriptural constraint in his account of doctrinal development.

> It may be objected that its [the Church's] inspired documents at once determine the limits of its mission without further trouble; but ideas are in the writer and reader of the revelation, not the inspired text itself; and the question is whether those ideas which the letter conveys from writer to reader, reach the reader at once in their completeness and accuracy on his first perception of them, or whether they open out in his intellect and grow to perfection in the course of time. Nor could it surely be maintained without extravagance that the letter of the New Testament, or of any assignable number of books, comprises a delineation of all possible forms which the divine message will assume when submitted to a multitude of minds.[27]

Several things are worth noting here. First, note that Newman suggests that the only alternative to his view is to believe that "those ideas which the letter conveys from writer to reader, reach the reader at once in their completeness and accuracy on his first perception of them." As is often the case, his rhetoric is grossly misleading, for those who reject Newman's account of development obviously need not assume anything as absurd as the notion that the full meaning of scripture is instantly understood at first sight. Second, note that he suggests that on his view, the truths in scripture only "grow to perfection in the course of time." Now it is one thing to say our understanding of scripture grows closer to perfection over the course of time and reflection, but it is another matter altogether to say *the message itself* grows to perfection. Third, notice his claim that the ideas in the Christian revelation are not in the text but "in the writer and reader of the revelation." This is a telling observation in its own right, but it also leads to the fourth point, which I particularly want to emphasize. He apparently wants to legitimize "all possible forms which a divine message will assume when submitted to a multitude of minds."

This is the sort of claim Newman recognizes he must make to support his contention that the whole Roman panoply represents authoritative doctrinal development. He is keenly aware that the express teaching of scripture

27. Newman, *Essay*, 56–57.

will not support those "large accretions," nor will the early history of the church. But he thinks they can be legitimized if one accepts as true development "all possible forms a divine message will assume when submitted to a multitude of minds."

Later on in the same chapter, Newman advances a similar claim.

> It is in point to notice also the structure and style of Scripture, a structure so unsystematic and various, and a style so figurative and indirect, that no one would presume at first sight to say what is in it and what is not. . . . Of no doctrine whatever, which does not actually contradict what has been delivered, can it be peremptorily asserted that it is not in Scripture.[28]

Again, Newman is highly tendentious in his rhetoric when he speaks of presuming "at first sight" to know what is in scripture, or "peremptorily" determining what is not. We can certainly agree with him that the meaning of scripture cannot be so easily and quickly ascertained. However, this observation does not rule out that a community of well informed, thoughtful, patient readers can determine what is and what is not in scripture. Notice also Newman's appeal to the "figurative and indirect" style of scripture. The reason for this is obvious, namely, that the Marian dogmas have little if any "direct" support from scripture, so any viable claim to biblical support must come by way of various figurative interpretations of scripture.

But most significant, notice how difficult it is on Newman's terms to show a doctrine is not in scripture. No doctrine can be ruled out if it "does not actually contradict what has been delivered." The only test is outright logical contradiction. We cannot determine that a doctrine is not in scripture by showing that it lacks express biblical support or by showing that it is not in any substantial sense necessarily connected with doctrines that do have such support. No, for Newman, one cannot show that a doctrine is not in scripture unless it actually contradicts what clearly is in scripture.

Given Newman's project of providing an account of doctrinal development that warrants all the claims of Rome, these sorts of moves are altogether understandable. But for those who are not committed to Rome they have little to commend them.

Indeed, it is precisely the sort of extravagance that Newman defends that the principle of *sola scriptura* intends to guard against. It is our minds (and imaginations) that must be submitted to the revelation and not the revelation to our minds. We are not warranted in thinking any idea that might be generated by a "multitude of minds" reflecting on Christian revelation is a viable candidate for a binding dogma. Again, this does not mean that our

---

28. Newman, *Essay*, 71.

minds do not play a key role in the reception and perception of divine revelation, particularly the corporate mind of the church. But it does mean that legitimate doctrinal development is constrained by clear scriptural support.

Clear scriptural support will be further reflected in the ecumenical sense of the corporate church, a consensus that goes beyond the Church of Rome. The *Catechism* recognizes the sense of the faithful as a crucial indicator of doctrinal truth because this sense is produced by the anointing of the Holy Spirit. "'The whole body of the faithful . . . cannot err in matters of belief. This characteristic is shown in the supernatural appreciation of faith (*sensus fidei*) on the part of the whole people, when from 'bishops to the last of the faithful' they manifest a universal consent in matters of faith and morals."[29]

It is precisely this sort of "universal consent" that is enjoyed by the doctrines of the Nicene Creed. I have been arguing that Protestants have perfectly good reasons on their own principles to affirm not only classic creedal orthodoxy, but the New Testament canon, reasons that do not in any way commit them to accept the claims of Rome. Accordingly, the argument of these chapters provides further reasons not to be a Roman Catholic.

---

29. *Catechism*, para. 92 (original ellipses). The paragraph is a quote from "*Lumen gentium*," 12.

CHAPTER SIX

IT ALL DEPENDS ON MARY

ONE OF THE MOST famous college landmarks in the world is the golden dome of the University of Notre Dame. "Notre Dame" is French for "Our Lady," so it is only fitting that standing atop the golden dome is a nineteen-foot-tall statue of the Virgin Mary that weighs four thousand pounds. I am a proud graduate of that great Roman Catholic university and I have seen the golden dome many times. Only a few years ago, however, I learned something about the statue of Mary from a close-up picture that I did not know before. What is not obvious from viewing the statue from a distance is that Mary is depicted as trampling on serpents.

The image of Mary trampling a serpent is a common one, but what is particularly interesting about these statues and images is that they were inspired by a famous mistranslation of scripture, namely, Genesis 3:15: "I will put enmity between you [the serpent] and the woman, and between your offspring and hers; he will strike your head, and you will strike his heel." These words were spoken by God to Adam and Eve after the fall, and they are considered the first promise of the coming of Christ. Christ is the offspring of the woman who would be attacked by the serpent, but who would prevail by crushing the serpent's head.

This important biblical prophecy was significantly mistranslated in the Roman Catholic Douay-Rheims version of the Bible. For "he will strike" it translated "she shall crush," and for "his heel" it translated "her heel." In other words, it substituted feminine pronouns for masculine ones, which makes it appear the prophecy is about a woman rather than a man. The translators of Douay-Rheims justify this translation on the grounds that a number of church fathers read it this way on the basis of the Latin translation of the

Bible. The Latin, however, is a mistranslation of this text, for the original Hebrew pronouns are masculine, not feminine.[1]

Roman Catholics have taken this text as a prophecy about Mary, even though it is a mistranslation of the original Hebrew. Indeed, the text was even cited in support of Marian dogma at Vatican II. So, this mistranslation has deeply influenced Roman Catholic piety and theology for centuries.

This story illustrates much of what Protestants find objectionable about Marian piety and theology as it has developed in the Church of Rome. Roman Catholics, it seems, have been more than willing to read far more into the biblical text than is there, to exaggerate its claims, and at worst even misrepresent it to justify the strong claims their church makes about Mary. Indeed, popular Roman Catholic piety may even devolve into worship of Mary even though official teaching insists that Mary should not be worshiped.

MARY AS CO-REDEEMER?

But even when worship of Mary is repudiated, Roman Catholics are often intent on playing up her role to such an extent that it almost invariably results in overreach. Consider, for instance, these lines from Roman enthusiast Peter Kreeft:

> Nothing is more Biblical than the historical fact that in God's providential plan, it was her free surrender to His will, her "Let it be to me according to your word," that made our salvation possible. . . . If Mary had said no, Christ would not have come. He spiritually seduces but does not rape. He Himself made His coming dependent on her choice. Thus, indirectly but really, she is a link in the chain of our salvation, in fact the link that most directly connects us with Christ. In this sense she is our active "co-operator in redemption" by her fiat. This is what is meant by the threatening-sounding term "co-redemptrix."[2]

Now we can readily agree that we should honor Mary for her part in bearing and raising the Son of God. For the plan of salvation designed by God to be executed, his Son had to take on human nature and be born of a human mother. The New Testament narrative, especially the Gospel of Luke, celebrates Mary's part in the story, and to be true to the word of

---

1. See Wells, *Revolution in Rome*, 129–37, esp. 133–35. Roman Catholic apologists acknowledge the mistranslation, but still defend the text as referring to Mary as well as Christ. See Akin, "Mary and Genesis 3:15."

2. Kreeft, *Catholics and Protestants*, 130.

scripture, we must gladly do the same. I wrote a poem several years ago, attempting to do just that.

CHRISTMAS EVE

> Adam's rib was Christmas Eve
> Foreshadow of a pierced side
> Who pulling down forbidden fruit
> Set fast in motion Yuletide.
>
> Joseph's bride was Second Eve
> Endowed with gift of pierced soul
> Who bowing down to own his will
> Joined God in making wounded whole.[3]

Mary's humble submission to the will and purposes of God is indeed a thing of great beauty and a model for us all. Protestants have no doubt shied away from properly honoring Mary partly in response to Roman Catholic excesses. But if scripture is to be our guide, we must give honor to whom honor is due, and the mother of our Lord deserves our honor and our emulation.

Still, Kreeft's comments above typify the sort of Marian piety that exaggerates her importance in the narrative of salvation. Mary's willing choice to bear the Son of God and to raise him does not in any way serve as a parallel to what Christ did in saving us or warrant calling her "co-redemptrix" (co-redeemer).

First, Christ played an indispensable role in our salvation that no one else could have played. No one but the Father's only begotten Son, the Word of God incarnate, could have died to atone for our sins and been raised for our justification. Mary, by contrast, does not play a role that no one else possibly could have played. Kreeft says: "If Mary had said no, Christ would not have come." But this claim goes way beyond what the Gospels tell us and is radically at odds with what we know about God and his resources to implement his purposes. No doubt God knew Mary's heart and character and knew she would agree to bear his Son. But that is no reason to assume that Mary is the only girl that could possibly have played this role, or that God could have providentially prepared to play it. God's plan of salvation was not "dependent on her choice" in anything like the way it was dependent on the choice of Christ to be "obedient to the point of death, even death on a cross" (Phil 2:8).

3. Walls, "Christmas Eve."

Second, Mary's suffering was in no way comparable to that of Christ. Indeed, sometimes her suffering is exaggerated as if her very willingness to bear and raise the Son of God was itself a great sacrifice. To the contrary, it was a singular honor and the accent in the Magnificat is on the fact that all generations would call her blessed (Luke 1:48). To be sure, her unique honor also entailed suffering, as indicated in Simeon's prophecy that "a sword will pierce your own soul" (Luke 2:36). But remarkably, while the Gospels describe the suffering of Christ in vivid detail, they tell us nothing about the suffering of Mary. It is only common sense, of course, to assume that she did suffer when her son was crucified, as any loving mother would. But the fact remains that the Gospels are silent on the matter and give no indication that Mary's suffering was an important part of the story. This is even more remarkable since Luke does comment on the fact that some of the women who followed Jesus "were beating their breasts and wailing for him" as he was led away to be crucified (Luke 23:37). Significantly, their suffering is highlighted, but Mary's is not. Indeed, only the Gospel of John unequivocally tells us that Mary was even at the cross (John 19:25), and none of the Gospels clearly inform us that Mary came to his tomb after his resurrection, though other women did, most notably Mary Magdalene.[4] Mary the mother of Jesus simply does not play a significant role in the Gospel narratives of Jesus' death and resurrection.

Third, there is nothing in the New Testament to suggest that Mary is the link in "the chain of our salvation" that "most directly connects us with Christ." Nowhere does the New Testament teach that our connection to Christ is mediated by Mary, but quite the opposite.[5] In fact, some of the strongest words in the New Testament that would discourage this line of thought come from Christ himself. On one occasion, his family (including, presumably his mother) attempted to restrain him because there were accusations that he had lost his mind (Mark 3:20–21). They were calling for him and sent for him to come with them, and this was his response:

> And he replied, "Who are my mother and my brothers?" And looking at those sitting around him, he said, "Here are my mother and my brothers! Whoever does the will of God is my brother and sister and mother." (Mark 3:33–5)

---

4. It is possible, though unlikely, that Mary the mother of Jesus is mentioned in Mark 15:40–41, 47; 16:1 and Matthew 27:56, 61; 28:1. See Licona, *Why Are There Differences*, 209–12.

5. It is worth noting that Mary is not explicitly mentioned even once in the epistles of Paul, or in the epistles of Peter and John. Galatians 4:4 alludes to Mary but does not name her.

Not only does Jesus say nothing here to indicate that Mary provides some sort of direct connection to himself, but he even encourages us to think in very different terms about who are his real mother and brothers. Indeed, most remarkably, he suggests *we can be* Jesus' mother and sister and brother by doing the will of God. Or consider the incident in Luke when a woman interrupted his teaching to praise his mother.

> While he was saying this, a woman in the crowd raised her voice and said to him, "Blessed is the womb that bore you and the breasts that nursed you!" But he said, "Blessed rather are those who hear the word of God and obey it!" (Luke 11:27–28)

If ever there were an occasion when we might have expected Jesus to give a nod in the direction of Marian devotion if he wanted to encourage it, this would be it. But again, he defines blessedness in an altogether different way than this woman does and discourages her would be Marian piety.

It is also worth noting that the book of Hebrews tells us that Jesus is not ashamed to call us his brothers and that he became like us in every way so he could be a merciful and faithful high priest for us (Heb 2:11, 17). Because he has shared our human condition and was tempted in every way we are, we are invited to "approach the throne of grace with boldness, so that we may receive mercy and find grace to help in time of need" (Heb 4:16). Again, there is no hint that we must rely on Mary to connect us to Christ or that she is our most direct connection to him. Rather, we have a direct connection to him and can approach God boldly because he is our merciful and faithful high priest who calls us brothers and sisters.

All in all, Kreeft stretches the truth to the breaking point, and makes claims about Mary that go far beyond the biblical narrative and what it teaches us about the mother of our Lord.

Before moving on, it is worth asking what motivates this sort of piety. Consider Eric Metaxas's account of Martin Luther's experience as a monk, part of which included regularly praying the *Salve Regina* (Latin for "Save Us, O Mary"). The prayer was as follows: "Save O Queen, Our Mother of Mercy, our delight, and our hope. To thee we exiled Sons of Eve lift up our cry. To thee we sigh as we languish in this veil of tears. Be Thou our advocate, sweet Virgin Mary, pray for us, Thou holy Mother of God." Metaxas explains how this sort of Marian piety often reflected a distorted view of God and his grace.

> Part of the difficulty that Luther would find as he trod this wellworn path was that God the Father and Jesus the Son were both principally thought of as fierce judges. So the role of comforter

fell to Mary, the human one who understood us and our trials, the soft mother full of grace who could protect her beloved child from harsh and unyielding men. Although Christian doctrine had always clearly taught that Jesus himself had been fully human and could therefore understand and sympathize with our trials and sufferings and temptations, the reality of church life at this point in history was that this part of Jesus had mostly been ignored, so that he was now thought of as every bit as distant and remote and terrible as God the Father ever had been. So only Mary, his entirely human mother, could comfort us. And not only that, but she could appeal to her harsh and perhaps indifferent son as only a dear mother could.[6]

Or consider the same point expressed in a single sentence by Steven Botterill, who explains that "by virtue of being closer to the human plane, she is more approachable by those who have reason to fear, or who cannot comprehend, the ineffable mystery of God or the stern authority of Christ."[7]

In short then, it is arguable that much Marian piety reflects a profound failure to understand the grace of God and his love for us as revealed in the incarnation of Jesus. Christ is the one who has been tempted in all ways as we are and can sympathize with our weakness. It is because of Christ that we can approach the throne of grace with boldness and find grace to help us in every time of need.

MARIAN MAXIMALISM: DOGMATIZING MARY

But perhaps the most vivid instances of excessive claims about Mary pertain to the two Marian dogmas that have been declared infallible by the pope. The first of these, dogmatized in 1854, recall, is the immaculate conception, the doctrine that Mary was not only conceived without original sin but also lived a sinless life. This dogma, it is important to emphasize, lacks clear scriptural warrant and was rejected by several of the church fathers. Indeed, it remained controversial into the Middle Ages, when it was rejected by a number of noted theologians and was still a matter of dispute at the famous post-Reformation Council of Trent.

The doctrine eventually prevailed due to a general line of argument that appealed to what seems most fitting to ascribe to Mary. Exactly stated, the formula was stated as follows: "Whatever was both possible and eminently

6. Metaxas, *Martin Luther*, 35.
7. Botterill cited by Pelikan, *Mary Through the Centuries*, 140.

fitting for God to do, that he did."[8] This basic method of reasoning was developed by Duns Scotus into a stronger form known as "maximalism." The idea here is that when we are considering possible claims about the Virgin, "if it does not contradict the authority of Scripture or the authority of the church, it seems preferable to attribute greater rather than lesser excellence to Mary."[9] By this reasoning, it is preferable to believe Mary was born without original sin altogether than to believe that she was cleansed of sin an instant after she was conceived, as Aquinas held, or even later in her life.

Now the notion of what seems most "fitting" for God to do as a criterion for theological dogma about Mary may seem rather speculative, if not given to pious fancy. Using the criterion of maximalism, should we believe Mary was the smartest person who has ever lived? Did she have the most perfect health of anyone ever? Was she the most beautiful woman who has ever lived? To the last of these questions, Denys the Carthusian, employing the "fitting" line of argument, returned a positive answer. He held that Mary is "lovelier, even in natural physical beauty, than those of her holy ancestors whose beauty is praised in the Scriptures (Rebecca, Rachel, Judith, and Esther), and the Christian maidens (Catherine, Agatha, Agnes, and the rest) praised in the acts of the early martyrs."[10]

In any case, we also see Marian maximalism at work in the dogma of Mary's bodily assumption. Like the immaculate conception, this doctrine also lacks clear scriptural warrant and took centuries to develop.[11] In the fourth century, Epiphanius speculated that Mary never died, but clear affirmation of her bodily assumption did not emerge until the late fifth and early sixth centuries.[12] But once declared infallible, it officially licensed extraordinarily exalted claims about Mary. Jaroslav Pelikan observes:

> Thus it became obligatory in 1950 for Roman Catholics to believe and teach that, as the Spanish Marian mystic Sister Maria de Jesus de Agreda had said in her Life of the Virgin Mary already in 1670, Mary "was elevated to the right hand of her Son and the true God, and situated at the same royal throne of the Most Blessed Trinity, whither neither men nor angels nor seraphs have before attained, nor will ever attain for all eternity. This is the highest and the most excellent privilege of our Queen

---

8. Pelikan, *Mary Through the Centuries*, 196.

9. Pelikan, *Mary Through the Centuries*, 196.

10. Saward, *Sweet & Blessed Country*, 140.

11. For an account of how these doctrines took centuries to develop, see Pelikan, *Mary Through the Centuries*, 189–213.

12. See Collins and Walls, *Roman but Not Catholic*, 306–8; Ortlund, "Why Mary's Assumption."

and Lady: to be at the same throne as the divine Persons and to have a place in it, as Empress, when all the rest of humanity are only servants or ministers of the Supreme King."[13]

Pelikan goes on to observe that the proclamation of Mary's bodily assumption caused an uproar among Protestant clergy and was widely perceived as provocative and divisive. This was even more so because it happened at a time when ecumenism was on the rise and there were hopeful signs of healing some of the breaches that had divided the Western church for centuries. "Almost as if to find new reasons to perpetuate the schism now that some of these earlier points of disagreement had begun to yield on both sides of the conflict, the Marian doctrines of the immaculate conception in 1854 and the assumption in 1950 came along to counter this trend."[14]

To get a sense of the sharp dogmatic edge of these Marian doctrines, consider the claims made by the respective popes when they were officially proclaimed. After defining the doctrine of immaculate conception, Pope Pius IX issued this warning to any who might be inclined to doubt it.

> Hence, if anyone shall dare—which God forbid!—to think otherwise than as has been defined by us, let him know and understand that he is condemned by his own judgment; that he has suffered shipwreck in the faith; that he has separated from the unity of the Church; and that, furthermore, by his own action he incurs the penalties established by law if he should dare to express in words or writing or by any other outward means the errors he thinks in his heart.[15]

A century later, after the assumption was defined, Pius XII issued a similarly severe warning.

> Hence if anyone, which God forbid, should dare willfully to deny or to call into doubt that which we have defined, let him know that he has fallen away completely from the divine and Catholic Faith.[16]

Now these claims may seem rather extreme. However, I would suggest that they are entirely understandable given the Roman Catholic view of authority. Indeed, we have here the makings of another "all or nothing" argument that is even more rigorous than the ones we looked at earlier.

---

13. Pelikan, *Mary Through the Centuries*, 204.
14. Pelikan, *Mary Through the Centuries*, 205.
15. Pius IX, "*Ineffabilis Deus*."
16. Pius XII, "*Munificentissimus Deus*."

ALL OR NOTHING REDUX

Recall the passages from the *Catechism* I quoted in a previous chapter, which assert a connection between scripture, tradition, and the Roman magisterium that is such that no one of them can stand without the others. Recall too the claim that: "The task of giving an authentic interpretation of the Word of God, whether in its written form or in the form of Tradition, has been entrusted to the living teaching office of the Church alone." The claim that the magisterium *alone* has the authority of "authentic interpretation of the Word of God" is a far reaching one with large implications. Consider now this claim:

> The Church's Magisterium exercises the authority it holds from Christ to the fullest extent when it defines dogmas, that is when it proposes, in a form obliging the Christian people to an irrevocable adherence of faith, truths contained in divine Revelation or also when it proposes, in a definitive way, truths having a necessary connection with these.[17]

And here is one more passage with large implications for the role of the magisterium in Christian knowledge. Here, the *Catechism* is expounding the Roman Catholic view that revelation comes to us both in the form of scripture and the form of tradition, including oral tradition.

> As a result, the Church, to whom the transmission and interpretation of Revelation is entrusted, "does not derive her certainty about all revealed truths from the Holy Scriptures alone. Both Scripture and Tradition must be accepted and honored with equal sentiments of devotion and reverence."[18]

Now these various claims from the *Catechism* give us the material to construct a more rigorous "all or nothing" argument. Think about the implications of these claims for Rome in relation to other Christian traditions. The Roman magisterium allegedly has exclusive authority to provide "authentic interpretation of the Word of God" whether in the form of scripture or tradition, including oral tradition. Moreover, dogma that is defined "in a form obliging the Christian people to an irrevocable adherence of faith" is equal in authority and certainty whether derived from scripture or tradition. These binding truths, again, may either be contained in revelation, or they may have a "necessary connection" with such truths.

---

17. *Catechism*, para. 88.
18. *Catechism*, para. 82. The passage quoted is from Paul VI, "*Dei Verbum*," para. 9.

So, consider again the Nicene Creed, the paradigmatic instance of a conciliar dogmatic determination that not only Roman Catholics but many other believers, including many Reformation Christians, would accept not only as an authentic interpretation of scripture, but one with binding authority. Now consider the fact that the Marian dogmas we have been considering have been given the highest level of dogmatic authority possible since they have been declared infallible by the Roman magisterium, particularly the pope. These dogmas have now been elevated to the same level of authority as the Nicene Creed.

Now this raises in a rather pointed way serious questions since these dogmas are typically rejected by Christians in the Reformation traditions.[19] The question is whether one can coherently affirm the Creed as a true interpretation of scripture, while rejecting the dogma of the Mary's bodily assumption. A closely related question is whether it is a coherent position to affirm the Creed but deny the bodily assumption *given Roman Catholic claims about magisterial authority.*

As we have noted, Roman Catholics often argue that Protestants cannot consistently accept or believe in the authority of the Bible and the classic creeds if they reject the authority of the Roman magisterium. Consider, then, the following argument as a rigorous version of this sort of "all or nothing" argument:

1. We can consistently believe that the Nicene Creed is a true interpretation of scripture only if we believe that the Roman Catholic magisterium (RCM) has infallible teaching authority.
2. If we believe that the RCM has infallible teaching authority, then we believe that what the pope proclaims *ex cathedra* is infallible truth.
3. If we believe that what the pope proclaims *ex cathedra* is infallible truth, then we believe that the dogma of the bodily assumption of Mary is infallible truth.
4. We can consistently believe that the Nicene Creed is a true interpretation of scripture only if we believe that the dogma of the bodily assumption of Mary is infallible truth.
5. If we do not believe that the dogma of the bodily assumption of Mary is infallible truth, then we cannot consistently believe that the Nicene Creed is a true interpretation of scripture.[20]

19. The immaculate conception is, however, accepted by some Lutherans, who find some support for the doctrine in Luther himself.

20. Thanks to Kyle Blanchette for suggesting this more efficient version of my argument, which has fewer steps than my original.

This argument is valid, so its conclusion does in fact follow from its premises with "stern logical necessity." The more interesting question, obviously, is whether all its premises are true, and whether it is thus a sound argument, as well as a valid one. The key premise, upon which the entire argument turns, is the first one. The other premises (2 and 3) are straightforward propositions that must be accepted by anyone who understands the teaching authority Rome claims for itself and knows the pope has declared *ex cathedra* that the dogma of Mary's bodily assumption is infallible truth. Premise 4 follows from 1 through 3 (by extended hypothetical syllogism), and 5 follows from 4 (by contraposition).

Protestants will deny premise 1, and in the previous chapter I showed why Protestants have excellent reasons to affirm the truth and authority of the Nicene Creed on their own principles. But the question remains whether this premise fairly states what Roman Catholics are committed to. Is this what is entailed in the claim that scripture, tradition, and the magisterium are so connected that one cannot stand without the others?

I will not attempt a definitive answer to that question: that is up to Rome. But here I want to identify some other variations on the argument that might be suggested instead of the one above. Another, slightly weaker claim would be the following:

> 1a. We can be rationally certain that the Nicene Creed is a true interpretation of scripture only if we believe that the Roman Catholic magisterium has infallible teaching authority.

The argument would be rephrased accordingly, and the conclusion would be as follows:

> 5a. If we do not believe that the dogma of the bodily assumption of Mary is infallible truth, we cannot be rationally certain that the Nicene Creed is a true interpretation of scripture.

Notice that the claim here pertains to rational certainty, not consistency. That is, it might be argued that one is not, strictly speaking, inconsistent in rejecting the claims of the Roman magisterium while believing that the Nicene Creed is a true interpretation of scripture. But one does not have solid grounds for rational certainty.

Another, stronger version would be the following.

> 1b. We can *know* that the Nicene Creed is a true interpretation of scripture only if the Roman Catholic magisterium *has* infallible teaching authority.

Again, the argument would be rephrased accordingly, and the conclusion would be as follows:

5b. If the dogma of the bodily assumption of Mary is not infallible truth, we cannot know that the Nicene Creed is a true interpretation of scripture.

This version is stronger because it claims that the very possibility of knowing that the Creed is a true interpretation of scripture hinges on the Roman Catholic magisterium having infallible authority. The issue here is not whether one can be consistent or rational or rationally certain in believing that the Creed is a true interpretation of scripture if one does not believe that the magisterium has infallible teaching authority. What is at stake in this claim is not the consistency or rationality of anyone's beliefs but *the very possibility* of having knowledge about the true interpretation of scripture.

Before moving on, it is worth noting that these various all-or-nothing arguments so beloved by Roman Catholic apologists are strikingly similar to certain arguments sometimes deployed by conservative, usually fundamentalist, Protestant apologists. Consider this argument and the ways it is parallel to the ones above.

1. We can consistently believe in the bodily resurrection of Jesus only if we believe that the Bible is the infallible word of God.

2. If we believe that the Bible is the infallible word of God, then we believe what it teaches in every detail.

3. If we believe what the Bible teaches in every detail, then we believe that the earth is only thousands of years old.

4. We can consistently believe in the bodily resurrection of Jesus only if we believe that the earth is only thousands of years old.

5. If we do not believe that the earth is only thousands of years old, then we cannot consistently believe in the bodily resurrection of Jesus.

While the parallel is not exact, the fundamental similarity is that this argument, like the ones preceding it, appeals to a far-reaching claim about infallible authority, and on this basis it tries to establish that certain doctrines are equally supported by this authority.[21] Those doctrines are consequently on

---

21. Claiming that the Bible teaches that the earth is only thousands of years old depends, of course, on a rather literalistic reading of the Old Testament chronologies. Yet the young earth view probably has more direct biblical support than the bodily assumption of Mary. On such a literal reading, Archbishop Ussher's famous chronology dated creation at 4004 BC.

an epistemic par, and we have no rational right to accept one without also accepting the other. To do so is to fall into irrationality or inconsistency of some sort.

IF MARY BE NOT BODILY ASSUMED INTO HEAVEN, OUR FAITH IS VAIN?

The fundamental similarity of these arguments explains why many Roman Catholic apologists, like their fundamentalist counterparts, are so driven to try to demonstrate some glaring contradiction in the views of the persons they have targeted for conversion to their position, or to claim that their position alone is fully consistent. (Indeed, it is perhaps telling that some of the most zealous Roman Catholic apologists are former Protestant fundamentalists.) While this argumentative strategy unsettles many people who naturally want to maintain their cherished beliefs, and many convert under the pressure of thinking they need to do so in order to preserve their faith, the sense of being settled that is gained by such "consistency" is a fragile one.

Indeed, I suspect that those who employ these "all or nothing" arguments, by insisting that one cannot affirm the Creed without affirming these distinctive claims of Rome, realize that those distinctive claims of Rome are on tenuous grounds otherwise. Unfortunately, this strategy for shoring up those beliefs puts the whole faith in jeopardy.

Consider the young person who is convinced that his basis for believing in the bodily resurrection of Jesus has the same ground as his belief that the world is only thousands of years old. When confronted with powerful scientific evidence that the earth is in fact much older, his faith in the resurrection of Jesus is thereby threatened. He faces the unsettling choice of rejecting that scientific evidence or having his faith in the resurrection of Jesus undermined.

Similarly, there is something obviously wrong when an argument can be mounted that we cannot consistently or rationally believe in classic creedal doctrines without accepting the Marian dogmas and similar claims. Think about it. These arguments claim that we cannot rationally believe doctrines that are utterly central to the Christian revelation, doctrines that have enormous biblical support, unless we believe certain doctrines that have only the most tenuous, if any, clear biblical support, or even grounding in early tradition.

There is to be sure an inner coherence and logical relationship between those classic creedal doctrines that comprise the heart of our faith. Everything starts in the order of *knowing* from the bodily resurrection of Jesus, as we observed in the first chapter. "And if Christ has not been raised, your faith is futile; you are still in your sins" (1 Cor 15:17). The resurrection was the explosive event that eventually propelled and gave shape to the historic Christian faith. It is the definitive evidence for the deity of Jesus, which leads us straight to the doctrines of atonement and incarnation.[22] And these doctrines, along with the revelation of the Holy Spirit at Pentecost, lead to the doctrine of Trinity.[23] There are, moreover, logical relations among these doctrines and an inner coherence that weaves them together as a single garment. To deny any of these doctrines is to begin to unravel the whole.

But here is the question: Can it seriously be maintained that the Marian dogmas have a similar relation to these doctrines? Is denial of the bodily assumption of Mary really tantamount to denying the incarnation and the Trinity? If one doubted transubstantiation, would doubts about the resurrection inevitably follow? Does rejection of these Marian doctrines unravel classic creedal Christianity, as the pope warned when he defined these dogmas? If one looked into the historical foundations of the papacy and found them wanting, would that person's faith in Christ begin to crumble as well?

Protestants, I have argued, have principled reasons for affirming the authority of scripture and the Creed, while rejecting the claims of the Roman magisterium. The coherence of catholic Reformation Christianity in no way depends on accepting the Marian dogmas or other claims of Roman Catholicism, such as papal infallibility.

For Roman Catholics, however, it is far from clear that their faith in classic creedal doctrines can coherently stand without the Marian dogmas. Again, the basic logic is straightforward: if the bodily assumption of Mary is not infallibly true, the doctrine of papal infallibility is not true; and if the doctrine of papal infallibility is not true, the claims of the Roman magisterium to have exclusive authority to define dogma are not true. And the claim to such exclusive authority by Rome is apparent in the claim we have been examining in this chapter that "sacred Tradition, Sacred Scripture, and the magisterium of the Church are so connected and associated that one of them cannot stand without the others." In short, then, the credibility of the entire Roman Catholic authority structure hinges on the infallible truth of Mary's bodily assumption, and in turn papal infallibility. Those who are not dogmatically committed to Rome may see here a house of cards waiting to fall.

---

22. This is not to insist that any particular *theory* of atonement is essential. The Creed does not settle that.

23. The order of *being* is exactly the opposite of the order of *knowing* these central Christian doctrines. God was a Trinity from all eternity; the Son of God became incarnate, then atoned for our sins, and then was resurrected.

Finally, we might take a cue from C. S. Lewis who was once asked by one of his correspondents what he thought about saying "Hail Mary." Here was his response.

> My own view would be that a salute to any saint (or angel) cannot in itself be wrong any more than taking off one's hat to a friend: but that there is always some danger lest such practices start one on the road to a state (sometimes found in Roman Catholics) where the Virgin Mary is treated really as a deity and even becomes the centre of the religion. I therefore think that such salutes are better avoided.[24]

What we have seen in this chapter is evidence of what Lewis warned against. Popular Marian piety in Roman Catholicism has morphed into infallible dogmas that make Mary far more central to the faith than scripture warrants.[25] Not only has she been elevated into a virtual female counterpart of Christ, but popes warn us that our faith in Christ cannot stand without assent to Roman Marian dogma. The fact that Roman theology is so badly off center in this regard is yet another reason not to be a Roman Catholic.

It is important to emphasize that more is at stake here than an intellectual debate about logical consistency. This is a pastoral issue as well as a philosophical and theological one. For believers who think their right to believe in the resurrection of Jesus depends on their believing the earth is only several thousand years old, or who think their right to believe in the incarnation and atonement of Jesus requires them to believe in Mary's bodily assumption, are not only caught up in an intellectually dubious position but a spiritually precarious one as well. The "right" to believe the saving truths of the gospel should never be held hostage by other beliefs that are peripheral at best. Those who press such arguments on vulnerable believers to pressure them to "convert" to their church or theological position are not only setting them up for intellectual implosion but spiritual shipwreck as well.

---

24. Ford, *Yours, Jack*, 183.

25. For more on this, see Collins and Walls, *Roman but Not Catholic*, 280–320; Arbour, "Evangelical Protestant's Reflections," 21–38.

CHAPTER SEVEN

CATHOLIC CONVERSION AND COERCION

RECALL FROM THE PREVIOUS chapter that both times when the Marian dogmas were defined the pope issued severe warnings against anyone who might be disposed to openly question or reject those dogmas. Here again is the warning from Pope Pius IX concerning the immaculate conception.

> Hence, if anyone shall dare—which God forbid!—to think otherwise than as has been defined by us, let him know and understand that he is condemned by his own judgment; that he has suffered shipwreck in the faith; that he has separated from the unity of the Church; and that, furthermore, by his own action he incurs the penalties established by law if he should dare to express in words or writing or by any other outward means the errors he thinks in his heart.[1]

To suffer "shipwreck in the faith" is a serious matter because what is ultimately at stake is nothing less than eternal salvation.

These warnings reflect an interesting aspect of Roman Catholic history and practice, namely, a willingness to employ various forms of coercion to convert people or to keep them in the fold. At one level these warnings might be taken as a form of intellectual coercion, since they demand that no one "think otherwise than as has been defined by us" on pain of damnation. The sort of coercion I will focus on here, however, goes beyond these sorts of threats and involves the use of physical force and other punishments to impose the acceptance of beliefs on the unwilling. Notice in the passage

---

1. Pius IX, *"Ineffabilis Deus."*

above that in addition to suffering "shipwreck in the faith," such persons also incur "the penalties established by law."

Pope Pius IX is also the author of the famous *Syllabus of Errors* that was issued in 1864. One of the "errors" that document condemned was the following: "Every man is free to embrace and profess that religion which, guided by the light of reason, he shall consider true."[2] With the rejection of religious freedom comes the right to punish those who do not think and believe as prescribed by the church.

NO SALVATION OUTSIDE THE CHURCH (OF ROME)?

One of the deepest roots of this whole matter goes back to the dictum affirmed by the church fathers that "outside the church there is no salvation." At one level, this claim is one that any Christian should affirm. The church, after all, is the body of Christ. Salvation comes through Christ, the head of the church. So to be in Christ is to be in his body, the church.

However, this rather straightforward claim of the church fathers can also be understood in a more controversial sense that pits Roman Catholics against other Christians. In short, "the church" can be identified with "the Roman Catholic Church," so that the claim is interpreted to mean that there is no salvation outside the Roman Catholic Church. In previous centuries, this claim was understood in a rather exclusive sense that would have condemned not only unbelievers but also Protestants to hell. Since Vatican II, however, the Roman Catholic Church has been more generous in its assessment of other Christians. Here is the contemporary understanding of the patristic dictum that "outside the church there is no salvation":

> Basing itself on Scripture and Tradition, the [Second Vatican] Council teaches that the Church, a pilgrim now on earth, is necessary for salvation: the one Christ is mediator and the way of salvation: he is present to us in his body which is the Church. He himself explicitly asserted the necessity of faith and Baptism, and thereby affirmed at the same time the necessity of the Church which men enter through Baptism as through a door. Hence they could not be saved who, knowing that the [Roman] Catholic Church was founded as necessary by God through Christ, would refuse either to enter it or to remain in it.[3]

---

2. Pius IX, "Syllabus of Errors."
3. *Catechism*, para. 846.

CATHOLIC CONVERSION AND COERCION

The first two sentences here are entirely unobjectionable for any orthodox, biblical Christian. Only when we come to the last sentence do we encounter claims that are contentious. Although the claim is qualified in significant ways, as we shall see, it still asserts the necessity of entering the Roman Catholic Church in order to be saved.

One qualification comes immediately after this paragraph, and it makes explicit that this "affirmation is not aimed at those who, through no fault of their own, do not know Christ and his Church." Such persons fail to know Christ and his church due to "invincible" ignorance that is in no way their fault, so they are not in any way to blame for their failure to know Christ and his church.[4] They have simply not had the opportunity, due to circumstances beyond their control, to learn about Christ and his church, so they cannot be held responsible for their ignorance. It is clear then, that the strong claim above affirming the necessity of entering or remaining in the Roman Catholic Church for salvation applies only to those "in the know" about Christ and his church.

WHAT ABOUT PROTESTANTS AND FORMER CATHOLICS?

It is only reasonable not to blame people for things they cannot avoid, so this qualification is hardly surprising. What is a bit surprising, however, is that Protestants are also seen as exceptions to the general rule that entering the Roman Catholic Church is necessary for salvation. The passage below from the *Catechism* comes after paragraphs that assert that the Roman Catholic Church is the sole church founded by Christ and that in it alone can the fullness of salvation be found. The next section, headed "Wounds to Unity," describes and warns against "certain rifts" that are censured as "damnable" because of the divisions they create in the body of Christ. Protestants, it might seem, would fall under this condemnation, as they have in earlier centuries. But here is how Protestants are viewed since Vatican II:

> However, one cannot charge with the sin of the separation those who at present are born into these communions [that resulted from such separation] and in them are brought up in the faith of Christ, and the Catholic Church accepts them with respect and affection as brothers. . . . All who have been justified by faith in Baptism are incorporated into Christ; they therefore have a

---

4. For a definition of invincible ignorance, see *Catechism*, para. 1793.

right to be called Christians, and with good reason are accepted as brothers in the Lord by the children of the Catholic Church.[5]

Now this is not only a welcome development from earlier attitudes, but a fascinating one as well. How exactly are we to understand this? Are Protestants under a cloud of invincible ignorance from their upbringing that prevents them from seeing that the Roman Catholic Church is the one true church, which all Christians, if properly informed, should enter? Since Protestants are typically taught an account of the Christian faith that is at odds with some essential claims of Roman Catholicism, is it not their fault that they do not believe the claims of Rome? And if they do not even believe the distinctive claims of Rome, presumably they do not "know" that the Roman Catholic Church was uniquely founded by Christ as necessary for salvation. Most would agree that if you do not even *believe* a claim, you do not *know* it. Sincere belief is a necessary condition for knowledge.

However, there is a large group of contemporary Protestant believers who do not fit the description in the paragraph above. Notice that it specifies persons who "are born into these communions [that resulted from such separation] and in them are brought up in the faith of Christ." So, the question is, what about all those contemporary Protestants who were not born and raised in Protestant communions? Consider the fact that the Roman Catholic Church in the United States is losing members faster than any other church.[6] Now many of these persons have left the faith altogether, but many of them are now active in various Protestant churches. Or consider the millions of former Roman Catholics in South America who have left the church where they were baptized and confirmed, but are now active members of evangelical or Pentecostal churches. What about them? Are they also accepted with "respect and affection as brothers"?[7]

SANCTIONED RELIGIOUS COERCION?

In raising these questions, we bring into sharper focus the more troubling form of religious coercion that has played a significant role in Roman Catholic theology and practice, and has been the subject of considerable controversy. As we approach this issue, it is important to acknowledge Roman Catholics have not been the only ones who have used coercion in the

---

5. *Catechism*, para. 818.

6. See O'Loughlin, "Pew Survey"; Kandra, "New Gallup Poll."

7. For a very interesting discussion of this, see Collins and Walls, *Roman but Not Catholic*, 112–24.

form of physical force. Other Christians have done so, and they have left embarrassing stains on their history. But what is of particular interest here is that Rome has officially affirmed religious coercion as a matter of magisterial teaching. This poses a distinctive sort of problem for Roman Catholics.

One of the most famous of these formal affirmations of coercion was in response to an opinion of Erasmus that endorsed a significant measure of religious freedom. In particular, Erasmus held the view that those who were baptized as children should be asked to publicly re-affirm their baptism when they had grown up. If they declined to do so, however, Erasmus held that they should not be subject to any other punishment or coercion than exclusion from receiving the sacraments.

It was this opinion of Erasmus that was strongly repudiated. For example, in 1528, the theologians of the Sorbonne in Paris formally censured Erasmus as follows: "Whence those baptised as children can be compelled to retain the Christian faith no less than Jews circumcised as children could once be compelled to keep the laws of Moses."[8]

This same conviction was affirmed in 1547 in a more definitive dogmatic fashion at the council of Trent in session 7 canon 14.

> If anyone says that when they grow up, those baptized as little children should be asked whether they wish to affirm what their godparents promised in their name when they were baptized; and when they reply that they have no such wish, they should be left to their own decision and not, in the meantime be coerced by any penalty into the Christian life except that they be barred from the eucharist and the other sacraments, until they have a change of heart: let him be anathema.[9]

Notice the view of Erasmus—that children who, when grown, decline to affirm the faith should not be punished in any way beyond withholding the sacraments from them—is roundly condemned by an anathema! This canon emphatically affirms that further punishment should be exacted.

Indeed, the means of coercion that were approved could be rather extreme. For instance, the noted theologian and cardinal Francisco de Toledo went so far as to insist that, "Those baptized as infants before the use of reason are certainly to be compelled when they reach the age of reason to retain the faith, even on penalty of death."[10]

The use of coercion to compel religious assent remained officially approved as late as the nineteenth century. Recall that Pope Pius IX rejected as

8. Cited by Pink, "John Finnis's Alternative History."
9. Cited in Pink, "John Finnis's Alternative History," 1–2.
10. Cited in Pink, "John Finnis's Alternative History," 3.

an "error" the idea of religious freedom that allows everyone to embrace and profess the religion they judge to be true.

A GOOD REASON TO REJECT ROME'S CLAIMS OF AUTHORITY?

Now then, for those who believe such coercion is clearly wrong, the fact that the Church of Rome has dogmatically affirmed such coercion is a good reason to reject the teaching authority of Rome. Political philosopher Kevin Vallier has provided an elegant version of the argument from coercion.

1. If the Catholic Church is the true church, then she has infallible teaching authority.
2. If the Catholic Church has infallible teaching authority, she has a limited right of religious coercion over the baptized.
3. But the Catholic Church lacks a limited right of religious coercion over the baptized; for its exercise would violate the dignity of the person.
4. The Catholic Church lacks infallible teaching authority.
5. The Catholic Church is not the true church.[11]

The stark claim of those who defend religious coercion is that such coercion is justified for validly baptized persons. If such persons preach heresy or forsake the faith, then the Roman Catholic Church can rightly direct a Catholic ruler of a Christian state to employ coercion to impose punishment on these persons to motivate them to give up their heresy, or to return to the Church. Such punishments can include imprisonment and execution, even execution by fire, a widely practiced method of punishment for heretics for centuries. Protestants, obviously, would be fair game for such punishment.

Vallier's argument is valid, so everything depends on the truth of the premises. Given Rome's claims to infallible teaching authority, premise 1 is clearly true. If indeed Rome is the true church, she has the infallibility she claims. Premise 2 is perhaps the most controversial premise, but the passages cited above show beyond reasonable doubt that Rome has claimed the right to religious coercion in dogmatically authoritative documents. Premise 3 is the central moral judgment upon which the argument hinges. While almost everyone today would agree with it, those who defend religious coercion as morally acceptable will dispute it. This argument is aimed at those who judge religious coercion to be clearly wrong. 4 follows from a 2 and 3; and 5 follows from 1 and 4.

---

11. Vallier, "Best Argument," 1.

Again, those who want to challenge this argument and its conclusion should challenge premise 3.

RADICAL REVERSAL?

Now it is more than a little interesting that contemporary Roman Catholic theologians emphatically reject religious coercion. Indeed, the Vatican II document "Declaration on Religious Freedom" (*Dignitatis Humanae*) insists that religious freedom is a fundamental human right. The opening paragraph of chapter 1 reads as follows.

> This Vatican Council declares that the human person has a right to religious freedom. This freedom means that all men are to be immune from coercion on the part of individuals or of social groups and of any human power, in such wise that no one is to be forced to act in a manner contrary to his own beliefs, whether privately or publicly, whether alone or in association with others, within due limits.[12]

Given this affirmation of religious freedom, the document later goes on to observe that "a wrong is done when government imposes upon its people, by force or fear or other means, the profession or repudiation of any religion, or when it hinders men from joining or leaving a religious community."[13]

It is particularly noteworthy that coercion is roundly and repeatedly repudiated in this document, almost as if to repent of past coercion and distance itself from previous dogma. And yet, all of this is only implicit. There is no explicit acknowledgment that official dogma affirms the moral legitimacy of coercion, nor is there any overt rejection of that dogma. Indeed, given Rome's claims to infallible authority, the dogmatic authority of the Council of Trent cannot simply be denied.

So this creates a quandary for Roman Catholics who want to respect the authority of official dogma but also believe that religious coercion is morally wrong. For there certainly appears to be a clear contradiction between the Council of Trent and the *Syllabus of Errors,* on the one hand, and the "Declaration on Religious Freedom," on the other. Indeed, this contradiction has been acknowledged by Roman Catholic theologians for decades. The distinguished theologian John Courtney Murray, SJ, for instance, pointed out the problem faced by Vatican II shortly after the Council concluded:

---

12. *Documents of Vatican II*, 392.
13. *Documents of Vatican II*, 395–96.

The notion of development, not the notion of religious freedom, was the real sticking-point for those who opposed the Declaration even to the end. The course of development between the *Syllabus of Errors* (1864) and *Dignitatis Humanae* (1965) still remains to be explained by theologians.[14]

Notice the Declaration was controversial and was opposed by some of the participants of Vatican II all the way to the end. But the issue was not whether coercion was wrong; that was a matter of agreement. The problem, rather, was how the repudiation of coercion and the strong affirmation of religious freedom could be construed as a "development" that was fully consistent with earlier dogma. It is a hard sell to pass off a patent contradiction as a matter of mere "development." Indeed, as Terrence Tilley observes, this development was quite a turnaround from just a decade earlier.

> In 1955 Murray was silenced by Roman authorities because he advocated freedom of religion as a positive political good rather than a (barely) tolerable political evil. Less than a decade later, Murray's position would be in large part vindicated by the promulgation of *Dignitatis Humanae* at the Second Vatican Council. This is not only a radical reversal, but given that "the Church thinks in centuries," a practically instantaneous turnaround.[15]

So what are faithful Roman Catholics to do in the face of this quandary? Should they simply bite the bullet and defend religious coercion as morally justified, or should they face up to the fact that their church was wrong on this matter and now holds a position that is the complete opposite of previous magisterial teaching?

A THIRD OPTION OR A REVISIONIST RUSE?

Or is there a third option? Recently, some have argued that there is. According to this third option, magisterial teaching, properly understood, did not in fact license religious coercion. A notable defender of this view is John Finnis, the great Roman Catholic legal scholar who has taught for many years at Oxford and Notre Dame. Finnis offers a creative historical re-construction of the events surrounding the famous canon 14 of session 7 of the Council of Trent intended to show that canon 14 does not in fact condemn the views of Erasmus. What actually happened at Trent, he says, was a subtle rejection of religious coercion, not an affirmation of it.

14. Murray cited by Tilley, *Inventing Catholic Tradition*, 116.
15. Tilley, *Inventing Catholic Tradition*, 117.

It would take us too far afield to examine the historical details of this debate, but interested readers should read both Finnis's essay and Pink's critique.[16] At any rate, I found Pink's critique to be altogether convincing, and I think it shows there is no plausible third option for those who want to reject religious coercion as immoral and also want to affirm the authority of magisterial teaching. I think Pink shows that such options require a sort of historical revisionism that is simply not true to the facts. Indeed, even conservatives who aspire to submit to magisterial authority engage in a subtle sleight of hand, according to Pink:

> For these Catholics, history cannot be doctrinally irrelevant. But still they do not submit their theology to history. Rather the reverse. Their view of history turns out to be an ideological product of their theology.... Religious liberty, Church and state, the death penalty, Jewish salvation, the dependence of salvation on the sacraments generally, the nature and function of the liturgy—any of these can be reconceived even in official circles within the Church in radically new terms that would most certainly have been condemned by past authority as damnandus, haereticus or falsus. But then this official theology's notional loyalty to the historical magisterium kicks in—not to block the revisionary theology itself, but to block the frank admission of its revisionary nature. The full extent to which official theology has actually contradicted past magisterial doctrines in these areas is simply not admitted. Change has to be disguised—and one way is through some inventive myth about what the Church "has always taught." The revisionary theology of the "conservatives" is prone to camouflage itself in revisionary history. John Finnis's account of Trent is an ingenious but unconvincing exercise in such revision.[17]

Notice particularly this line: "The full extent to which official theology has actually contradicted past magisterial doctrines in these areas is simply not admitted." By not admitting what is really happening, these conservatives can propagate a myth about what the Church "has always taught."

Of course, in fairness we must acknowledge that these documents are rather complex and the meaning of them is open to some degree of interpretation. Perhaps with sufficient effort and ingenuity, what appears to be a patent contradiction between earlier magisterial teaching and today's official theology can be shown not to be. But insofar as such efforts rely on strained

---

16. For Finnis's essay, see John Finnis, "John Finnis on Thomas Pink," in George and Keown, *Reason, Morality and Law*, 566–77.

17. Pink, "John Finnis's Alternative History," 14–15.

interpretations that are historically dubious, as that of Finnis appears to be, we have good reason to reject them.

Before concluding this brief chapter, it is worth noting that the issue remains unclear whether Rome embraces as "separated brethren" those persons who were born and baptized into the Roman Catholic Church but have now converted to Protestant churches and are actively involved in them. Since these persons no longer believe the Church of Rome is the one true church, presumably they could not be fairly charged with "knowing that the [Roman] Catholic Church was founded as necessary by God through Christ." Again, belief is a necessary condition for knowledge, so no one can *know* a given claim if he does not sincerely *believe* it. And if so, it seems such persons should not be judged culpable for choosing not to remain in the Roman Catholic Church. One might conclude then, that Roman Catholics should accept these Protestant converts with "respect and affection as brothers," just as they now accept as brothers those who were born into Protestant churches and raised in them. That, of course, is for Rome to decide, and I will leave it at that.

In any case, what remains clear is that there is a serious problem for Roman Catholics who reject religious coercion as immoral, but want to respect the authority of magisterial teaching. This difficulty counts against the teaching authority of Rome and provides another reason not to be a Roman Catholic.[18]

---

18. It is likely no accident that the world's greatest democratic republic to date that is founded on freedom of religion and freedom of speech has been predominantly Protestant since its inception. For some of the ways modern ideals of freedom are due to Protestantism, see Miller, *Religious Roots*; Ryrie, *Protestants*.

CHAPTER EIGHT

"YOU ARE YOUR OWN POPE"

The Tu Quoque *Objection*

THE PHRASE "TU QUOQUE" literally means "you too," and is the Latin name for the informal fallacy that occurs when one accuses his critic of the same thing of which his critic is accusing him. "*Tu quoque*" is thus in one sense a diversionary tactic that aims to turn the tables on one's critic instead of answering his criticism. "I'm a scoundrel, huh? Well, so are you!"

While it is recognized as an informal fallacy, those who make the *tu quoque* move sometimes have a point. For instance, if one is accused of lying, the charge loses at least much of its force if the person leveling the accusation is himself a known liar. While that does not show you are not a liar, it does at least show you are in the same boat as your critic, and he loses the high moral ground if he is guilty of the same thing you are.

It is in this sense that Reformation Christians may make the *tu quoque* move in response to certain criticisms from their Roman colleagues pertaining to authority. In this chapter, I will examine a statement of the argument by Roman Catholic philosopher and apologist (and former Evangelical) Bryan Cross, who attempts to show that Roman Catholics are not in the same boat as they contend their Protestants friends are, and thus that the *tu quoque* argument against them has no force.

Cross prefaces his response to the *tu quoque* objection by summarizing an argument about the nature of authority that he thinks poses problems for Protestants. Here he reiterates a variation on the familiar claim that those who do not accept Roman Catholic claims about apostolic succession are bereft of any principled reason to accept the authority of creeds and confessions. As Cross puts it, each Protestant is left to "pick" the confession that most closely resembles his personal interpretation of scripture. But he is not bound by that confession, for if his interpretation of scripture changes, he can simply pick another one that lines up better with his new perspective.

The important principle he wants to emphasize is that if we only submit to an authority when we agree with it, we are in reality only submitting to ourselves. "In other words, agreement with oneself cannot be the basis for authority over oneself. Therefore, a creed or confession's agreement with one's own interpretation of scripture cannot be the basis for its authority. And this is why without apostolic succession, creeds or confession have no actual authority."[1]

In other words, if you do not accept Roman claims about apostolic succession and the authority of the magisterium, you are your own pope, as one of my Roman Catholic friends insisted to me![2] So the charge is that every Protestant elects himself to the office of pope over the domain of his own personal interpretation of the faith.

OH YEAH? YOU TOO!

Here is where Reformation Christians want to lodge the *tu quoque* objection. Aren't those who embrace Rome in the same boat? Aren't they choosing the denomination or church that best fits their own understanding of scripture, history, and tradition?

> But if picking a confession on the basis of its agreement with one's own interpretation of Scripture entails that this confession has no authority over oneself, then picking the Catholic Church on the basis of its agreement with one's own interpretation of history, tradition, and Scripture entails that the Catholic Church has no authority over oneself. In short, the conclusion of the *tu quoque* objection is that either the Catholic Church likewise has no authority, or the Protestant confessions can truly have authority.[3]

Cross, however, denies that Reformation and Roman Catholic Christians are in the same boat in this regard. Indeed, as he apparently sees things, Reformation Christians are buffeted about in a leaky little sail boat, whereas Roman Christians are aboard a majestic ocean liner. His reply to the *tu quoque* objection is given in three key points, which I summarize in the next section.

1. Cross, "Tu Quoque," I (numbers refer to sections of this paper).
2. This came from Mike Allen, a former student of mine.
3. Cross, "Tu Quoque," II.

NOT US, JUST YOU!

First, he spells out the course of study that should be followed by those who seek to join the Church of Rome, and what he believes will be the outcome of that study. "Apart from a supernatural experience, ideally, an adult would come to seek full communion with the Catholic Church only after careful study of the motives of credibility, Church history, the Church Fathers, and Scripture."[4] The "motives of credibility" are the external proofs of the Christian revelation, such as "the miracles of Christ and the saints, prophecies, the Church's growth and holiness, and her fruitfulness and stability."[5]

The study of church history would be a "decade by decade" exploration, starting with the time of the apostles, down to the present day. The study would pay particular attention to schisms, and in each case, the prospective Roman Catholic would note the criteria by which it was determined that in each case, the party in schism was guilty of dividing the church. Now here is the expected outcome: "By such a study, and by the help of the Holy Spirit, he would discover that the Catholic Church is the one, holy, catholic and apostolic Church that Christ founded in the first century, and that has continued to grow throughout the world over the past two millennia."[6]

The key word here is "discovered," a word that he continues to employ over and over. In particular, Cross thinks his prospective convert "discovers" the Roman Catholic Church, whereas the Protestant only "discovers" a confession that agrees with his personal interpretation of scripture. And that, he alleges, explains why the former can have real authority, while the latter cannot. "The difference lies fundamentally neither in the discovery process nor in the evidence by which the discovery is made, even though these may be different. The difference lies fundamentally in the nature of that which is discovered."[7]

Second, Cross highlights the reason why there is a difference between the authority of scripture and Protestant confessions. Whereas scripture has intrinsic, binding authority because God himself is its source, all confessions are "merely" human interpretations of scripture, and thus they do not bear the same authority. He reiterates this claim over and over, using some form of the word "mere" at least nine times while making this second point in order to underscore the contrast he wants to draw between Roman Catholic "discovery" and Protestant "interpretation." There is no "guarantee

---

4. Cross, "Tu Quoque," III.A
5. *Catechism*, para. 156.
6. Cross, "Tu Quoque," III.A
7. Cross, "Tu Quoque," III.A

of protection from error" since these confessions are "essentially human opinion" that have no more authority than a systematic theology written by a theologian. "This is why a Protestant confession has its 'authority' only on the basis of the individual's agreement with its interpretation of Scripture, not because of who wrote that confession."[8]

This puts Protestants in a rather precarious position, according to Cross, for if the only basis for the authority of a confession is the individual's agreement with its interpretation of scripture, that authority could shift at any time. The individual may agree with it now, but perhaps not tomorrow.

> This shows that the confession has no intrinsic authority; it is not the confession that is authoritative over his beliefs; rather, his present beliefs make the confession to be "authoritative," by containing the interpretation he presently believes to be required of himself. . . . He picks this particular confession because it conforms to his interpretation; it does not oblige him to conform to it, or, once picked, to remain conformed to it.[9]

Third, Cross draws a contrast between what he takes to be the difference between the authority of the Church of Rome and Protestant confessions. And here his case hinges crucially on his claim that the convert to Rome "discovers" something that is not a mere interpretation. What the convert finds through his study of history, tradition, and scripture is the true church.

> He finds the one, holy, catholic and apostolic Church and its magisterial authority in succession from the Apostles and from Christ. He does not merely find an interpretation in which the Church has apostolic succession; he finds this very same Church itself, and he finds it to have divine authority by a succession from the Apostles. In finding the Church he finds an organic entity nearly two thousand years old with a divinely established hierarchy preserving divine authority.[10]

And this he takes to be the crucial difference between the church found by the Roman Catholic convert and any Protestant confession. Whereas Protestant confessions have "mere" human authority, the church is of divine origin and authority, and consequently can bind the conscience.

Indeed, Cross compares the discovery of the church through study of scripture, tradition, and history to the discovery of Christ himself through

---

8. Cross, "Tu Quoque," III.B
9. Cross, "Tu Quoque," III.B
10. Cross, "Tu Quoque," III.C

reading the scriptures. The reader who discovers Christ in the scriptures has discovered a divine person, someone who has authority over him. To discover Christ in this fashion is not to "pick" him as an authority, so this discovery is nothing like adopting a Protestant confession.

> Just as discovering Christ through the study of Scripture is not subject to the *tu quoque* objection, so for the same reason discovering the Body of Christ through the study of Scripture, tradition and history is not subject to the *tu quoque*. In both cases, it is the same Christ he has discovered, in His physical body which has ascended into Heaven, or his mystical body, the Church.[11]

Now this is a remarkable claim: discovering Christ in scripture is essentially the same as discovering the church through scripture, tradition, and history. Indeed, immediately after these lines, he cites the following quote from St. Joan of Arc that he thinks sums up the faith and good sense of both the holy doctors and ordinary believers: "About Jesus Christ and the Church, I simply know they're just one thing, and we shouldn't complicate the matter."[12]

By contrast, he alleges that Protestants define the church not in terms of divine authority that is handed down in succession from the apostles but rather in terms of agreement with one's personal interpretation of scripture. This undercuts any meaningful ecclesial authority "because for each disputant, if 'the Church' rules against his interpretation, for him she ceases to be 'the Church,' and hence, he need not submit to her." This, moreover, amounts to "nothing less than an implicit denial of a visible catholic Church."[13]

This means, Cross alleges, that Protestants cannot claim that they have "discovered" the church in any sense like Roman Catholics can. All that their claim amounts to, he says, is "that they have discovered other persons who have faith in Christ, a faith in Christ that is sufficiently similar to their own."[14]

To make matters even worse, Protestants cannot appeal to the fact that they have discovered the gospel to solve their individualistic authority problem. While the scripture surely has authority, any interpretation of scripture that goes beyond repeating the exact words of the Bible is a merely human product and has no conscience binding authority. "So, for that reason, what Protestants refer to as 'the gospel,' insofar as it is not an exact re-statement

---

11. Cross, "Tu Quoque," III.C
12. This quote is from *Catechism*, para. 795.
13. Cross, "Tu Quoque," III.C
14. Cross, "Tu Quoque," III.Q1A

of Scripture, has no more authority than a systematic theology text, being a merely human opinion."[15]

THE TRUE CHURCH WITH APOSTOLIC SUCCESSION

Cross mounts an impressive effort to stave off the *tu quoque* objection, but unfortunately for him, his case has numerous problems. As a preliminary matter, notice how much Cross has invested in the Roman Catholic claim to apostolic succession as providing warrant for its exclusive claims to teaching authority. He wrote: "He [the inquirer] does not merely find an interpretation in which the Church has apostolic succession; he finds this very same Church itself, and he finds it to have divine authority by a succession from the Apostles." There are a couple of problems with this claim.

First, the Roman claims about apostolic succession, like their claims about the early papacy, are lacking in historical credibility. Here is the assessment of Raymond Brown, the distinguished Roman Catholic New Testament scholar, after an examination of the evidence.

> The presbyter-bishops described in the NT were not in any traceable way the successors of the twelve apostles.... It is quite plausible that when churches without presbyter-bishops ultimately established them, they did so in imitation of churches that already had them, but many times without any special apostolic appointment. And so the affirmation that all the bishops of the early Christian Church could trace their appointments or ordinations to the apostles is simply without proof—it is impossible to trace with assurance any of the presbyter-bishops to the Twelve and it is possible to trace only some of them to apostles like Paul.[16]

But even leaving matters of critical history aside, there is another problem for any appeal to the discovery of apostolic succession to ground the exclusive claims of Rome. As anyone with even a casual knowledge of church history is aware, there are two other major churches that claim apostolic succession, namely, the Eastern Orthodox Church, and the Anglican Church. So, both critical history and basic church history pose challenges for any notion that a discovery of apostolic succession secures the claims of Rome to be the one true church with exclusive teaching authority.

---

15. Cross, "Tu Quoque," III.Q2A
16. Brown, *Priest and Bishop*, 72–73.

AN UTTERLY IMPRACTICAL IDEAL

Next, consider what his "ideal" inquirer must study before conversion: the "motives of credibility," scripture, the church fathers, and church history. The problem here is that if he means serious study of all these matters to the point that one has any sort of sound understanding of the controverted issues, of the arguments and counter-arguments, then he is asking for something that is utterly unrealistic.

Take scripture for a start. If the prospective convert is to intelligently weigh in on disputed issues of biblical interpretation, must he learn Greek and Hebrew? Must he at least read the best Protestant and Eastern Orthodox biblical scholarship, along with the best Roman Catholic scholarship, and master this material well enough to render an informed judgment? Doing this with anything approaching even competence, let alone expertise, would require years of intensive study.

Then there are two thousand years of church history to examine. Recall that Cross envisions a "decade by decade" study of the history of the church from the apostles to the present day. Such a study that would be anything beyond the most superficial survey would be beyond the competence of most persons. Consider just the issues involved in patristic scholarship and the controverted issues that separated Roman Catholics from Eastern Orthodoxy. Most prospective converts are hardly equipped to grasp these issues in any sort of depth, let alone to pronounce upon them. Another set of complex issues are involved in the medieval period of church history, ranging from penance to indulgences to purgatory to transubstantiation. Then there are the issues of the period of the Reformation. Again, is the prospective convert really to become an expert in Reformation history? Skipping over a few centuries, we come to the difficult issues that arise with the Modernist controversy and the rather significant changes of Vatican II. What I have mentioned here represents just a few of the bare bones of church history, and even to understand these issues with anything approaching competence would require massive time and effort.

We have not even mentioned the complex philosophical and historical issues involved in exploring with real insight the "motives of credibility" or the issues surrounding tradition and the various ways it is understood in the three major branches of the Christian Church. But the point for now is clear: Cross's "ideal" inquirer is just that, an ideal that seldom if ever exists.

SCRIPTURE'S NOT CLEAR, BUT ALL THAT IS?

But here is the deeper problem with Cross's suggestion. Roman Catholics are sharply critical of the Protestant principle of *sola scriptura* and the attendant claim about the clarity of scripture. Roman apologists love to point out that commitment to the authority of scripture is no guarantee of orthodoxy, that groups ranging from fundamentalist Baptists to contemporary cults affirm the Bible as their sole authority. Moreover, Evangelicals of different stripes disagree about various issues, such as the sacraments, predestination, church polity, and so on. If scripture is clear, the question is pressed, how can all these groups differ so much since they all claim to accept the authority of the Bible?

In response to this question, it is important to remember that the clarity of scripture is not a claim that everything in scripture is clear, or equally clear. As St. Peter observed about the letters of Paul, "There are some things in them hard to understand" (2 Peter 3:16). But the fact that some things are hard to understand suggests that much is not. And the principle of the clarity of scripture pertains to those things. *The Westminster Confession* puts it as follows:

> All things in Scripture are not alike plain in themselves, nor alike clear unto all; yet those things which are necessary to be known, believed, and observed for salvation, are so clearly propounded and opened in some place of Scripture or other that not only the learned but the unlearned, in a due use of ordinary means, may attain unto a sufficient understanding of them.[17]

Now here is the point I am driving at. While Cross apparently denies the Protestant principle of the clarity of scripture, he appears to believe clarity is to be found in something vastly more complex, namely, scripture plus the church fathers plus church history. In other words, while appeal to the authority of scripture is not adequate to provide Protestants with a sufficiently clear source of doctrinal authority, appeal to the threefold criterion cited above is.

Now if this is what Cross is claiming, it is not only a remarkable claim but also a wildly implausible one. The clarity that scripture lacks as a doctrinal authority is to be supplied by the far more extensive body of material that adds to scripture the church fathers and two thousand years of church history. All of that is supposed to generate clarity in a way that scripture does not?!

---

17. Westminster Divines, "Confession," 1.7.

Indeed, the utter impracticality of trying to understand, let alone master, this massive body of literature can actually be a strategic ploy for Roman Catholic apologists. If prospective converts are convinced that they need to master all this material, and have even a remote idea what that involves, they will be completely overwhelmed. In this condition, they may welcome any answers that purport to make sense of this enormous welter of material they are not qualified to assess.

Now, by contrast with such utterly unrealistic ideals, let us turn to the book of Acts and the famous example of the Bereans. When they heard the preaching of Paul and Silas they "welcomed the message very eagerly and examined the scriptures every day to see whether these things were so" (Acts 17:11). Notice, it was only after examining the scriptures that they believed. But more important for our concerns, this implies that they could understand the meaning of scripture well enough to render this judgment. This examination, moreover, was done communally and not merely as individuals. But there is no suggestion that there was anything special about the Bereans other than a sincere fidelity to scripture and a desire to measure the preaching of Paul and Silas by that standard. It is clear, however, that their response to the apostles is described approvingly.

Examining the scriptures in this fashion, while a demanding task, is at least reasonably practical. Testing a claim that purports to be God's ultimate good news against the standard of scripture is within the reach of ordinary seekers who diligently study scripture, especially as they do so in community. But it is hard to imagine an equivalent story where prospective converts would be expected to examine not only the scripture but also two thousand years of church history and theological controversy before rendering a judgment.

TRIVIALIZING PROTESTANT "AUTHORITY"

Next, Cross's account of how Protestants come to acknowledge authority is highly tendentious and misleading. Recall that his charge is that Protestants have no real authority because each person "picks" the confession or church that matches his current interpretation of scripture. Consequently, the confession has no authority since his present beliefs are what give the confession its authority. If he changes his mind, or his interpretation varies, he is not bound, and he can simply "pick" another church or confession.

There are several problems in these claims. First, his description of individuals "picking" their beliefs is hardly true to how Protestants typically come to affirm a confession or church. Protestants do not, despite the common caricature, typically arrive at their beliefs by going into the desert with their Bible so they can be alone to figure out its meaning for themselves. Rather, they are more typically reared in churches where they are taught the scriptures in the context of Christian community and hear biblical preaching, often for years, before they embrace the faith for themselves. It is in this sort of context that Protestants are formed and, not unlike the Bereans, discern a match between what scripture teaches and what their church teaches. They do not simply "pick" a church or confession after constructing their own personal version of the faith.

At the heart of Protestant preaching and teaching is the gospel, which Paul summed up as the wonderful news that Christ died for our sins in accordance with the scriptures, that he was buried and on the third day was raised from the dead and appeared to numerous witnesses, starting with Peter and the other disciples (1 Cor 15:1–7). It is this straightforward message that Paul says he received and, in turn, passed on to the Corinthians. This is the gospel that has been passed down from generation to generation to the present day. It is not mere opinion, but the very word of salvation in which we stand, and through which we are being saved.[18]

Moreover, core creedal orthodoxy, abundantly attested in scripture, is affirmed not only in magisterial Protestantism but also other Evangelical churches. Thus, Protestants are in fact schooled and formed by apostolic truth that has been affirmed for over two thousand years, and it is with this sort of formation that they "pick" their confession/church. It would be far more accurate to say, however, that the truth of the gospel has gripped them, and their acceptance of it is simply a matter of acknowledging that reality. (I will say more about this in the last section of this chapter).

Here we come to one of the fundamental problems in Cross's article. It is completely misleading, if not outright caricature, to say that a Protestant's present beliefs "make" a confession authoritative. Recall Cross's explanation of why a Protestant's confession has no intrinsic authority: "It is not the confession that is authoritative over his beliefs; rather, *his present beliefs make the confession to be 'authoritative,'* by containing the interpretation he presently believes to be required of himself" (emphasis added).

This is to confuse what makes a claim authoritative and the mental act of recognizing or discerning an authority. What makes a theological truth claim authoritative is that it is either a direct revelation from God, or a faithful statement of that revelation, or a clear inference from it. My beliefs do not make any of these authoritative. However, my belief can reflect that authoritative truth when I recognize it and assent to it. But that hardly

---

18. See especially verses 1–2.

means my belief is what makes that truth authoritative. It is completely the other way around. The truth elicits our belief, but our belief does not create or establish truth.

AN EXTREME RESTRICTION

Here Cross may protest that any element of human judgment undermines authority and renders it a matter of "mere" human opinion. Indeed, recall that he even goes so far as to insist that any claim that goes beyond stating the "exact" words of scripture must be a matter of mere human authority.

Once again, this is an extreme claim that leads to some rather absurd implications. Recall that scripture was originally written in Hebrew and Greek. So, if Protestants cannot take anything as authoritative except the "exact" words of scripture, then we are confined to the original Hebrew and Greek. Every translation involves some degree of human judgment, and indeed, this even goes for the Hebrew and Greek text, for we do not have the original autographs and the manuscripts in our possession have suffered some degree of corruption, however slight. So once again, Cross is demanding something that is utterly unrealistic.

Consider the common Christian practice of sharing our faith with unbelievers. Are we restricted to citing the exact words of scripture when we do so? Or may we explain the meaning of scripture, paraphrase it, and so on? Surely we may do this, and we can be faithful to scripture in doing so.

Even more, it is certainly reasonable to believe that Bible translations can accurately, even if imperfectly, communicate God's revelation to us in authoritative form. God did not intend his word only for the original recipients, and it is certainly reasonable to think human language is an adequate medium to convey God's revelation in scripture to different ages and cultures. Again, confidence in the essential clarity of scripture, and the more foundational belief that God has successfully revealed himself in scripture, leads us to this conclusion.

DEGREES OF AUTHORITY AND ROOM FOR DISAGREEMENT

But even if scripture is essentially clear, there is still considerable room for Protestants to disagree on some pretty important issues. And here, it seems, the element of mere human judgment comes to the fore to undermine Protestant claims to authority. Consider one of the most famously contested issues among Protestants, namely, the issue of how predestination relates to free will and responsibility. Calvinists and Arminians have sharply disagreed on that issue for centuries and vigorously debate it to this day, and that difference will be reflected in conflicting Protestant confessions.

Well, here it is highly instructive to note that Roman Catholics have their own version of this same dispute, particularly the historic controversy between the determinist Dominicans and the libertarian Molinists. This controversy was hotly contested, and the opponents of Molina pressed for his condemnation, and in fact when Molina died there were numerous rumors that his views would be condemned by Rome. The pope, however, declined to condemn Molinism, but he did issue a decree forbidding the contending parties from calling each other heretics and promised to resolve the matter at an opportune time. Alfred Freddoso, who translated Molina into English, wryly observed: "It stands as a tribute to the prudence of Paul V and his successors that this 'opportune' time has yet to arrive."[19]

While we may agree with Freddoso in admiring the pope and his successors in one way, in another way we might wonder what the alleged advantage of having a pope amounts to if controversies like this one are left unresolved. Clearly, the issue is an important one, and both sides cannot be right. One might wonder why the pope did not pronounce more definitively on the matter, unless perhaps it shows that such disagreements and disputes are altogether legitimate and maybe even integral to a growing understanding of biblical truth, whether in Roman Catholicism or Protestantism.

THAT'S ALL THAT INFALLIBILITY GETS YOU?

Here it is worth underscoring that infallible proclamations are relatively few and far between. To be sure, Roman Catholicism makes more claims to infallible teaching than Orthodoxy and Protestantism, and this is part of its appeal to many people. Many of these doctrines are shared by Protestants, such as the classic creeds and the repudiation of Pelagianism. Even if Protestants do not typically identify these creeds as infallible, the central doctrines they affirm are normative for most in a way that is functionally the same.

Indeed, Protestants could take a stronger line here and argue that the first seven ecumenical councils are essentially infallible. The leadership of the Holy Spirit may be assumed to guarantee truth in an ecumenical undivided church in a way that no longer holds in a divided church. Once the church divided between East and West in 1054 and set forth conflicting truth claims, the warrant of infallibility no longer holds. This would be a

---

19. Molina, *On Divine Foreknowledge*, viii.

plausible way to affirm infallible interpretation of scripture without reliance on apostolic succession.

In any case, the additional pronouncements that have been elevated to the level of infallibility by Rome are more dubious and controversial. The doctrine of transubstantiation and the post-Reformation decrees on justification were the product of a divided church, and they do not carry the authority of truly catholic consensus. The same can be said of the Marian dogmas, which represent the two clear occasions when the pope has spoken *ex cathedra*. The Marian dogmas have no clear basis in either scripture or the earliest sources, and they do nothing to settle disputed issues of biblical interpretation, like the Molinist-Dominican controversy. So that's what papal infallibility gets you? The elevation of extra-biblical doctrines to the same level of dogmatic authority as the Nicene Creed, a move that has only hardened the divisions within the larger church.

In view of all this, the initial appeal of a larger body of infallible doctrine claimed by Roman Catholicism may lose much of its luster. Indeed, given that Roman theology elevates extra-biblical doctrine to the same level of authority as central Christological teaching and tends to generate an "all or nothing mentality," Protestants have good reason to think the Roman Catholic claim to infallibility is a serious liability rather than an asset.

MAKING DO WITH ORDINARY MAGISTERIUM

In any case, the reality is that in their day-to-day Christian discipleship, Roman Catholics do not have infallible pronouncements to guide them; rather, they have to make do with what is called the "ordinary magisterium." This "ordinary magisterium" is non-definitive teaching from popes, bishops, and priests that the faithful are expected to follow. As Aiden Nichols, a contemporary Roman Catholic theologian, explains, the faithful should give allegiance to this teaching even though it makes no claim to be the last word.

As Nichols recognizes, "the Second Vatican Council itself considerably modified certain elements in the ordinary papal teaching (faithfully echoed by the wider episcopate) of the last hundred years."[20] In view of this reality, Nichols contends that the guidance of the Holy Spirit in the church "justifies our confidence in the general reliability of the ordinary magisterium, even though we cannot deny a priori that some particular aspect of its teaching may eventually be perceived as needing mulching or pruning, cultivation or cutting back." Now here is the practical upshot of recognizing this reality.

20. Nichols, *Shape*, 250.

> From these considerations there derives the duty of Catholics to make a sincere, sustained effort to give *ex animo* assent to the teachings of the ordinary magisterium—teachings that are always more likely to be right than not. However, in a given case, they may find that, nevertheless, they are not convinced. . . . More than this, they find themselves in a state of moral certitude on some point in a manner that could not leave the magisterial teaching intact.[21]

Notice, these teachings are "more likely to be right than not." That is far from a guarantee of truth, let alone infallible truth. Indeed, as Nichols acknowledges, conscientious Roman Catholics my find themselves in a "state of moral certitude" that would be incompatible with some of this teaching.

So here is the question: Does the magisterium have authority, even when it is recognized that its teaching is not infallible, and may well require "pruning" of various kinds? Or does the magisterium function as "mere men" in such cases? Presumably, Cross would want to say they have genuine teaching authority despite the fallible nature of these pronouncements and directives.

Practically speaking, Roman Catholics are in the same situation here as Protestants who affirm, say, the Westminster Confession or the Methodist Articles of Religion. Protestants who affirm one of these confessions recognize it as authoritative because they believe it is essentially true to scripture since it was produced by devout believers who were also excellent theologians and biblical scholars. They need not think the confession is infallible or beyond question to affirm it or take it as a normative guide for their nurture and discipleship. Because they believe God is always reforming his church through his infallible word, Protestants are comfortable with some degree of ambiguity as they continue to grow in grace and understanding and seek to be ever more faithful to that living word.

"DISCOVERING" THE CHURCH

Cross's central contention is that the difference between the Roman Catholic convert and the Protestant lies fundamentally in the nature of what is discovered. What he thinks the prospective Roman convert discovers is that the Roman Catholic Church is identical with the church that Christ founded, and that it has maintained its magisterial authority ever since. "The Church he finds in history and in the present has its divine authority from Christ through the Apostles and the bishops by way of succession.

---

21. Nichols, *Shape*, 251.

Herein lies the critical difference between the Church the inquirer finds in the centuries following Christ, and a Protestant confession."[22]

Now here it is important to note that Cross's claim is profoundly question begging. For everything hinges for him precisely on whether the Roman Catholic Church is in fact what it claims to be. For Cross simply to state that this is what the inquirer will find is to presume what is very much at issue in these competing accounts of authority. This is not to say that he needs to make his case from history in his brief article, but that does not warrant him in a polemical article simply to take it as a given that the inquirer will "find" what he believes to be the case.

It is important to reiterate that what Cross professes to "find" or "discover" involves numerous controversial interpretations of biblical and historical evidence, and he cannot validate these personal judgements simply by labeling them a "discovery." Indeed, it is worse. What makes his interpretations even more precarious is the fact that what he claims about the origin of the Roman Catholic Church, the papacy, and so on flies in the face of the consensus of serious scholarship, both Protestant and Roman Catholic, as we have seen in an earlier chapter.

Cross is obviously aware that most church historians, historical theologians, biblical scholars, and so on, who have given years to careful study of the evidence, have not "discovered" the Roman Catholic Church to be what he claims it to be. I will not reiterate what I have already detailed in earlier chapters, but there I have laid out some of the evidence and lines of argument that lead me to reject the claims of Roman Catholicism. The notion that Peter was the first pope is an anachronism, entirely lacking historical evidence. Likewise, the claims about unbroken lines of apostolic succession going back to the apostles do not hold up under critical historical investigation. Moreover, the Church of Rome is hardly blameless in the schisms that have occurred but must shoulder a portion of responsibility in these tragic events that have divided the church.

THE CLARITY OF CHRIST AND THE VISIBLE CHURCH

This brings us to Cross's claim that discovering Christ through the study of scripture is tantamount to discovering the church, the body of Christ, through the study of scripture, tradition, and church history. I think this is a dubious claim, misleading at best. Consider what we come to see when we discover Christ in scripture. We see that he is the very Son of God and that he came to provide salvation and eternal life. We see perfect humanity as

---

22. Cross, "Tu Quoque," III.C

well as deity. "No one has ever seen God. It is God the only Son who is close to the Father's heart, who has made him known" (John 1:18).

Consider again the luminous splendor of Christ as revealed in the pages of scripture. He is the spotless Lamb of God who could ask his critics, "Which of you convicts me of sin?" (John 8:46). Every word he spoke, as well as every action performed with his body, demonstrated God's holy love. We see a man who was never compromised by corruption or sinful motives, but who expressed God's character perfectly.

Can anyone honestly say that the body of Christ, in any of its manifestations, shows forth God's holy character in a comparable way? Indeed, specify this question to the Roman Catholic Church. Does the history of the Church of Rome display the "same" Christ with the same sort of clarity and luminous splendor with which Christ is displayed in the pages of scripture? The answer, I think, is apparent. We do not discover a church that is distinctly holy even by comparison with other churches, but one that has its own unsavory history marred by zeal for political power and other forms of scandal and moral corruption, continuing into the twenty-first century.[23] The reality of the morally ambiguous history of the Church of Rome further undermines Cross's claim that "the Church" can be discovered in scripture/history in a way that parallels how Christ is discovered in the pages of scripture.

Now if the church cannot be identified in scripture/history with the sort of clarity that Cross believes it can, does that mean we deny a visible catholic church, as he contends? Is an invisible church the only alternative to securing the true identity of the church through demonstrating an "unbroken" magisterial succession from Christ and the apostles?

It is a false dilemma to insist our only alternative to an invisible church is a demonstrable episcopal succession going back to Christ and the apostles. We can believe the church catholic is visible without insisting that it can be identified through magisterial succession. Consider an analogy. Imagine a first-time visitor to Oxford who wants to see the university for which that city is famous. "Where is the university?" he asks. Now anyone who is familiar with Oxford knows there is no simple answer to this question, since Oxford University is composed of several different colleges, some of which go back to medieval times, while others were founded much more recently. There is none of these colleges to which one can point and say "*that* is Oxford University" in the sense that that particular college is identical with Oxford University. If our visitor has a preconceived notion of what a

---

23. The sex scandals depicted in the Academy Award-winning movie *Spotlight* are only the most notorious of recent examples of moral corruption. More recently, see "Grand Jury Report."

university is or insists on a more definite answer to his question, he will be disappointed.

However, the fact that we cannot simply point to one college or one part of Oxford University to answer the question of the first-time visitor does not mean that Oxford University is invisible or that there is anything particularly mysterious about its identity. Nor does it undermine the essential unity of purpose that is common to every college that is part of Oxford University, nor the fact that the university was founded in 1096.

Likewise, the catholic church that was founded by Christ is composed of any number of churches, some ancient, some more recent, but all of them united by commitment to the gospel and rooted in classical Christian faith as expressed in the ecumenical creeds. Christ is the invisible head of the visible church, and it is his Spirit that baptizes all Christians into one body and unites all the various churches into one church (1 Cor 12:12–13). All of them are now products of historical splits and divisions, but they can all trace their roots back to Christ and the apostles. There is no doubt ambiguity with respect to some of these churches and some members of each of these churches. But the ambiguity does not override the impressive unity that runs through the various branches and parts of the church.

Given this ambiguity, it is inevitable that our judgment will sometimes be mistaken about the extent and location of the church. But the main point remains that we need not resort to the notion of an invisible church if we reject the claims of Rome.

SUSTAINING THE OBJECTION: INESCAPABLE INDIVIDUAL JUDGMENT

The central argument running through this chapter can perhaps be summed up like this: Cross not only exaggerates the individualism of Protestants but also downplays the individualistic aspect of conversion to Rome. There are places in his article, however, when he acknowledges this issue. One of them is in response to this question: "But isn't the person who becomes Catholic using his own private judgment just like the Protestant?" Here is his reply:

> We cannot but use our intellect and will in interpreting evidence, drawing conclusions, discovering truths, and making decisions. In that respect, inquirers who eventually become Protestant or Catholic start in the same epistemic situation. . . . With the help of the Holy Spirit, the inquirer who uses his intellect and will to examine history, tradition, and Scripture, discovers this divinely founded entity bearing divine authority, and at that point

submits to it. His own interpretation has no divine authority. But he discovers something beyond his own interpretation, something to which his interpretation points, and which does have divine authority. He discovers the Church. The Protestant can understand this in some sense, because in discovering Scripture the Protestant too has discovered something having divine authority, even while using his own intellect and will.[24]

This is a crucial point. The rhetorical force of Cross's essay very much depends on the contrast he continually attempts to draw between the Protestant's individual, personal "interpretation" and the Roman Catholic's "discovery" of objective, divine authority. Throughout most of his essay, Cross's claim to his "discovery" of the one true church, with its exclusive claim to apostolic succession, suggests he has a silver bullet that elevates him and his fellow Roman Catholics above the "epistemic situation" of other fallible human beings. In this quote, however, he at least broaches the hard reality that must be kept squarely in view in discussing these issues, namely, that *all of us* start in a similar epistemic situation and rely on the same fallible faculties as we render our judgment on these vital matters. Indeed, throughout our inquiry, we must rely on those same faculties.

This is particularly important to keep in mind because of the extraordinary range and complexity of issues Cross thinks the ideal inquirer should investigate and presumably master to the point of rendering an informed judgment. In other words, Cross's view makes remarkable demands on individual judgment on a vast body of literature and issues. As these inquirers render their judgment, it must be kept squarely in view that they "cannot but use [their] intellect and will in interpreting evidence, drawing conclusions, discovering truths, and making decisions."

In other words, the key point here is that there is an inescapable element of individual judgment involved for all those who join any church or convert to one of them. This is true for Roman Catholics no less than Protestants. This is not to deny or downplay the reality that all such individual choices and judgments take place in community and are formed and shaped by our participation in various communities. Our judgments and decisions may be very much influenced by other persons, but when we join a church or convert, we are exercising an element of personal judgment and doing what seems right to us (assuming we do so sincerely with even a modicum of thought). Both the individual as well as the communal aspects of these decisions need to be frankly recognized by all sides.

24. Cross, "Tu Quoque," III.Q4A

In short, there is no escaping personal responsibility here. In *this* sense, all of us are "our own pope," including Cross and his followers.

NOTHING TO COMPEL

It is also important to emphasize here that a decision to accept the authority claims of Rome is no guarantee that converts will not later change their mind. Cross seems to think Protestants are uniquely vulnerable to changing their mind because their churches have no interpretive authority to forbid them from joining another church. A Pentecostal, for instance, might become a Calvinist and join a church that subscribes to the Westminster Confession. Or a Calvinist might become an Arminian and join a church that subscribes to a Wesleyan confession of faith. Their former churches cannot forbid them from leaving and their confessions of faith only have authority over them insofar as they choose to remain united to the church that subscribes to that confession.

Of course, the fact is that many Protestants faithfully submit to the authority and discipline of their church even when they find it unpleasant or difficult. They do so because they recognize the church as a legitimate authority, even when it is inconvenient. Such submission is a moral act of the will, but it depends on the prior judgment that the church is a legitimate authority. Protestant churches do not resort to coercion to retain members who choose to leave, and there is nothing to compel them to stay if they no longer believe what their church professes.

Curiously, Cross seems to think Roman Catholics, with their exclusive claim to interpretive authority, are not vulnerable in the same way to their members leaving to join another church. The fact is, however, that Roman Catholics can also come to reject the authority of their church and choose to join another church. Indeed, many Roman Catholics have done just that, often converting to Evangelical Protestantism, most notably in South America.

But my point here is not a mere sociological observation. Rather, the point is that a Roman Catholic may convert to a different church for the same sorts of reasons Protestants do. Roman Catholics cannot prevent persons from leaving their church merely by appealing to their alleged exclusive interpretive authority. For that appeal only has force for those who believe Rome actually has that authority. But suppose, say, a Roman Catholic were to explore the historical foundations of the early papacy and discover that they are quite lacking. Suppose he became convinced that Rome's distinctive claims simply are not true and decided to convert to another church. In such a case, Rome has no more authority to compel the person to stay than a Protestant church has in a similar situation. Both may try to persuade the person not to convert and may even issue threats that those who convert are endangering their salvation, but if their efforts fail, they cannot compel them to remain.

To be sure, Roman Catholics in the past have licensed religious coercion in magisterial teaching to keep wayward members in the fold, as we saw in a previous chapter. Perhaps this is why Cross thinks Roman Catholics are not free to change their minds in the same way Protestants are. If Rome is willing to employ coercion, then it does indeed have a means to compel its members not to convert. But as we also saw in the previous chapter, since Vatican II, Rome apparently no longer endorses the use of religious coercion, so its members are just as free to convert as Protestants are if they no longer believe the distinctive claims of their church.

SUSTAINING THE OBJECTION: PARALLEL DISCOVERIES

In any case, the point remains that there is no escaping personal responsibility here. This reality cannot be evaded by insisting that the Protestant is trusting only in his "interpretation," while the Roman Catholic has truly "discovered" divine authority. The fact is that both sides judge that they have discovered divine truth and authority, and both have plausible claims to having done so. Notice in the quote above that Cross concedes that Protestants "have discovered something having divine authority" in their discovery of scripture. Recall too his claim that discovering Christ in scripture is not subject to the *tu quoque* objection.

Here again we have parallel claims, despite Cross's denial. To discover in scripture something having divine authority is to grasp the central claims of scripture and their truth. To find Christ in scripture, as Cross observes, is to discover "the second Person of the Divine Trinity."[25] It is important to emphasize that this discovery about divine authority is not merely formal but a substantial one; one that involves discernment of the truth that we must acknowledge, believe, and obey. If scripture is not essentially clear in its central claims, the claim that we discover divine authority in it is effectively vacuous. On the other hand, if it is not vacuous, if we do in fact discover "the second Person of the Divine Trinity" in scripture, this supports the Protestant conviction that we find in its pages a stable core of divine truth by virtue of its essential clarity.

25. Cross, "Tu Quoque," III.C

Furthermore, and for similar reasons, Protestants believe they have discovered that these central truths represent a broad consensus among all the main branches of the church, including the various Evangelical churches. It is not a matter of enormous historical complexity beyond the reach of ordinary believers to discover classic creedal Christianity, or what C. S. Lewis identified as "mere Christianity," as a matter of essential agreement among Christians of different traditions. The widespread appeal of Lewis's account across denominational and international lines is a telling indicator that this essential truth is accessible and readily recognized by Christians throughout the world.

It is important to emphasize this point because it underscores the fact that Protestants do not have to determine the truth of each doctrine on a case-by-case basis using personal judgment. They do not construct the faith from the ground up, employing individual interpretation. Rather, they discern essential Christian truth not only in the pages of scripture but also in the consensus of the church catholic, understood as a reality that is more expansive and inclusive than the Church of Rome.

A DISCOVERY OR AN ENCOUNTER?

We have been using Cross's language of "discovery" in this discussion, language that may suggest an intellectual quest in which we play the primary active role. This is perhaps the deepest theological error running throughout his whole argument. For the reality is that coming to see Christ in scripture is more accurately described as a personal encounter than a "discovery." Indeed, it is an encounter in which Christ takes the initiative, and we come face to face with Christ himself. As St. Paul put it, those who read the scriptures have a veil over their minds, one that is only removed by those who turn to Christ. "For it is the God who said, 'Let light shine out of darkness,' who has shone in our hearts to give the light of the knowledge of the glory of God in the face of Jesus Christ" (2 Cor 4:6).[26]

In other words, we do not merely discover an abstraction called divine authority; we are encountered by a divine person! Indeed, we are encountered by three persons who take the initiative to reveal themselves to us and make their word clear to us. In seeing "the glory of God in the face of Jesus Christ," we encounter the Father of the Son who is "the reflection of God's glory and the exact imprint of God's very being" (Heb 1:3).

This encounter is mediated by the Holy Spirit, whom Jesus also calls the Spirit of Truth, who would glorify Christ and lead us into all truth (John

26. For the larger context, see 3:12—4:6.

16:12–15). Jesus taught that the testimony of the Holy Spirit along with that of the apostles convinces us of truth about himself. "When the Advocate comes, whom I will send to you from the Father, the Spirit of truth who comes from the Father, he will testify on my behalf. You also are to testify because you have been with me from the beginning" (John 15:26–27). The apostles also invoked this twofold testimony when they gave witness to the resurrection of Jesus: "And we are witnesses to these things, and so is the Holy Spirit whom God has given to those who obey him" (Acts 5:32).

The witness of the Holy Spirit to Christ and the gospel has been essential to Reformation accounts of the authority of scripture.[27] Again, what this highlights is the illuminating power of the Holy Spirit and the crucial role he plays in grounding biblical authority and the clarity of its central message. The clarity of scripture is not merely a matter of the verbal or grammatical features of a document but of the truth, beauty, and power of the God who is revealed as we personally encounter him through his inspired word.

Indeed, following the lead of Alvin Plantinga, we may hold that when our faculties are functioning properly, we will find ourselves believing "the great truths of the gospel" as we read scripture or hear it preached and the Holy Spirit witnesses to its truth. Not only are we warranted in these beliefs, but we can also know them to be true in these circumstances.

It is noteworthy that Cross appeals to the "help of the Holy Spirit" in his description of how his inquirer "discovers" the Catholic Church. It is not clear if he means to suggest that the Holy Spirit witnesses to the truth about the church as discovered in the fathers plus church history plus scripture in the same sort of way the Bible clearly teaches that the Holy Spirit witnesses to the truth about Christ and the gospel. Perhaps he does. Recall, moreover, his quotation of Joan of Arc: "About Jesus Christ and the Church, I simply know they're just one thing, and we shouldn't complicate the matter."

With all due respect to Joan of Arc, it's not that simple. To insist otherwise is to distort the truth about both Christ and his church. Christ should not be identified with his church in any way that makes our knowledge of him and of the way of salvation hinge on any one particular ecclesial or theological tradition.

I conclude then, that the *tu quoque* objection is sustained. Roman Catholics are not above the fray, and they cannot seize the high moral or epistemic ground by insisting that they have "discovered" objective

---

27. Alvin Plantinga has developed this in philosophical detail in his epistemology of Christian belief. Plantinga contends that essentially the same view was held by both Aquinas and Calvin. See Plantinga, *Warranted Christian Belief*, esp. chapters 6–9. More recently Plantinga has published a more concise version of his account of Christian epistemology under the title *Knowledge and Christian Belief*.

authority, while their Protestant counterparts are mired in "mere" subjective "interpretations." Those who see this will recognize that Cross does not in fact provide good reason to be a Roman Catholic.

CHAPTER NINE

PROTESTANTS IN THE CROSSHAIRS
Popular Roman Catholic Apologetics

IN THIS BOOK MY focus has primarily been on official Roman Catholic documents and standards, along with other scholarly authors and sources. In this chapter, however, I want to take a look at a different kind of literature that has had a large impact on these discussions, namely, popular Roman Catholic apologetic books. There have been a number of such books written, many of them by former Protestants, with a notable zeal to convert Protestants and Evangelicals to Rome. Indeed, as a longtime observer of this phenomenon, I have often thought that if Roman Catholics were even half as interested in renewing the faith of their own many inactive members as they are in converting Protestants, the world might witness a great revival!

Be that as it may, there is a steady stream of such books being published by Roman Catholics. Several of these books are conversion narratives that detail the reasons the authors converted from Evangelical Christianity to Roman Catholicism. Although many of them are not by scholars or academics, some have been endorsed and promoted by respected Roman Catholic academics. This chapter will look at a couple such representative books by former Protestants, both of which have been endorsed by noted Roman Catholic scholars. The first, entitled *The Protestant's Dilemma*, is by a single author, and the second, entitled *Surprised by Truth*, contains the conversion stories of eleven different persons who are described in the Foreword by Scott Hahn as "theological step-children who have finally come home."[1] The popularity of these books is suggested by the fact that the latter book advertises on the front cover that it has sold over 250,000 copies.

---

1. Madrid, *Surprised by Truth*, 10.

My aim in this chapter is first is to get a sense of the sort of arguments and claims that thrive in popular Roman apologetics, especially given the fact that these books apparently have a rather large circulation and are taken quite seriously by their many enthusiastic readers. I also want to point out not only the weakness of these arguments but also the problems they pose for the larger project of Christian apologetics and Christian unity. I will conclude with some advice for readers of these books, who may have contracted "Roman fever."

PROTESTANTISM IS IMPOSSIBLE . . .

A good place to begin to get a sense of the tone of popular Roman Catholic apologetics is this quote from Devin Rose in the introduction to his book *The Protestant's Dilemma*, where he describes the outcome of his critical examination of his Protestant commitments. In doing so, he emphasizes that he came to his investigation with a commitment to reason and evidence, and this is what he discovered:

> I brought such an analysis with me into my newfound faith, and I discovered that Protestantism's tenets led to untenable conclusions. It was simply not possible to maintain a reasonable basis for my Christian faith while remaining a Protestant. At least one *ad hoc* leap was required—accepting a given set of books as inspired Scripture—but once I chose to endorse such a leap, I had no basis to criticize some who made a different leap (say, for instance, that the book of Mormon or the Koran was also inspired by God).[2]

Now there are a number of interesting and characteristic claims here worth noting, but I especially want to highlight his claim that it was "simply not possible to maintain a reasonable basis for my Christian faith while remaining a Protestant." This is an extraordinary claim. Does he really mean to say that no reasonable basis for Christian faith is *possible* on Protestant principles? It certainly sounds like it. Later, on the same page, he writes that Protestant premises "result in logical absurdities." Logical absurdity is a decisive indicator of incoherence and therefore falsity.

Now if Rose is correct in this claim, then no Protestant who is true to Protestant premises has ever succeeded in maintaining a reasonable basis for his faith. What is "simply not possible" cannot be done, after all. None of the notable Protestant theologians, biblical scholars, or philosophers have

---

2. Rose, *Protestant's Dilemma*, 18.

ever maintained a reasonable basis for their faith: not John Calvin, not John Wesley, not Leibniz, not Jonathan Edwards, not Thomas Reid, not C. S. Lewis, not N. T. Wright, not Wolfhart Pannenberg, not William Lane Craig, not Alvin Plantinga. None of them, brilliant and learned as they are, can do the impossible.

Now here it might be objected that Rose is not claiming anything as strong as this. Perhaps all he means to say is something much more modest and personal. Recall that he says that it "simply was not possible to maintain a reasonable basis for *my* Christian faith" (emphasis added). Perhaps the key word here is "my" and he is merely making a claim about himself, not about the logical absurdity of Protestant faith per se.[3] Moreover, on the next page, he makes a more modest claim, when he writes that his ultimate goal is "to demonstrate that the Catholic Faith is more plausible than Protestantism."

Now if this was all Rose meant to claim, he should have been clearer in his language. Certainly the rhetorical force of his claim depends on taking him to be making the stronger claim. Suppose Rose had said something like the following: "As a relatively young believer, and as an amateur theologian and apologist, I did not have the resources to maintain a rational basis for my Protestant faith." If he had said something like this, his statement would be a trivial piece of autobiography. It would be a statement about the limitations of his own personal capacities or his own personal understanding of Protestantism, but would tell us nothing whatever about whether it is possible for other Protestants to maintain a rational basis for their faith. It is a safe bet that most of his readers take him to be doing something much more interesting and significant than registering an autobiographical fact about himself and his own limitations.

In any case, the remainder of his paragraph is interesting in its own right and perhaps also telling. Notice that he thinks that an "*ad hoc* leap" is required for Protestants to accept as inspired scripture the sixty-six books that they believe are canonical. Indeed, he suggests that there is no principled difference between accepting those books as inspired scripture and accepting the Book of Mormon or the Koran. Again, this is a striking claim. Does Rose not think the intrinsic moral authority and the "divine qualities" of those books is more clearly evident than the Book of Mormon or the Koran? Since Protestants reject the claims of Rome, are they left to make a blind, arbitrary leap in the dark when it comes to discerning the true revelation of God? Does Rose think the objective historical credentials of the New Testament are no more substantial than the historical credentials of the book of Mormon or the Koran?

---

3. Rose indicated as much in a Facebook exchange involving his views.

If Rose really thinks this, it is not surprising that he could not maintain a rational basis for his previously Protestant faith. But again, this tells us nothing whatsoever about whether it is possible for Protestants who are better informed on these matters to judge them differently than he did.

CANONICAL CARICATURE

Let us look a little more at Rose's account of the Protestant view of the canon. At the outset of one of his chapters on this issue, he writes: "If Protestantism is true, the canon of Scripture is subject to every Christian's personal discernment." Later, on the same page, he expounds what he takes to be Calvin's theory of the self-authenticating authority of scripture.

> This theory did away with the need for trusting the corrupted early Church or for tracing the messy history of the canon's development. Instead, you as a faithful Christian simply picked up your Bible, read the books, and listened for the inner witness of the Spirit telling you that the books were inspired by God.[4]

Rose's account of Calvin here is a laughable caricature, at best, of what follows from Calvin's view of the authority of scripture. Recall from an earlier chapter the sketch of contemporary Reformed theologian Michael Kruger's account of the canon with its emphasis on understanding "the messy history of the canon's development" and the crucial role of the church in discerning the canon. Calvin's theory hardly dispenses with those factors as irrelevant.

Nor does Calvin's view license the sort of individualism that Rose depicts here. He goes on to quote a passage from Calvin in which the reformer affirms the self-authenticating power of scripture, while denying that its certainty depends on the church. Among the lines quoted are these:

> It is utterly vain, then, to pretend that the power of judging Scripture so lies with the church and that its certainty depends on churchly assent. Thus, while the church receives and gives its seal of approval to Scripture, it does not thereby render authentic what is otherwise doubtful or controversial.[5]

Rose proceeds to charge Calvin with presenting us with a false dilemma:

> Either the Church, by discerning the canon, imagines itself in authority over Scripture, or the canon is self-evident to

---

4. Rose, *Protestant's Dilemma*, 75.

5. Rose, *Protestant's Dilemma*, 76. The lines cited are from *Institutes of the Christian Religion* 1.7.2.

any Christian. Calvin replaces the belief that God guided the Church in selecting the canon with the belief that God guides me or you in selecting it. He forces the reader to choose between these options, but in fact they are both false.

But again, this is a caricature of Calvin's view. It hardly follows from the self-authenticating power of scripture through the witness of the Holy Spirit that any given Christian has the discernment on his own to sort out the entire canon, or that every book would be "self-evident" to every Christian. Even more obviously, the absurd notion does not follow that Protestants believe "God guides you or me in selecting it."

The canon has already been determined and Protestants do not labor under the notion that it is up to them to keep selecting it as individuals. Indeed, Protestants can readily concur that God guided the church, not in "selecting" the canon, but in correctly *discerning* it. As Calvin remarks, the church gives its "seal of approval" but that approval is not the ultimate source of our certainty that it is true.

Consider an analogy. Suppose a math professor writes a textbook that includes many complicated proofs. The fact that they are included in the book is good reason for a student to believe the proofs are sound. However, the truth of the proofs does not ultimately reside in the fact that they are included in this book or the fact that the professor chose to include them. Rather, it resides in the very nature of mathematical truth. Students who work the proofs and come to see them for themselves know their truth more directly and certainly than do those students who accept that they are true simply because they are in the book. The role of the church is like that of the professor. His seal of approval does not make the proofs correct, nor is it the ultimate basis for the certainty that they are true.

Protestants have perfectly good reasons, moreover, on their own principles to believe that, since God providentially guided the church in the formation of the canon, it is closed.[6] So again, Rose's claim is quite wide of the mark when he alleges that for Protestants, "the possibility remains that there may be future public revelation—like the Book of Mormon—leading to confusion and chaos among God's people."[7]

---

6. See Kruger, *Canon Revisited*, 94–97, 280–81, 286–87.
7. Rose, *Protestant's Dilemma*, 109.

SILLY *SOLA SCRIPTURA* STRAW MAN

The aim in challenging the Protestant account of canon, of course, is to make the case that the Roman Catholic Church gave us the Bible, so Protestants cannot consistently appeal to the authority of scripture without acknowledging the infallible authority of the Church of Rome. Bob Sungenis puts it like this:

> I found an indisputable example of the infallibility of the Catholic Church when I began to reflect on the question of the canon of Scripture—how the books of the Bible were determined, an issue often ignored by Protestants. There is no inspired "table of contents" anywhere in Scripture. . . . Since the Bible does not indicate which books belong within it, and since Protestants do not believe the Church has any authority to infallibly determine which books belong and which books don't, Protestants are left with an epistemological dilemma. . . . The issue of the canon is an unsolvable epistemological problem for Protestants.[8]

I have discussed the canon elsewhere and why Protestants have principled reasons for accepting as scripture the books we do. But here again, I want to point out the gross exaggeration and rhetorical overkill in these claims. First, the author claims to show us an "indisputable" instance of the infallibility of the Roman Church. We are then informed that the canon is "an unsolvable epistemological problem for Protestants." The problem, moreover, is unsolvable because the Bible does not give us a table of contents. The only way out is to accept the claims of Rome.

As noted previously, I readily grant the crucial role of the early ecumenical church (the church that existed before the split of East and West in 1054) in discerning the canon and can even agree that they had infallible guidance from the Holy Spirit in doing so. This does not, however, entail that the church was infallible, only that God infallibly directed the church in the crucial matter of receiving scripture. Indeed, guiding the church to correctly recognize scripture is integral to the whole purpose of inspiring it as an infallible authority in the first place. It would make little sense for God to inspire scripture as a source of infallible teaching and moral instruction and then leave it to happenstance whether or not it was accurately recognized as such by those for whom it was intended. But this hardly requires us to accept the infallibility of the Church of Rome in all its dogmatic pronouncements.

Nor is our only recourse to deal with this allegedly unsolvable epistemological dilemma to have a table of contents that identifies which books

---

8. Madrid, *Surprised by Truth*, 123.

are canonical. Indeed, this is a curious claim, and it is not clear how it would help even if we had such a list, as Michael Kruger has noted. Suppose there were a twenty-eighth book that listed the twenty-seven books of the New Testament. Would this satisfy the concerns Roman Catholics raise about *sola scriptura* and convince them that we need not affirm the infallibility of the Church of Rome? Not at all, Kruger contends, for the question would just arise all over again, for how can we know that the twenty-eighth book has actually come from God?

> The Catholic objection about the need for a "table of contents," therefore, misses the point entirely. Even if there were another document with such a table, *this document would still need to be authenticated as part of the canon*. . . . Such a "table of contents" would never satisfy their concerns, even if it were to exist, because they have already determined *a priori*, that no document could ever be self-attesting. In other words, built into the Roman Catholic model is that any written revelation (whether it contains a "table of contents" or not) will require external approval and authentication from an infallible church.[9]

In any case, *sola scriptura* comes in for frequent attack in popular Roman Catholic apologetics as part of this same web of arguments pertaining to canon and the claim that the infallibility of the church is necessary to establish the canon. Here again is Sungenis, with the same sort of overinflated rhetoric. "If Protestantism's fundamental doctrine was nowhere to be found in Scripture the implications are devastating to Protestantism: if sola scriptura is not taught in the Bible then it is a self-refuting proposition."[10] And then several pages later, he characterizes his experience with those who hold to *sola scriptura* as follows. "My seventeen year experience with Protestant biblical scholars had made one thing clear to me: Sola scriptura is a euphemism for 'sola ego.'"[11]

A couple of comments are in order. First, *sola scriptura* is not Protestantism's fundamental doctrine. The fundamental doctrine of Protestantism are the essential claims of the gospel, that Christ died for our sins, that he was raised from the dead, that we are saved by grace through faith, and the like. *Sola scriptura* is a fundamental claim about the nature of authority, but it is not a first-order doctrine in the same sense as the incarnation, the resurrection, and the Trinity.

---

9. Kruger, *Canon Revisited*, 43.
10. Madrid, *Surprised by Truth*, 103.
11. Madrid, *Surprised by Truth*, 119.

Next, it is not necessary for *sola scriptura* to be stated in so many words for it to be found in scripture. As John Peckham has argued, all we need to show is that it can be derived from scripture. In particular, we can derive *sola scriptura* from the fact that scripture presents itself as uniquely authoritative over other sources, namely, reason, experience, and tradition.[12]

To be sure, *sola scriptura* has been abused and misused by both its critics as well as its proponents, and certainly criticism is warranted when that is the case. Roman Catholic apologists make lots of hay highlighting the diversity within Protestantism, and indeed they seem to revel in depicting Protestants as strident individualists who concoct their own personal versions of the faith. T. L. Frazier, for instance, colorfully describes Protestants as a "bunch of individualists running around with Gideon Bibles and 'Just Me and Jesus' attitudes."[13] In a similar vein, Devin Rose alleges that, "In a sense, every Protestant since the Reformation has been a new reformer: sifting, interpreting, and assembling his own potpourri of doctrines to profess."[14]

No doubt there are individuals who could be pointed to who would meet these descriptions. The question, however, is whether they are good representatives of the principle of *sola scriptura*. Roman Catholic apologists like to suggest that they are and indeed that they are the very embodiment of what Protestantism is all about. Indeed, Rose points to heretical bishop John Shelby Spong as someone who really "gets" Protestantism.[15] As Rose sees things, there is no principled reason for Protestants why the likes of Spong "could not start a new Reformation that would do for the Christianity of today what Luther's Reformation did for the Church in the 1500s since, by Protestant acclaim, rejecting traditional doctrines can be a noble thing."[16]

Spong has proposed that his radical departures from core Christian doctrines are in the spirit of the Reformation, and Rose agrees. For Rose, there seems to be no difference between Luther's biblically driven reform of a church that was undeniably corrupt in many ways and Spong's radical departure from clear, consensual biblical doctrine that is agreed on by all major Christian traditions.

I have argued in previous chapters that *sola scriptura*, properly understood, does not in any way undermine classic consensual Christian orthodoxy but rather firmly undergirds it. But here is the point for emphasis

---

12. Peckham, "Sola Scriptura," 10–13.
13. Madrid, *Surprised by Truth*, 209.
14. Rose, *Protestant's Dilemma*, 203–4.
15. Rose, *Protestant's Dilemma*, 205.
16. Rose, *Protestant's Dilemma*, 207.

now. These popular Roman Catholic apologetic works give readers the impression that *sola scriptura* is not only a frivolous doctrine that is obviously self-defeating and incoherent but also one that inevitably leads to absurd consequences. One would never get the impression that the doctrine represents a serious option for any thoughtful person or that countless brilliant biblical scholars and theologians have been operating with this conviction for centuries, producing outstanding works of Christian scholarship and continue to do so at the present. To the contrary, it is presented in cartoonish fashion for the purpose of discrediting Protestant Christianity and promoting Rome as the only alternative.[17]

SIMPLISTIC HISTORY AND QUESTION BEGGING

Another problem with these books is that they rely on simplistic, uncritical historical claims as well as question-begging assertions. Such claims are frequently made about the Roman Catholic doctrine that Jesus appointed Peter as the first pope and established the bishop of Rome as the head of the church. Popular Roman Catholic apologetics often presents this as a straightforward historical fact that is beyond serious dispute. Consider, for instance, the following from Devin Rose, cited in a previous chapter: "The Church had a pope, a visible head, from the beginning. In fact, we know the names and approximate dates of all of the popes, all the way back to the first century: Peter first, then Linus, Anacletus, and Clement I."[18]

As we have seen in an earlier chapter, this claim is entirely lacking in terms of solid historical evidence. There is no good evidence of a monarchical bishop in Rome until the late second century. This is the consensus of serious historians, whether Protestant, Orthodox, or Roman Catholic.

But notice now his claim that "we know the names and approximate dates of all the popes." Who does he mean to include in the "we" who allegedly know these things? The phrase "we know" in a controversial context like this is typically employed when referring to something that is a matter of broad agreement or scholarly consensus. One argues to more disputed claims on the basis of what it can be fairly said to be a matter of agreement that "we know." But since Rose's claim here is hardly a matter of scholarly consensus, even among Roman Catholic historians, for him simply to say "we know" these claims about the papacy is not only misleading but question begging as well. He is simply assuming to be true the very claims that

---

17. For a defense of *sola scriptura* against popular objections, see Peckham, "Sola Scriptura." See also Allen and Swain, *Reformed Catholicity*, 49–93.

18. Rose, *Protestant's Dilemma*, 35.

are at issue between Protestants and Roman Catholics, which is obviously question begging.

For another instance of this, consider these lines from Julie Swenson.

> John Henry Newman, the famous Evangelical Protestant convert to Catholicism, once said, "Knowledge of Church history is the death of Protestantism." He was right. My study of the early Church showed clearly that it was Catholic in its beliefs and practices—in fact, had begun calling itself "Catholic" at least as early as the end of the first century.[19]

Newman's famous line (paraphrased by Swenson) is of course a favorite among Roman Catholic converts, as we have noted before. And while many of them may fondly imagine that Protestants can only maintain their Protestant faith if they remain blissfully ignorant of church history, the many learned church historians and historical theologians in the ranks of Protestantism should be sufficient to discredit this myth once and for all (see Irena Backus, Roland Bainton, Gerald Bray, Henry Chadwick, Owen Chadwick, Justo L. Gonzalez, Charles Hill, Michael W. Holmes, Kenneth Scott Latourette, J. B. Lightfoot, Morwenna Ludlow, George Marsden, Alister McGrath, Mark Noll, Heiko Oberman, Thomas Oden, Alex Ryrie, and Philip Schaff, for a start).[20] But Newman's claim remains a popular notion, apparently, and was cited a number of times by other authors in the book in which Swenson's essay appears.

Notice, moreover, that she deems it "clearly" to be the case that early church history supports the claims of Roman Catholicism, as attested partly by the fact that the term "catholic" was used to describe the church by the end of the first century. But again, this is question begging, not least because the use of the word "catholic" in the first century hardly provides significant evidence in favor of the distinctive ecclesial claims of Rome. It is anachronism to import into the first-century use of the term all the later developments that came to predominate in the Church of Rome, and to distinguish it not only from Eastern Orthodoxy but also from Reformation Christians. The fact that the term "catholic" was used early in the history of the church does not even begin the settle the issue of whether the Roman Catholic Church of today is the "one true church" or the church that distinctively represents the contemporary embodiment of the first-century church. Indeed, it is more than a little ironic that those who cite Newman's famous line often make such simplistic historical claims.

19. Madrid, *Surprised by Truth*, 154–55.
20. We include Anglicans since Newman appears to do so in the context of his famous remark.

Later in the same volume, T. L. Frazier cites Ignatius to make a similar point. "'Where the bishop is to be seen, there let all his people be, just as where Jesus Christ is present, there is the Catholic Church.' That Ignatius called the Church 'Catholic' had a profound psychological effect on an anti-Catholic like myself."[21] While I will not dispute that seeing the church described as "catholic" in an early church father may have a "profound psychological effect" on a self-described "'born again' Fundamentalist,"[22] this says nothing whatever in favor of the notion that the use of the term here supports the claims of the Church of Rome. Indeed, notice that Ignatius says the catholic church is "where Jesus Christ is present." I heartily concur with that, but that does nothing to show that Jesus Christ is distinctively present in the Church of Rome in some sense that uniquely identifies it as the "one, holy, catholic church." Indeed, it is misleading that the word "Catholic" was capitalized in the quote from Ignatius, as that identifies the "catholic" church with the Roman Catholic Church. The Greek word simply means "catholic" in the sense of "universal."[23]

For one final example, consider the claim that Protestants, in effect, do not believe the promises of Jesus that he gave to his disciples to protect the church and guide her into all truth since they reject the claims of Rome. Marcus Grodi, detailing the reasons he "could no longer remain a Protestant" cited this as a crucial consideration. "To do so [remain a Protestant] meant I must deny Christ's promises to guide and protect his Church and to send the Holy Spirit to lead it into all truth (cf. Matt 16:18–19; 18:18; 28:20; John 14:16, 25; 16:13)."[24]

Again, this is deeply question begging. Grodi apparently identifies whatever the Church of Rome claims to be infallible teaching with the truth that Christ promised the church would be led into by the Holy Spirit. But that claim is hardly warranted unless we assume the Church of Rome is indeed the one true Church whose magisterium in fact has the unique teaching authority it claims to have.[25] And again, that is precisely what is at

---

21. Madrid, *Surprised by Truth*, 197.

22. Madrid, *Surprised by Truth*, 181.

23. The passage quoted is from the letter of Ignatius to the Smyrnaeans (8.2). The passage is translated by J. B. Lightfoot and J. R. Harmer as follows: "Wherever the bishop shall appear, there let the people be; even as where Jesus may be there is the universal Church." See "Epistle of S. Ignatius: To the Smyrnaeans," 158, in Lightfoot and Harmer, *Apostolic Fathers*, 156–59. More recently the passage has been translated: "Wherever the bishop appears, there let the congregation be; just as wherever Jesus Christ is, there is the catholic Church." See "Letter of Ignatius to the Smyrnaeans," 255, in Holmes, *Apostolic Fathers*, 248–61.

24. Madrid, *Surprised by Truth*, 53.

25. It is worth noting here that converts to Rome typically ignore the claims of the

issue. We can certainly believe the Holy Spirit has faithfully led the church into all truth, as Christ promised, without agreeing that everything the Roman Catholic Church claims as infallible truth is in fact infallible truth into which they were led by the Holy Spirit.

Protestants certainly believe that the Holy Spirit has led the church into the truth he intended by not only inspiring the apostles and others to write the scriptures but also helping the church to correctly discern the canonical books and accurately interpret their essential teaching. Despite the errors and corruption into which the church has undoubtedly fallen at various stages of history, including the present, God has preserved the church and the message of the gospel, and God will do so until the end of time. We need not agree on all the details of the narrative to affirm God's providential role in protecting the church and preserving the truth of the gospel. It is quite parochial to insist that Protestants cannot make these claims with integrity unless they accept the claims of Rome.

Examples of such question begging and other simplistic arguments could easily be multiplied, but let us turn now to another sort of argument that frequently recurs in popular Roman Catholic apologetics. Indeed, this is perhaps the argument that drives all the others I have surveyed.

CARTESIAN CERTAINTY SYNDROME

Descartes's very name has become identified with his attempt to secure an utterly secure foundation for his beliefs, a foundation so secure that it would be completely invulnerable to doubt and uncertainty. To do so, he engaged in his famous thought experiment in which he doubted all of his beliefs he could possibly doubt, and even imagined that an evil demon was trying to deceive him and lead him into error. In this thought experiment, he arrived at one belief that would be invulnerable to this most extreme onslaught, namely, his belief that he was thinking, and this led to one of the most famous lines in the history of philosophy: "I think, therefore I am."

Descartes then proceeded to rebuild the edifice of his beliefs from this secure foundation, arriving at what he believed to be an utterly certain system of knowledge. The sort of knowledge claims that aspire to such invulnerability to doubt are thus labelled claims of "Cartesian certainty."

Now it is worth noting that Descartes was a Roman Catholic who wrote his famous works in the aftermath of the Reformation, when competing truth claims by Protestants and Roman Catholics undermined the

---

Orthodox Church, and it is far from clear why they so readily accept the claims of Rome rather than those of Orthodoxy.

claims to certainty that were previously taken for granted by many believers. Descartes's project thus appealed to many of those whose sense of certainty had been shaken. Indeed, Descartes set the modern world on a centuries long debate about the nature and possibilities of knowledge.

The important point for emphasis now is that Cartesian certainty is generally recognized as an unrealistic standard to expect for human knowledge claims. In other words, many of the things we can rightly claim to know, such as basic sense perceptions, memory beliefs, historical beliefs, and so on, fall short of Cartesian certainty. The ghost of Descartes lives on, however, and his quest for a guarantee of absolute certainty continues to haunt many people.

Indeed, a big part of the attraction of Roman Catholicism is that many people see it as providing a degree of certainty that they did not find in Protestantism. For a characteristic instance of this, consider the following from Marcus Grodi, who was a Calvinist pastor before he converted to Rome.

> I struggled with the questions, "How do I know what God's will is for my life and for the people in my congregation? How can I be sure that what I am preaching is correct? How do I *know* what truth is?" . . . Since it was my duty and desire to teach the truth of Jesus Christ to my congregation, my growing concern was, "How do I *know* what is truth and what isn't?" . . . "Am I preaching truth or error?" I asked the Lord repeatedly. "I *think* I'm right, but how can I know for sure?" . . . I remember standing beside the hospital bed of a man who was near death after suffering a heart attack. His distraught wife asked me, "Is my husband going to heaven?" All I could do was mouth some sort of pious but vague "we-must-trust-in-the-Lord" reassurance about her husband's salvation. She may have been comforted but I was tormented by her tearful plea. After all, as a Reformed pastor I believed John Calvin's doctrines of predestination and perseverance of the saints. This man had given his life to Christ, he had been regenerated, and was confident that he was one of God's elect. But *was* he?[26]

The italicized words in this quote are all in the original, and they highlight the quest for certainty that drove Grodi's conversion to Roman Catholicism. Indeed, he apparently thought he should even have absolute certainty about the state of grace of persons who have died, and that his uncertainty in this matter was an argument against Protestantism.

---

26. Madrid, *Surprised by Truth*, 37, 39, 40.

Grodi apparently believes that embracing the claims of Rome solves all these issues and gives him the infallible certainty he craved. Near the end of his essay, he writes:

> All this wrangling of how to interpret Scripture gets one nowhere if there is no way to know with infallible certitude that one's interpretation is the right one. The teaching authority of the Church in the magisterium centered around the seat of Peter. If I could accept this doctrine, I knew I could trust the Church on everything else.[27]

On the very last page of his essay, he quotes Newman's line, "To be deep in history is to cease to be a Protestant" and then goes on to state with characteristic certainty that the Church of Rome is the true church:

> Newman was right. The more I read Church history and Scripture the less I could comfortably remain a Protestant. I saw that it was the Catholic Church—the Roman Catholic Church—that was established by Jesus Christ, and all other claimants to the title "true Church" had to step aside.[28]

The ease with which converts like Grodi attain "infallible certitude" about a whole host of exegetical, historical, and theological issues that are deeply contested among Anglican, Eastern, Protestant, and Roman scholars who share a deep commitment to the authority of scripture and classic Nicene catholic Christianity is striking indeed. It is also appealing, and all the more so in a chaotic world where conflicting claims abound. Whether this "infallible certitude" is warranted or corresponds to objective truth is another matter, however. But the promise to resolve these disputes with a guarantee of infallible certainty is a large part of the appeal in Roman apologetics.

Indeed, the quest for infallible certainty is a driving force behind the other arguments we have examined as well. The claim that it is "impossible" to maintain a rational basis for Protestant faith; the caricatures of *sola scriptura* and the notion that it is obviously incoherent; the suggestion that it is a knockdown argument against Protestantism that the church gave us the canon; the simplistic historical claims and the question-begging claims that *assume* the authority of Rome; all of these feed the hankering for infallible certainty and lead readers to think they can have it all if they simply accept the claims of Rome.

---

27. Madrid, *Surprised by Truth*, 53–54.
28. Madrid, *Surprised by Truth*, 56.

In all these respects, popular Roman Catholic apologetics is reflecting the worst tendencies of popular apologetics, period. I have no doubt that there is Protestant literature critical of Roman Catholicism that mirrors the worst arguments of Roman Catholic apologists. And more generally, popular Christian apologetics sometimes displays the same unfortunate tendencies.

Readers of popular apologetics are usually looking for answers, indeed, they are often looking for *easy* answers, and it is tempting to cater to their wishes by grossly oversimplifying the views one is criticizing and claiming easy victories over them and to exaggerate the strength and conclusiveness of one's own arguments.[29]

I do not mean to demean popular apologetics; indeed, I believe it plays a vital role. There is certainly a need for books that present apologetic arguments in a clear, engaging, and accessible fashion. But it does not serve the apologetic enterprise, and, even more importantly, it serves neither truth nor charity nor Christian unity to promote books that perpetuate simplistic caricatures.

PRESCRIPTIONS FOR ROMAN FEVER

It's likely that most people who read popular Roman Catholic apologetic books are exploring "conversion" to Rome. Indeed, they may be hanging around the banks of the Tiber and may have contracted a bad case of Roman fever, a condition that produces an alluring vision of what lies on the other side and a strong urge to plunge into the river and swim across as fast as one can, never looking back. In this final section, I offer some counsel to those in the grip of Roman fever.

First, take every care not to fall into the mindset of comparing the best of Rome with the worst of Protestantism. One of my Roman Catholic friends, wanting to score a point for his church quipped: "We have Dante's *Divine Comedy*, and you have the *Left Behind* series." He was, I think, only being mischievous since he has many Evangelical friends and often works closely with them on various projects. But his quip does reflect an attitude that often comes with Roman fever. Those in the grip of it tend to grab onto the worst practitioners or the most notable foibles of Evangelicalism, as if they are typical, and to extol the best of Rome (which is sometimes an idealistic illusion) by way of invidious comparison. And in fact the books we examined in this chapter do this repeatedly.

---

29. See Burson and Walls, *C. S. Lewis and Francis Schaeffer*, 239–44.

Of course, Protestants do not have to look too hard to find displays of popular piety in Roman Catholicism that are hardly worthy of celebration or emulation. Carl Trueman serves up a few examples with a humorous flourish:

> There are things which can be conveniently ignored by North American Roman Catholic intellectuals because they take place in distant lands. Yet many of these are emblematic of contemporary Roman Catholicism in the wider world. Such, for example, are the bits of the real cross and vials of Jesus' blood which continue to be displayed in certain churches, the cult of Padre Pio and the relics of Anthony of Padua and the like (both of whom edged out Jesus and the Virgin Mary in a poll as to who was the most prayed to figure in Italian Catholicism). We Protestants may appear hopelessly confused to the latest generation of North American Roman Catholic polemicists, but at least my own little group of Presbyterian schismatics does not promote the veneration of mountebank stigmatics or the virtues of snake-oil.[30]

Italy is rather close to the heart of Roman Catholicism, as it were, so the results of this poll mentioned by Trueman are more than a little telling.[31]

Trueman also comments on the irony of the fact that Rome has managed to advertise itself as the church for intellectuals and academics. A little historical perspective that looks beyond the last few decades reminds us that things were rather different not so long ago. Indeed, the infamous Index of Prohibited Books, first adopted in 1559, was not abolished until 1966, when Pope Paul VI finally got rid of it.

> I well remember being amazed when reading the autobiography of the analytic philosopher and one-time priest, Sir Anthony Kenny, that he had to obtain special permission from the Church to read David Hume for his doctoral research in the 1950s. At the start of the twenty-first century, Rome may present herself as the friend of engaged religious intellectuals in North America but she took an embarrassingly long time even to allow her people free access to the most basic books of modern Western thought. Women in Britain had the vote, Elvis (in my humble opinion) had already done his best work and the Beatles and Rolling Stones were starting to churn out hits

---

30. Trueman, "Pay No Attention."
31. For details about the poll, see "Padre Pio Tops Saints Poll."

before Roman Catholics were free to read David Hume without specific permission from the Church.[32]

The point here is that honesty, as well as charity, require us to recognize that both theological traditions have many strengths to celebrate and both have embarrassing weaknesses.

To fixate on the weaknesses of either tradition, while ignoring the strengths, in order to justify conversion, serves neither clarity nor charity. Indeed, as Steve Long has astutely noted, "Many Protestant conversions to Catholicism are themselves *protestant* conversions. On one occasion when I was tempted to convert to Catholicism, I did so because I was angry at the silliness of activities like puppet-and-clown Eucharists."[33] A little honest perspective that recognizes there is silliness on both sides, as well as much to be admired, can often cool Roman fever.

The practical question here may come down to this: Where do I go on Sunday morning? And it's a question that needs an answer. If one is attending a church that is primarily evangelistic in focus and offers little by way of nourishment for growing and mature believers, it may be advisable to change churches. If one's spiritual needs would be better met in a more liturgical church with an emphasis on classical forms of worship and hymnology, it may be advisable to change churches. But it hardly follows that Rome is the panacea for all ills or that Rome is the only alternative to the superficiality of some Evangelical churches.

Second, keep squarely in mind that one can embrace a fully catholic faith without going to Rome. Firmly resist any attempt to drive a wedge between traditional catholic orthodoxy and Protestantism. As I have argued throughout this book, the claim of Rome to be the one true church is poorly founded and reflects an unduly narrow vision of true catholicism.

Protestants need to understand their catholic legacy, and where it has been ignored or minimized, they need to recover and celebrate it. No doubt part of what produces Roman (and Eastern) fever is a desire to be part of a great tradition, and one of the weaknesses of Evangelicalism is that it has often failed to communicate this larger tradition. Protestants no less than Roman Catholics have roots that go all the way back to the apostles and the great ecumenical consensus represented in the classic creeds, and this was strongly emphasized by the great Reformers.[34]

---

32. Trueman, "Pay No Attention."

33. Long, "My Church Loyalties."

34. For some excellent sources here, see Stewart, *In Search of Ancient Roots*; Allen and Swain, *Reformed Catholicity*.

There is another side of the coin we need to recognize as well, namely, that Roman Catholics also have Reformation roots that are very much a part of their story. Roman Catholic historian Gary Macy puts the point as follows.

> Not a single Christian group in the west survived the Reformation unchanged. Even the Roman church emerged a very different entity than that of the medieval church. . . . Different churches retained different customs of the old medieval church, to be sure, and some of the churches, especially the Roman Catholic and Anglican churches, treasured their continuity with the medieval centuries. Yet it is important to remember that none of the churches that emerged from this great upheaval can claim the past as exclusively their own. The modern Roman Catholic church started in the sixteenth century just as surely as the Lutheran or Calvinist churches.[35]

So just as it is true that Protestants have a patristic catholic heritage, it is also true in an important sense that Roman Catholics have a Reformation heritage.

Third, in keeping with the previous point, it is vital to understand that those who embrace an understanding of the church catholic that is larger than Rome can celebrate and be spiritually and intellectually nourished by the whole host of theologians, saints, martyrs, and artists who have given witness to classic Christian faith in their lives, writing, painting, and music. All these riches are gifts of God to be received with gratitude and joy by *all* Christians.

The attitude I am recommending here is very much at odds with that of some Roman Catholic apologists, who want to claim Christians of their tradition as their exclusive property. Indeed, Devin Rose deploys the saints in yet another variation on the "all or nothing" argument to contend that Protestants cannot claim them. He writes: "If I were drafting baseball players as a Protestant Christian, I would want St Augustine on my team for his great love of scripture, the honesty of his Confessions, his Protestant-friendly ideas on justification and predestination, and his philosophical wisdom."[36] Rose goes on however, to contend that Augustine also held a number of views Protestants typically reject, so he could not be on the Protestant team. Similarly, he argues that St Athanasius, St Cyprian, St Thomas Aquinas, and St Francis de Sales are also disqualified.

---

35. Macy, *Banquet's Wisdom*, 170.
36. Rose, *Protestant's Dilemma*, 196.

Leaving aside the anachronistic problems with this claim, I want to highlight how remarkably parochial it is. Rose does not celebrate these great saints as members of the Christian "team" who have much to teach all of us; rather, his primary concern is to draft these great saints to score points for team Rome.

The view of the church catholic I have been commending in this book is one that recognizes that the church fathers belong to *all* of us, that the saints and heroes of our particular traditions are not to be jealously claimed as our exclusive possession but rather as treasures to be joyfully shared for the enrichment of the whole church. C. S. Lewis, Protestant though he certainly was, is a gift to believers in "mere Christianity" of all traditions. J. R. R. Tolkien, Roman Catholic though he certainly was, is no less a gift to all Christians. The same can be said about the music of Bach; the poetry of George Herbert and Dante; the sermons of Wesley, Spurgeon, and Newman; the theological brilliance of Barth and Balthasar; the masterful biblical scholarship of Joseph Fitzmyer and N. T. Wright; the philosophical genius of Thomas Aquinas, Thomas Reid, Alvin Plantinga, and Richard Swinburne; the missionary zeal of Francis Xavier and Amy Carmichael; the social reforming passion of Wilberforce and Dorothy Day; the fiction of Flannery O'Connor and Marilynne Robinson; the piety of Thomas à Kempis, Catherine of Genoa, Oswald Chambers, and Dallas Willard. None of these are gifts to be hoarded as the exclusive property of any particular Christian tradition.

It is surely appropriate to take pride in the great exemplars of one's tradition even while recognizing that they were partisans of particular traditions and would defend their distinctive theological convictions. But one need not agree with any of these persons on all points, even important points, in order to embrace them wholeheartedly as fellow believers in Christ and to have an open heart and mind to receive what they have to teach us about loving him more faithfully.

In any case there is ample reason to resist Roman fever and to think twice before taking the Tiber plunge.

CHAPTER TEN

THE WORLD'S LARGEST PLURALIST CHRISTIAN DENOMINATION?

MUCH OF THE APPEAL of Roman Catholicism for many people, no doubt, is due to the claim that it provides rock solid, uncompromising commitment to unchanging truth. A common refrain of Roman apologists and converts is that Protestantism, by contrast, is hopelessly divided, unstable, and confusing. Often, this includes the claim that Protestantism is composed of thousands of denominations and sects.[1] Consider these words from former Evangelical pastor and Gordon Conwell Seminary graduate Steve Wood describing some of the questions he was wrestling with before he converted to Rome:

> How could Protestantism be his [Christ's] "church" when Protestant is nothing but disintegration, splintered, not unified, a frightening proliferation of squabbling, competing denominations, many masquerading under the title "non-denominational." The disunity and doctrinal chaos with [sic] Protestantism became deeply unsettling to me.[2]

Wood's internal struggle came to a head one Sunday morning when he was deeply disturbed about giving the sacrament of Communion to members of his church who were divorced and remarried:

---

1. A popular claim by Roman Catholic apologists is that there are thousands of Protestant denominations; indeed, the specific number thirty-three thousand is often cited. For an incisive critique and refutation of this popular myth, see Peoples, "Protestant Bogeyman." Roman Catholic apologist Scott Eric Alt acknowledges that Peoples's analysis is correct, and he urges his fellow Catholics to stop making this "outlandishly false" claim. See Alt, "We Need to Stop."

2. Madrid, *Surprised by Truth*, 89.

> My heart was flooded with conviction and sorrow. I felt God was telling me I had no right to administer the Lord's Supper in this situation. I realized that as a pastor, I couldn't continue to overlook the unbiblical marriages in my congregation.[3]

He was so distressed by these feelings that he walked to the Communion table, and to the shock and confusion of his congregation, announced that he was unprepared to administer the Lord's Supper that day. Not long after, he converted to Rome, which held out the promise of silencing the cacophony of conflicting voices and contradictory theological claims by providing a clear and palpable display of unity. "The Catholic Church has bishops who claim apostolic succession, and can back it up biblically and historically; the Catholic Church, unlike Protestantism, possesses visible doctrinal unity."[4]

Leaving aside Wood's remarkably simplistic claims about the biblical and historical grounds for the claims of Rome, it is hard to see how anyone who is reasonably informed can maintain such an idealistic picture of its unity. Anyone who has even compared, say, the claims asserted by Pope Pius IX's "Syllabus or Summary of the Main Errors of Our Age" with Vatican II knows that the Church of Rome is a dramatically different church than it was in the nineteenth and early twentieth century. More importantly, those very changes did not come about by seamless "development" or easy consensus. Rather, they were due to significant internal divisions and the desire to come to terms with them.

Even with all the dramatic changes Rome has undergone, it still often projects a powerful image of unshaken consistency and singular unity. This image, however, is largely an illusion when examined more closely. In the pages that follow I will show that the unity of the Church of Rome is not what it appears to be by highlighting some important facts about its actual nature. In particular, I will show that the Church of Rome is in reality more like a pluralist Protestant denomination than the bulwark of unbroken consistency its popular apologists purport it to be.

ARE MOST ROMAN CATHOLICS FUNCTIONAL PROTESTANTS?

I want to begin to make this case by drawing on personal experience. As I noted in the introduction, my time at Notre Dame as a graduate student not only provided me with a great philosophical education but also something

---

3. Madrid, *Surprised by Truth*, 94.
4. Madrid, *Surprised by Truth*, 90.

of an education about Roman Catholicism. I had had relatively little direct interaction with Roman Catholics before that time, so my three years there gave me at least something of a window into American Catholicism. While my data here was naturally piecemeal, anecdotal, and informal, I did come to some interesting impressions about American Catholics from my conversations with fellow students, faculty, and so on. In short, I came to the conclusion that most of them were not much different from Protestants except they identified as Catholics.

Indeed, I argued this case briefly in an article I wrote for the student newspaper, *The Observer*. In that article, I noted three different kinds of Roman Catholics I had encountered. First, there were a fair number of conservatives, who I described as follows: "Those who belong to this group like to characterize themselves as thoroughly Catholic. They stress the teaching authority of the Church and are quick to defend the official Roman position on all points. For such persons, papal encyclicals are not to be debated; they are to be accepted and obeyed."[5] I met a number of students who were actively involved with Opus Dei who met this description, as well as several others.

I also encountered some rather liberal Catholics, who were not only openly skeptical about the distinctive claims of their church but even basic creedal orthodoxy. They would be as dubious of the virgin birth as the immaculate conception (if they even knew the difference), but they would still identify as Catholic, even proudly so, especially on football Saturdays.

But my impression at the time was that most Roman Catholics fit into a third group somewhere between these two, a group I called "functional Protestants." I wrote: "When I say most Catholics are functional protestants I simply mean that most Catholics do not accept the authority claims of their Church. In actual belief and practice, they are much closer to the protestant view."[6] Many of the Catholics I knew at Notre Dame did not accept papal infallibility and were dubious of the Marian dogmas. Moreover, many of them rejected their church's stance on birth control. They were fundamentally orthodox in the classic creedal sense and took their faith in Christ seriously, but the same could not be said for many of the distinctive claims of their church. While they still had a loyalty to their Roman Catholic heritage and very much identified themselves as Catholic, their theological views were pretty much the same as mine.

---

5. Walls, "Reformational Theology," 8. My title for the article, as I recall, was "Are Most Catholics Functional Protestants?" but the editors changed it.

6. Walls, "Reformational Theology," 8.

The reaction to my article was telling. My conservative Roman Catholic friends applauded me and agreed that many of their fellow Catholics did not deserve the name. Others thought my conclusions were off target because I was defining Catholicism in traditional terms that were not true to the diversity in the contemporary Catholic Church. (Rumor had it this was the reaction in the theology department.) Still others essentially agreed with my analysis, but thought I was operating with too narrow an understanding of what is involved in being a faithful Catholic.[7]

One of the most interesting reactions to my article came from Professor Ralph McInerny, the distinguished medieval scholar and philosopher. In addition to teaching at Notre Dame and writing both scholarly and popular books as well as detective novels, Professor McInerny had co-founded with Michael Novak *Crisis Magazine*, which described itself as "A Voice for the Faithful Catholic Laity." In one of his articles in that magazine, McInerny not only agreed with my claims but saw them as further evidence that illustrated his concerns about the direction of his church. In the second paragraph of that article he wrote: "It was not clear to me four and a half years ago, when Mike Novak and I began this journal, how deep the divisions among Catholics were nor how much deeper they were destined to become. Nowadays, the very term 'Catholic' has become equivocal."[8] McInerny went on a few paragraphs later to summarize my article, and then went on to comment as follows.

> Now if Walls has a point, and surely he does, things have come to a pretty pass among us Catholics. As often before, I am reminded of Newman's "A Form of Infidelity of the Day." The most insidious enemy is the enemy within, and the heretic who claims to be a Catholic. It is such people, we are told, who are now in charge—readers will remember Thomas Sheehan's triumphalist victory statement on behalf of what he calls the liberal consensus.
>
> Wasn't it Karl Rahner who said that it had become necessary to think of Hans Küng as a Protestant in order to make sense of him?
>
> A few years ago I would never have described the foe in terms he now uses of himself. The days are far darker than once dreamed.[9]

---

7. Payne, "Letter to the Editor," 5.
8. McInerny, "'Quodlibets.'"
9. For more on the "Liberal Consensus," see McInerny, "Liberal Consensus."

Now what is particularly striking here is McInerny's confession that he had underestimated the depth of the divisions within his church when he first founded *Crisis Magazine*, and his assessment that things were "far darker than once dreamed." Moreover, the only way to make sense of some "Catholics" is to think of them as Protestants.

It is important to emphasize here that McInerny was not an extremist but rather a highly sophisticated Catholic intellectual who was very gracious and likeable. I remember him fondly from my days at Notre Dame. But it is most telling that he judged the Roman Catholic Church in 1987 to be much farther down the road toward liberalism than he had imagined only four or five years before.

Similarly, I have now come to the conclusion that my judgment in 1987 that most Roman Catholics are "functional Protestants" was far too optimistic. I had the sense then that most Roman Catholics were pretty firmly committed to core Christian orthodoxy and conservative moral convictions and could be counted on as Evangelical allies on these matters. As I have continued to assess the matter, I have come to the conclusion that most Roman Catholics are functional liberal Protestants, and that the Church of Rome is functionally the world's largest pluralist Protestant denomination.

Putting the matter this way is of course somewhat provocative, but I think it is not inaccurate. To see why, let me say more about what I mean by a pluralist Protestant denomination. For an example, let us consider the United Methodist Church.[10] At one time the Methodist Church was vibrantly growing, was the largest Christian denomination in the United States, and was thoroughly orthodox and evangelical in its theological commitments. This began to change in the late nineteenth century, and especially in the twentieth, when various forms of liberal theology gained acceptance and even dominance in Methodist seminaries. As a result, more and more clergy were trained in liberal schools of thought, and the Methodist theological identity became confused and equivocal. By the sixties, this was so much the case that when the United Methodist Church was formed in 1968 by merging the Methodist Church and the United Brethren, the Church was in reality radically pluralistic in terms of the theological diversity within the ranks of the clergy and the theological seminaries. At its General Conference in 1972, the Church made the move to affirm "theological pluralism" within its ranks as a "principle," thereby officially endorsing what had been the reality for several decades.

---

10. The United Methodist Church has recently split, and many of the conservative churches and pastors have left and formed The Global Methodist Church.

Fortunately, this experiment that many hailed as a bold harbinger of vitality and growth was soon recognized as a disastrous mistake.[11] In 1988, the United Methodists repudiated the pluralism they had embraced sixteen years before by adopting a new theological statement that reaffirmed the classic orthodoxy represented in their official doctrinal standards. And indeed, the United Methodist Church has been moving in the same direction ever since, as was made clear in the 2016 General Conference when the Church not only re-affirmed its traditional stance on sexuality but also adopted more conservative positions on abortion and other social and moral issues. At stake in these recent developments is the identity of the United Methodist Church as a global orthodox Christian church, a debate that is significant in its own right, though it is not my concern in this chapter.[12]

But here is an important point to make clear what I mean by a pluralist Protestant denomination. Throughout the time radical theological pluralism had been tolerated within the ranks of United Methodist clergy, even during those sixteen years when it was explicitly endorsed as a principle, its *official* doctrinal stance remained quite orthodox. All along if one wanted to know the doctrine of the United Methodist Church, the *official* answer could be found by consulting the Articles of Religion and Wesley's Standard Sermons, which affirm not only the substance of classic creedal orthodoxy, but also distinctively Reformed and Wesleyan claims about justification, sanctification, and the like. So a pluralist denomination is not necessarily one that officially gives up its official orthodox doctrinal standards. To the contrary, they may retain and continue to affirm those standards on paper.[13]

What is it then that characterizes a pluralist denomination? I would suggest three things. First there is large divergence between official doctrine and the actual beliefs and practices of significant numbers of the members of those denominations. Second, pluralist denominations are marked by tolerating clergy and academics who ignore or even deny the official teaching of their church and espouse theological views that are radically at odds with their doctrinal standards. The seminaries and other schools of pluralist denominations have no binding confessional requirements for their professors. Third, members of these denominations, particularly clergy, not infrequently ignore church law and engage in practices that are officially prohibited.

11. Walls, *Problem of Pluralism* [1988].

12. Given the recent split, the prospects of this are dim.

13. So the official doctrinal standards in the *Book of Discipline* of the United Methodist Church play a similar role to magisterial doctrinal statements in the Roman Catholic Church. But in both cases, official doctrine is one thing, actual belief and practice may be quite another.

Consider again the United Methodist Church. Not only do many of its clergy and seminary professors espouse views contrary to official doctrine, but they ignore church law. The most controversial instances involve homosexual behavior and marriage. Despite the official teaching and policy of the Church, a number of United Methodist clergy have performed gay weddings and most of the time they do so with impunity. So there is a glaring gap between official doctrine or policy and actual belief or practice in many cases.[14]

It is with regard to these three characteristics that the Roman Catholic Church may be functionally the world's largest pluralist Protestant denomination. So let us turn now to explore this claim in more detail.

COMPARING CATHOLIC CONVICTIONS

We can make some initial headway by comparing the beliefs of Roman Catholics with the beliefs of mainline Protestants, who are the epitome of pluralist denominations, and Evangelicals, who are more orthodox and conservative in their convictions. A good place to begin is with a Pew Research poll from 2014 that compared the beliefs of various religions, including different Christian traditions.[15]

For a start, consider how these three groups answered when queried about absolute standards for beliefs about right and wrong. They were asked whether there are clear standards for right and wrong or whether right and wrong depends on the situation. 30 percent of Roman Catholics said there are clear standards, while 67 percent said it depends on the situation. 32 percent of mainline Protestants said there are clear standards, while 65 percent said it depends on the situation. There is a marked difference with Evangelicals; 50 percent said there is a clear standard, while 48 percent said it depends on the situation.

These broad differences also appear when we consider more specific moral beliefs. Consider first abortion, where there is a significant gap between Roman Catholics and mainline Protestants. 48 percent of Roman Catholics said abortion should be legal in all or most cases, and 47 percent said it should be illegal in all or most cases, compared to 60 percent of mainline Protestants who said it should be legal in all or most cases, while 35

---

14. As I write, the UMC continues to hold conservative views officially on this issue but remains deeply divided. As noted above, many of the conservative churches have left the United Methodist Church.

15. The statistics that follow are from the Pew Research Center's "Religious Landscape Study."

percent said it should be illegal in all or most. Again, Evangelicals returned the most conservative numbers, with 33 percent saying it should be legal in all or most cases, and 63 percent saying it should be illegal in all or most.[16]

When we turn to what is perhaps the most volatile moral issue in contemporary America, we see Roman Catholics again aligning more with mainline Protestants than with Evangelicals. When asked about homosexuality, 70 percent of Roman Catholics said it should be accepted, while 23 percent said it should be discouraged. This is slightly more liberal than mainline Protestants, 66 percent of whom said homosexuality should be accepted, while 26 percent said it should be discouraged. Evangelicals were considerably more conservative, with 36 percent saying it should be accepted, compared to 55 percent who said it should be discouraged. On the issue of same-sex marriage, Roman Catholics and mainline Protestants are virtually identical. 57 percent of Roman Catholics favor or strongly favor same-sex marriage, and 34 percent oppose or strongly oppose it, compared to 57 percent of mainline Protestants who favor or strongly favor it, while 35 percent oppose or strongly oppose it. Again, the numbers for Evangelicals are significantly different. 28 percent favor or strongly favor same-sex marriage, whereas 64 percent oppose or strongly oppose it.

There is one interesting matter of traditional doctrine where the Pew Research poll found Catholics were very close to Evangelicals, and that is belief in heaven. 85 percent of Catholics said they believed in heaven, while 10 percent said they did not. This compares to 88 percent of Evangelicals who affirmed belief in heaven while 5 percent did not. Mainline Protestants are somewhat less confident of heaven, with 80 percent affirming belief in it, while 12 percent did not. However, when we turn to the less popular doctrine of hell, once again we see Roman Catholics more in line with mainline Protestants than with Evangelicals. 63 percent of Catholics affirm belief in hell, while 29 percent do not, while 60 percent of mainline Protestants said they believed in it, compared to 29 percent who said they did not. 82 percent of Evangelicals said they believed in hell, while 11 percent did not.

It is worth emphasizing here that the liberal convictions we have noted are not held only by Roman Catholics in the United States but in many other parts of the church as well. While Catholics in some parts of the world are much more conservative than they are in the American church, they are also more liberal in other parts of the world. A dramatic example of this

---

16. It is worth noting that a significant majority of Roman Catholics voted for the most pro-abortion president in American history, Barack Obama, in 2008 (54 percent of Roman Catholics voted for him compared to 45 percent of Protestants overall). Only 26 percent of Protestant Evangelicals voted for Obama in 2008. See, "How the Faithful Voted."

was on display recently in the Republic of Ireland, one of the most traditionally Roman Catholic countries in the world, with one of the highest percentages of Roman Catholics on the planet. In a national referendum on same-sex marriage in 2015, the Republic became the first country to legalize it through a popular vote, and they did so overwhelmingly, with 62 percent of the population supporting it.

A recent worldwide poll of Roman Catholics was also telling, not only of the liberal beliefs of many Catholics but also of the extreme diversity in the Church.[17] While same-sex marriage is supported by a significant majority in several countries, it is opposed by 99 percent of African Catholics. The poll also found that 78 percent of Catholics overall support the use of contraceptives, but over 90 percent do so in Argentina, Columbia, Brazil, Spain, and France.

Another issue of particular interest given recent developments in the Church of Rome is the question of whether divorced and remarried persons should be permitted to receive Communion. The official teaching is that they should not. The survey found that only 19 percent of European Catholics and 30 percent of South Americans agree with this. 75 percent of Africans do, however.

Now these statistics tell an interesting story. A significant majority of Roman Catholics are at odds with the teaching of their church on important issues. On some of these issues, they may be aligned with conservative Protestants (and Eastern Orthodox). Many conservative Protestants and Orthodox believe that contraception is morally acceptable. Likewise, many conservative Protestants (and Orthodox) believe that there are biblically justified reasons for divorce and remarriage.[18] To this extent, then, many Roman Catholics are functionally Protestant.

However, there is more to the story. Many, if not most, Roman Catholics also hold views that are more in line with liberal Protestants, as the Pew Research Poll demonstrated.[19] Over and again, we saw that Roman Catholic

---

17. Boorstein and Craighill, "Pope Francis."

18. The Orthodox Church excommunicates divorced persons for a time to emphasize that divorce is a serious sin. After that, they may be restored to full participation in the community, including receiving the sacrament of Communion. Such persons may then be remarried with the blessing of the Church.

19. It might be wondered whether educational differences account for the more liberal views of Roman Catholics. This does not appear to be the case, as the differences in education between Evangelicals and Roman Catholics are negligible. For Catholics, 46 percent only graduated from high school or less, compared to 43 percent of Evangelicals; 27 percent of Catholics had some college, compared to 35 percent of Evangelicals; 16 percent of Catholics graduated from college, compared to 14 percent of Evangelicals; 10 percent of Catholics had a postgraduate degree, compared to 7 percent

views on various moral and religious issues align very much with mainline Protestants and diverge from the majority of Evangelicals. This is one good reason, then, to suggest that many if not most Roman Catholics are not only functional *Protestants* but also functional *liberal* Protestants.

BIRTH CONTROL AND PAPAL AUTHORITY

The fact that Roman Catholics overwhelmingly reject their church's teaching on birth control is emblematic in more ways than one that most Catholics are functional Protestants. Indeed, it reflects the deeper reality that many Roman Catholics reject the distinctive authority claims that characterize their church, claims that are clearly at the heart of the divisions between Protestants and Roman Catholics.

To understand the connection between birth control and papal authority, we need to look back to the momentous events of Vatican II. As many analysts have observed, there was a majority of delegates who supported the "progressive" theology that was having a growing influence in the Church, along with a conservative minority who represented the traditional theology favored by the pope and the curia (the power structure in Rome). The documents of Vatican II were thus crafted, as much as possible, to satisfy both sides. Sometimes this resulted in language that was sufficiently ambiguous that both sides could assent to it, and at other times both views were presented in such a way that it was not clear how they could be mutually consistent.

A famous instance of this occurs in the very first document of Vatican II, Dogmatic Constitution of the Church (*Lumen Gentium*), specifically in chapter 3, "On the Hierarchical Structure of the Church and in Particular the Episcopate." This chapter, while asserting traditional claims about the papacy and episcopal authority also emphasized a strongly collegial view of the relationship between the pope and the college of bishops and the power they shared. Pope Paul VI, however, thought the document had compromised papal authority and made an unusual move to rectify the situation, as we saw in chapter one. After the document had already been passed, recall, he inserted a "Note of Explanation" that asserted a stronger view of papal authority than the document seemed to support.

> It is up to the judgment of the Supreme Pontiff, to whose care Christ's whole flock has been entrusted, to determine, according

---

of Evangelicals. Mainline Protestants were slightly more educated than both Catholics and Evangelicals. 37 percent only had high school or less; 30 percent had some college; 19 percent had a college degree; and 14 percent had a postgraduate degree.

> to the needs of the Church as they change over the course of centuries, the way in which this care may be best exercised—whether in a personal or a collegial way. The Roman Pontiff, taking account of the Church's welfare, proceeds according to his own discretion in arranging, promoting, and approving the exercise of collegial activity.
>
> As Supreme Pastor of the Church, the Supreme Pontiff can always exercise his power at will, as his very office demands.[20]

Since this "Note of Explanation" was added after the Council had completed its work, it was not voted on like other parts of the document.

This clash of authority came to the fore after Vatican II on the issue of birth control, an issue many hoped the Council would resolve. In 1963, Pope John XXIII had appointed a commission to study the issue. After the death of John, Paul VI increased the Pontifical Commission on Birth Control to seventy-two members, including several theologians and medical professionals. In 1966, the commission completed a report in which they concluded that artificial birth control is not inherently evil and that Roman Catholics should be permitted to use it. Their recommendation was rejected, however, and the minority report prevailed, resulting in the 1968 papal encyclical *Humanae Vitae*, a document that reaffirms the traditional Roman Catholic view that contraception is sinful.

Now what is most telling about this episode is that the arguments for the minority report seemed less concerned at times with the morality of birth control than with the concern that accepting it would undermine magisterial and papal authority. Given the many times the Catholic Church had condemned birth control in very strong terms, to accept it now would be an admission that the magisterium had been mistaken in the past. Consider these lines from the minority report:

> If contraception were declared not intrinsically evil, in honesty it would have to be acknowledged that the Holy Spirit in 1930 (Encyclical, Casti Connubi), 1951 (Address of Pius XII to midwives) and 1958 (Address to the International Congress of Haematologists in the year of Pius XII's death), assisted Protestant Churches, and that for half a century Pius XI, Pius XII and a great part of the hierarchy did not protest against a very serious error, one most pernicious to souls; for it would be suggested that they condemned most imprudently, under pain of eternal punishment, thousands upon thousands of human acts which are now approved. Indeed, it must be neither denied nor

---

20. *Documents of Vatican II*, 76.

ignored that these acts would be approved for the same fundamental reasons which Protestantism alleged and which they (Catholics) condemned or at least did not recognize.[21]

Particularly interesting for our concerns is the recognition that to regard the use of contraception as morally acceptable would not only call into question previous papal pronouncements but also legitimize Protestantism over against Rome.

Despite the fact that the conservative position prevailed officially, the decision by Paul VI hardly went uncontested. Those who took issue with the pope's decision thought he should have called a meeting of the bishops and the matter should have been resolved by collegial action. This claim, of course, goes back to the document on the church at Vatican II and the pope's decision to insert his "Note of Explanation," asserting his authority to act alone. Apparently, not all bishops agreed with the claims he made in that "Note." David Wells describes what happened later on:

> When the bishops eventually got together in Rome after Pope Paul's encyclical had been issued, they took him to task for not consulting with them. Leo Suenens, the Belgian cardinal and leader of the progressives, was most forthright in this matter, letting the pope know that he had acted unconstitutionally. Whether this was so, of course depends on how the document is interpreted. There are two ways of looking at it. From one perspective, Pope Paul acted quite within his power, while from the other perspective, he did not.[22]

In any case, our key point here is that the overwhelming majority of Roman Catholics side with Protestants on the issue of birth control, and their doing so is emblematic of the fact that most Catholics reject the claims to papal authority that Paul VI tried to re-assert at Vatican II. While conservatives rightly feared that accepting birth control would both undermine papal authority and give credence to Protestantism, the reality is that papal authority as Rome wanted to maintain it had already been lost.

THE BEWILDERING VARIETY OF ROMAN CATHOLIC THEOLOGY

The larger reality, however, is that Roman Catholics have far bigger theological fish to fry than any worries they may have about contraception.

21. Cited by Küng, *Truthfulness*, 132–33.
22. Wells, *Revolution in Rome*, 111.

Recall again McInerny's admission in 1987 that it was not clear to him "how deep the divisions among Catholics were nor how much deeper they were destined to become" when he and Michael Novak founded *Crisis Magazine* four years earlier. What had become clear to McInerny has become all the more evident in the years since then, and that is that the Roman Catholic Church is not only deeply divided but also radically pluralistic in the range of theological views represented in the Church. Indeed, it is not putting it too strongly to say that every theological novelty spawned by liberal Protestantism has been replicated or reproduced within Roman Catholic theology. And now Catholics have invented some of their own.

If I may draw on my Notre Dame experience again, my conservative friends complained that the theology department there represented the liberal sort of approach to the discipline that they thought destructive to Catholic orthodoxy. A good measure of the pluralism represented at Notre Dame is the book *Catholicism,* a widely used textbook by Richard P. McBrien, who was chairman of the theology department there for many years. His book, a "classic" that sold over 150,000 copies in its first edition, was intended by the author to be a "bridge between the Church of yesterday and the Church of today, and between conservative, traditionally minded Catholics, on the one hand, and progressive, renewal minded Catholics, on the other, even if some in the former group seem determined to resist and depreciate such an effort."[23]

The enormous popularity of McBrien's book suggests that the picture he paints of Catholicism is one that resonates with many contemporary members of his church. The book has been controversial, however, and has drawn criticism from Catholic Church officials, both in its earlier editions, as well as the 1994 version. In 1996, the National Council of Catholic Bishops Committee on Doctrine released a critical review of the book after expressing disappointment that McBrien had not corrected the defects they had pointed out in earlier editions. The review was published because the bishops judged that the book posed pastoral problems, so their reflections would be of value to the larger Roman Catholic community as well as an expression of concern to McBrien. The review identified three broad areas of concern with the book:

> First, some statements are inaccurate or at least misleading. Second, there is in the book an overemphasis on the plurality of opinion within the Catholic theological tradition that makes it difficult at times for the reader to discern the normative core of that tradition. Third, *Catholicism* overstates the significance

---

23. McBrien, *Catholicism*, xli.

of recent developments within the Catholic tradition, implying that the past appears to be markedly inferior to the present and obscuring the continuity of the tradition.[24]

Particularly interesting here for our concerns is the "overemphasis on the plurality of opinion within the Catholic theological tradition." The bishops were especially concerned that the book would be confusing when used as a college textbook for beginners or by Roman Catholic lay persons. Here is part of what they said about the concern with plurality: "The book gives an overview of the theological scene in all of its variety and presents numerous brief summaries of many positions.... The book requires the reader to find his or her own way through what is sometimes a bewildering number and variety of positions."[25]

To be sure, this does pose a pastoral problem, as the bishops note. But the deeper problem for the Church of Rome resides in the fact that there is a "bewildering number and variety of positions" within Roman Catholic theology to begin with. The reality is that McBrien's book is simply a reflection of the deep division and radical diversity that already prevails in contemporary Roman Catholic theology.

A MANDATE FOR THEOLOGIANS?

Before moving on from the state of theology in Roman Catholicism, it is worth noting that in 1990 Pope John Paul II issued the document *Ex Corde Ecclesiae* (From the Heart of the Church) in an attempt to call Catholic colleges and universities to some basic standards of accountability in order to preserve their identity as Catholic schools. Among the requirements of the document was the following:

> In ways appropriate to the different academic disciplines, all Catholic teachers are to be faithful to, and all other teachers are to respect, Catholic doctrine and morals in their research and teaching. In particular, Catholic theologians, aware that they fulfil a mandate received from the Church, are to be faithful to the Magisterium of the Church as the authentic interpreter of Sacred Scripture and Sacred Tradition.[26]

---

24. NCCB, Review of *Catholicism*.

25. It is worth noting that McBrien also surveys various Protestant views in some of his chapters, but the fact remains that the "bewildering" variety remains if only Catholic positions are included.

26. John Paul II, "On Catholic 'Universities'" 4.3.

Of particular interest here is the claim that theologians have a mandate from the Church, and the passage ends with a note that refers to a number of Church documents, and quotes canon law 812, which reads as follows: "It is necessary that those who teach theological disciplines in any institute of higher studies have a mandate from the competent ecclesiastical authority."

Given the state of contemporary Roman Catholic theology, it is hardly necessary to comment that this requirement for Roman Catholic theologians to have a mandate from the "competent ecclesiastical authority" and to "be faithful to the Magisterium of the Church" has not been widely followed. Indeed, Anne Hendershott described the reaction to the document as follows.

> Defiant from the earliest days of the release of *Ex Corde Ecclesiae*, many Catholic college presidents have refused to implement it. Notre Dame's then-president Fr. Edward Malloy, along with Fr. Donald Monan, chancellor of Boston College, responded to the release of the document by publishing an article in *America* calling the document "positively dangerous." Warning of "havoc" if it were adopted, the faculty senate at Notre Dame voted unanimously for the guidelines to be ignored.[27]

What we have seen then, is that the Roman Catholic Church is not only marked by extreme pluralism among its theologians, but that official efforts to hold them accountable to magisterial teaching have little force or effect. In both these respects, the Church of Rome very much resembles pluralist Protestant denominations.

IGNORING CHURCH LAW

Another defining marker of pluralist Protestant denominations is that liberal clergy not infrequently disregard church law with little if any disciplinary action from church leaders. As noted early in this chapter, the most notorious example of this reality pertains to official church teaching about homosexuality and same-sex marriage. Some pluralist denominations have officially changed their policy on this controversial issue, but others have maintained their traditional position, but have been lax in enforcing it. Here, again, the Church of Rome is not exempt from this difficulty.

A high level instance of this played out several years ago in Germany. In April of 2015, a woman who headed a Caritas day care center in Bavaria

---

27. Hendershott, "New Front." See also Mirus, "*Ex Corde Ecclesiae*"; McBrien, "Why I Shall Not."

had been asked to resign because she had announced that she was going to marry a woman. The decision was then reversed with the blessing of Church officials. William Oddie explains:

> Cardinal Reinhard Marx, Archbishop of the Diocese of Munich, has agreed to implement immediately new regulations approved by the German Bishops' Conference at the end of April 2015, drastically liberalising the Catholic Church's disciplinary rules in Germany. In the past, employees who deliberately and persistently did not live according to the Church's moral teaching would (as at first happened in this case) have been asked to leave their position in institutions of the Church.[28]

Oddie went on to cite the opinion of German Cardinal Reinhard Marx, who expressed the view that the Catholic Church in Germany is not simply a branch of Rome. "Each conference of bishops is responsible for pastoral care in its cultural context and must preach the Gospel in its own, original way." Oddie was incredulous of this claim, and went on to insist that all Catholics are members of churches that are branches of Rome, which is why they are called "Roman Catholics":

> And all this talk of being responsible for care of its own part of the Church "in its pastoral context" is a weasely way of saying that the German bishops have a right to determine what their own version of Catholic DOCTRINE is: when Marx says the German church "must preach the gospel in its own, original way" he is unambiguously declaring unilateral doctrinal independence from the teaching authority of the Church.

Oddie went on to give vent to the wish that many conservative Roman Catholics no doubt share, namely, that the pope would fire and replace all dissenting bishops. He concedes, however, that even if the pope were so disposed, he lacks the authority to do so. To resort to that measure or anything like it would lead to open schism. To make matters worse, Oddie realizes that lay opinion runs heavily in a liberal direction, even in many parts of the Church where conservative bishops are trying to remain faithful to official doctrine and policy.

I could easily belabor this point with other examples and illustrations, but there is no need to do so. The hard reality is that a significant majority of the membership of the Church of Rome is so far out of step with its official views that any hope of consistently enforcing Church doctrine and policy is

---

28. Oddie, "German Bishops."

A CONSERVATIVE CATHOLIC CRITIQUE

Consider the analysis of conservative Roman Catholic Ross Douthat with respect to the controversy surrounding *Amoris Laetitia*, especially with respect to whether the document permits married and divorced Roman Catholics to take the sacrament. The official position is starkly clear. "Contracting a new union, even if it is recognized by civil law, adds to the gravity of the rupture: the remarried spouse is then in a situation of public and permanent adultery."[29] Adultery is a mortal sin, so to be in a state of permanent adultery is to be in a state of permanent mortal sin. To freely remain in mortal sin is to remain in a state that leads to damnation if the sin is not repented of and forgiven. Such persons accordingly are excommunicated and unable to receive the sacrament of Communion so long as they remain in this situation.[30]

There is, however, a remedy for persons in these adulterous marriages that allows them to be reconciled to the community, namely, through the sacrament of penance. What this penance requires, however, is rather severe. "Reconciliation through the sacrament of Penance can be granted only for those who have repented for having violated the sign of the covenant and of fidelity to Christ, and who are committed to living in complete continence."[31] The couple can remain married and be welcomed again to receive the sacrament of Communion so long as they are totally committed to a sexless marriage. The only way to be restored to the community and to escape the state of perpetual mortal sin is to live together thereafter in perpetual continence, the way Roman Catholics believe Joseph and Mary did.

What is also starkly clear is that the overwhelming majority of Roman Catholics reject the Church's teaching on this matter, as indicated by statistics cited at the beginning of this chapter. More telling, however, is that apparently a significant number of Roman Catholic priests, including those in the hierarchy, also think the Church's stance on this issue is too stringent. Apparently that includes the current pope.

Douthat notes that his church has managed to remain officially united despite its deep divisions by a sort of truce between conservatives and liberals. "That coexistence depends on a tension between doctrine and practice,

---

29. *Catechism*, para. 2384.
30. It is worth noting that some Evangelicals share this view.
31. *Catechism*, para. 1650.

in which the church's official teaching remains conservative even as the everyday life of Catholicism is shot through with disagreement, relativism, dissent."[32] This arrangement, he notes, allows conservatives to feel reassured, even as it allows liberals to remain in the Church as they wait for it to "evolve" even more in their direction. Douthat thinks, however, that the terms of the truce have now changed with *Amoris Laetitia*. While the document does not provide a *formal* path for the divorced and remarried to receive Communion (without committing to total continence), it still marks a significant new policy. In effect, it endorses what is already "the existing practice in many places—the informal admission of remarried Catholics to communion by sympathetic priests."

In other words, the new document represents a highly significant development because it is essentially "a teaching in favor of the truce itself." Instead of merely tolerating the profound split between actual practice and official doctrine for the sake of formal unity, the split "now has a papal imprimatur." Douthat sees this new variation on the truce as even shakier than the earlier one between conservatives and progressives. "In effectively licensing innovation rather than merely tolerating it, and in transforming the papacy's keenest defenders into wary critics, it promises to heighten the church's contradictions rather than contain them." He concludes his article with these words.

> Francis doubtless intends this language as a bridge between the church's factions, just dogmatic enough for conservatives but perpetually open to more liberal interpretations. And such deliberate ambiguity does offer a center, of sorts, for a deeply divided church.
> But not one, I fear, that's likely to permanently hold.

Before concluding this section I should also mention here again the recent and similarly controversial Vatican Declaration *Fiducia Supplicans*.[33] This document, like *Amoris Laetitia*, has also come under fire from conservatives, in particular, because it affirms that blessings can be given to persons who are divorced and remarried (and therefore living in adultery, according to Rome) as well as to same-sex couples. Conservatives see this document as one that will inevitably, in time, lead to a more tolerant and even accepting attitude toward these practices. To see what has changed and how profoundly will not be immediately apparent. But the revolution has already occurred.

---

32. Douthat, "New Catholic Truce," 1
33. I also discuss this document in chapter 3.

VISIBLE UNITY OR DEEP DIVISION?

Anyone who understands the deep divisions in the Church of Rome that have been growing ever deeper since the pre-Vatican II era also understands that the image of unity Rome projects is just that, an *image*. I fully concur with Douthat in doubting that the "deliberate ambiguity" that comprises the center of his church will hold in decades to come.

As I have followed these recent controversies, I could not help but think about the story of Steve Wood and his conversion that I sketched at the beginning of this chapter. Recall his crisis of conscience because divorced and remarried persons were invited to receive the sacrament of Communion in his church. I have no idea where Wood is today, but I wonder what he thinks of the recent developments in his new church. Does he support his pope and believe that what he found so troubling in his church decades ago is now okay decades later if the pope approves of it? Or does he hold fast to the official teaching of his new church and think (like Douthat and many other conservatives) that the changes Francis has subtly embraced generate deep inconsistencies in official teaching?

Either way, the point is clear. Protestant converts to Rome who imagine they are joining a church that is free of the divisions and disagreements that plague Protestantism are quite mistaken. Indeed, far from escaping those problems of Protestantism they disdain, they are in fact joining a church that is *functionally* a radically pluralist Protestant denomination.

It is worth remarking here that Evangelical Protestantism, with all its denominational diversity, represents a far more impressive model of true unity than does the Church of Rome. The National Association of Evangelicals is comprised of some forty different Evangelical churches. Despite their differences on secondary issues, there is genuine agreement and substantial unity on classic orthodox catholic doctrine. Most of them, moreover, are in communion with each other. In the same vein, it is a safe bet that there is far more genuine agreement about catholic Christianity among the members of the Evangelical Theological Society than there is among, say, members of the Catholic Theological Society of America. This bet is further supported by the Reforming Catholic Confession I described in the Introduction.

Curiously, when these sorts of facts are pointed out, converts to Rome often dismiss them with little more than a wave of the hand. As Gerald Bray has observed, "Intellectual Protestant converts either ignore these unpleasant facts or make excuses for them in a way that they would never do for the Protestant denominations they have left."[34] This is more than a little tell-

---

34. Bray, *Church*, 236–37.

ing. Regardless of how they try to excuse it, and the double standard that may be at work here, the hard truth is that the permanence and unity that Roman apologists and converts like to project over against Protestantism is an idealistic illusion, at best. This reality, of course, is one more reason not to be a Roman Catholic.

CONCLUSION

FREE TO BE MORE CATHOLIC THAN CATHOLICS

THE PRECEDING CHAPTERS HARDLY exhaust the reasons I am not a Roman Catholic. Readers may wonder why I did not discuss justification by faith or the doctrine of assurance or various exegetical issues that divide Protestants and Roman Catholics. Moreover, what about issues in sacramental theology, such as the Roman Catholic doctrine of transubstantiation?[1] If my aim was to explain all my reasons, I would have to deal with these questions and more. However, my goal here was to focus on a set of issues that are central to why I reject the claims of Rome and to do so in a relatively concise fashion. In particular, I have focused on issues of authority and related issues of ecclesiology and catholicity.

I have given considerable attention to the papacy since so much rides on that institution for the Roman Catholic claim to exclusive teaching authority. Indeed, the pope has a unique role and singular power as the head of the ascending Roman magisterial hierarchy. An incident from Vatican I, where the dogma of papal infallibility was formally defined, is instructive. The bishops had proposed that it was the papal magisterium, not the person of the pope, that was infallible. In response Pius IX emphatically fired back, "I, I am the tradition! I, I am the church."[2] Whatever one thinks of this incident, it is telling that Pius IX would not hesitate to make such a claim for himself. What seems undeniable is that the papacy and the claims that have

---

1. For excellent discussion of these issues by my co-author, see chapters 9, 10, 17–19 in Collins and Walls, *Roman but Not Catholic*.

2. O'Malley, *Vatican I*, 212. This book is an excellent account of Vatican I and the issues that drove it.

been made for it are utterly essential to the Roman Catholic Church. In that sense at least, the pope is indeed the Church.

Given how crucial the papacy is to Rome, the fact that it faces so many severe difficulties altogether undermines the claims of Rome in my view. As we have seen, the papal doctrine is exegetically dubious, at odds with critical history, and profoundly compromised by a legacy of conspicuous corruption. Indeed, if the papacy were my only objection to Roman Catholicism, it would likely be enough to convince me that the Roman Catholic Church is mistaken in its claim to be the one true church.

I find it incredible to believe that a doctrine that is allegedly so vital to the church and its teaching authority rests on claims that the consensus of historians judge to be simply false. It is important to emphasize that this has nothing to do with a Protestant paradigm or Protestant assumptions. Rather, it is the consensus of critical historians, including Roman Catholics, that there was no monarchical bishop in Rome until sometime late in the second century, let alone anyone who had the sort of authority traditional papal theology claims for the alleged successors of Peter. In view of this, I am altogether as dubious of the distinctive claims of Roman Catholicism that hinge on claims about the early papacy as I would be about orthodox Christianity if the overwhelming consensus among serious scholars was that the bodily resurrection of Jesus did not happen and is only a pious myth.

These historical problems are exacerbated by the deep corruption that is an undeniable part of the story of the papacy. To make this observation is not to demand perfection, nor is it to subscribe to Donatism, the notion that the validity of sacraments depends on the character of the one administering them. But it is to say that it is a reasonable expectation that the "chief shepherd" should consistently meet some minimal standards of integrity and genuine piety, to say the very least.

This is all the more plausible if God has guaranteed an unbroken succession beginning with Peter, to this day, as Rome claims. It seems odd that God would be concerned to preserve such an unbroken chain (dubious though this is to historians) but would be apparently much less concerned with the quality of the links that comprise the chain. Indeed, when we examine the actual history of the papacy and the motives and behavior of many of the men who have held the office, those facts are better explained if the papacy is a very human institution rather than one designed by God for the lofty spiritual purposes Rome claims.

Moreover, the fact that there is no assurance (according to many Roman Catholics) that the men chosen as pope are actually God's choice further weakens the claim that the papacy plays as vital a role as Roman Catholic theology holds. The robust claims that are initially made about the papacy dwindle down to very modest assurances when we press the question of God's providential role in the papacy. Bad popes raise a serious problem on both weak and strong accounts of providence.

Of course, Roman Catholics can dismiss this line of argument by insisting that the history of corruption is, strictly speaking, irrelevant to the truth of traditional papal theology. Even if *all the popes* had been corrupt, it might be argued, and will continue to be, the truth of papal theology would remain unfazed. Now this is an extreme position, but unless a Roman Catholic is willing to embrace it, then in principle, a sufficient degree of corruption should be recognized as counting heavily against, if not entirely undermining, traditional papal claims. Perhaps it is hard to say how much corruption is required to reach this conclusion, but a rational person might believe a sufficient amount of corruption has in fact occurred, even if there is no simple way to decide that question.

Consider a recent example from the highly publicized sexual abuse scandals in the Roman Catholic Church, scandals that go all the way to the Vatican. Andrew Sullivan, a liberal Roman Catholic, describes his experience in reading a controversial book that aimed to expose the corruption and its ongoing cover up in the Vatican.

> As for me, someone who has wrestled with the question of homosexuality and Catholicism for much of my adult life, this book has, to be honest, been gutting. All the painful, wounding Vatican documents on my "objective disorder" that I have tried to parse and sincerely engage . . . I find out they were written, in part, by tormented gay men, partly to deflect from their own nature. Everything I was taught growing up—to respect the priests and hierarchs, to trust them, to accept their moral authority—is in tatters. To realize that the gay closet played a part in enabling the terrible, unimaginable abuse of the most vulnerable is a twist my psyche is having a hard time absorbing. . . . This may seem like hyperbole, but in my view, the last drops of moral authority the Vatican might hope to have evaporate with this book. It is difficult to express the heartbroken rage so many of us in the pews now feel.[3]

Sullivan's reaction here is not only understandable, but also rational. At a certain point, corruption can be so extensive and so treacherous that it undermines the authority of those who display it. In a similar way, I am suggesting, the history of corruption that has marred the papacy may lead to a similar conclusion. Again, how much corruption is required to reach this

---

3. Sullivan, "Corruption." The book referred to here is Martel, *In the Closet*.

conclusion is not easy to say. But in my judgment, the recurring corruption that has besmirched the papacy is sufficient to count significantly against traditional papal claims, to say the least.

Apart from the sordid side of the story, there is another aspect of papal history that raises serious questions for the claims of Rome, namely, the fact that the papacy has been a source of deep division and controversy in the church at large. It remains a matter of contention not only with Protestantism but also with Eastern Orthodoxy. Indeed, to make matters even worse, the papacy is sometimes a flashpoint of sharp conflict within the Roman Catholic Church itself, as the recent controversies surrounding Pope Francis vividly demonstrate. So the papacy has not in fact been a source of unity but, in many cases, quite the opposite.

In short then, the Roman Catholic claim to authority essentially depends on traditional papal theology, but that theology is poorly founded, to put it mildly. Traditional papal claims are exegetically dubious, undermined by critical history, clouded by deep and recurring corruption, and deeply divisive within the larger church. A church that stands or falls with such claims rests on a very flimsy foundation.

Similar problems for the Roman authority structure are also evident in the two Marian dogmas that have been declared infallible, the highest level of dogmatic authority. To deny a Marian dogma, as we saw in an earlier chapter, is to deny papal infallibility, and with it the whole Roman Catholic authority structure. It is telling that both popes, when dogmatically defining these dogmas, insisted that to deny these dogmas is tantamount to denying the whole Catholic faith. Again, an authority structure that makes the whole faith dependent on doctrines that have neither clear scriptural warrant nor the backing of the classic ecumenical creeds is badly off center and has placed far too much emphasis on something that cannot bear the weight.

The attempt to hold the whole faith hostage in order to compel assent to distinctively Roman Catholic claims is arguably part and parcel of the Roman pattern of religious coercion that we explored in an earlier chapter. It is worth noting in this connection that some of the most dramatic claims of papal power were made by some of the most corrupt and politically ambitious popes in history. Recall from an earlier chapter Boniface VIII, one of the popes Dante had in hell, who engaged in an ongoing power struggle with the king of France and insisted he had supreme power in both the spiritual and the temporal realm. The climax of his assertion of power over political rivals came in the form of the papal bull *Unam Sanctum*, which concludes with this line: "Furthermore, we declare, we proclaim, we define that it is absolutely necessary for salvation that every human creature be subject to the Roman Pontiff."[4]

It is altogether incredible that one's salvation could depend on submission to such a corrupt pope, not to mention many other popes down the centuries. And it was the overreaching of such popes and the unchecked corruption of the Church that led to the Protestant Reformation. Here it is important to reiterate that the aim of the great reformers was not to reject catholicism, as Peter Leithart reminds us: "Contrary to the mythology that one sometimes hears from Roman Catholic apologists, the Reformation was not individualistic but catholic. It was an effort not to destroy Catholicism but to restore it."[5]

In the same vein, I repeat that my quarrel is not with what is truly catholic, in the sense of what is universal, but with the distinctive and exclusive claims of the Church of Rome. It is precisely there, ironically, that the Church of Rome is not truly catholic. C. S. Lewis put the matter rather pointedly: "In a word, the whole set-up of modern Romanism seems to me to be as much a provincial or local variation from the central, ancient tradition as any particular Protestant sect is."[6]

Despite the large barriers that remain, Leithart expresses a hopeful vision of a united church in years to come. Developments in the global church, including the remarkable growth of Pentecostalism, hold out the prospect that divisions that have separated us for centuries might finally be healed. Concisely put, Leithart believes "it opens an opportunity for Reformational Catholicism."[7] Indeed, he even dares to dream that this united church will overcome the divisions that have fractured Protestants and Roman Catholics: "I believe that the future of the church is a catholic one and that nothing less than full reunion and fully committed communion will please our Lord. Only union in faith, sacraments, ministry, and mission will express the full unity to which the Spirit drives us."[8]

The vision of a united church that is both fully reformed and deeply catholic is as enticing as it is bold. More than ever believers in "mere Christianity" need to stand united against the pressures of a culture that is increasingly hostile to traditional Christian faith and morality. But I must say I am less sanguine than Leithart that the sort of unity he envisions can

---

4. Boniface VIII, "*Unam Sanctam.*" For discussion of this papal bull, including the contrived biblical exegesis used to support it, see Collins and Wall, *Roman but Not Catholic*, 227–30.

5. Leithart, *End of Protestantism*, 40. See also Barrett, *Reformation as Renewal*.

6. Hooper, *Collected Letters*, 647.

7. Leithart, *End of Protestantism*, 122.

8. Leithart, *End of Protestantism*, 166–67.

be realized, though I share his hope. It is hard indeed to see how Rome could accept the necessary reformation, given how much it has invested in its exclusive dogmatic claims. But then again, it would have been hard to imagine the changes that were made at Vatican II only decades before that momentous council. Perhaps a future Vatican III will hold similar surprises.

In any case, I very much agree with Leithart that going to Rome is not the way forward to promote true catholicism and unity in the body of Christ. Consider his striking observations about the divided Communion table that Roman Catholicism maintains:

> In important respects, Protestants are free to be more catholic than Catholics. Here is the question for Protestants considering a move into Catholicism or Orthodoxy: what are you saying about your past Christian experience by moving to Rome or Constantinople? Are you willing to start eating at a eucharistic table where your Protestant friends are no longer welcome? How is that different from Peter's withdrawal from table fellowship with gentiles? Are you willing to say that every faithful Protestant or Pentecostal saint you have known is living a sub-Christian existence because they are not in churches that claim apostolic succession, no matter that they live lives fruitful in faith, hope, and love? . . . To become Catholic, I would have to begin regarding my Protestant brothers as ambiguously situated "separated" brothers rather than full brothers in the divine Brother, Jesus. Why should I distance myself from other Christians like that? Reformational Catholics are too catholic for that.
> . . . To become Catholic I would have to *contract* my ecclesial world. The communion I acknowledge would become smaller, less universal. I would have to become *less* catholic—*less catholic than Jesus.*[9]

Leithart asks searching questions for prospective converts, questions that demand an honest and forthright answer. And the answers we give will have large implications, both theologically and practically. Another reason I am not a Roman Catholic is that I find incredible, both biblically and from personal experience, that only Roman Catholics can enjoy the fullness of God's saving and sanctifying grace.

William Abraham has recently argued for an account of the church in which "we begin with the proposition that where the Holy Spirit is, there is the church and the fullness of grace."[10] The Holy Spirit is the bond of unity, the ground of the ontological reality that the church, though composed of

---

9. Leithart, *End of Protestantism*, 170–71.
10. Abraham, *Systematic Theology*, 191.

many churches and individual persons, is ultimately one body. "For just as the body is one and has many members, and all the members of the body, though many, are one body, so it is with Christ. For in the one Spirit we were all baptized into one body—Jews or Greeks, slaves or free—and we were all made to drink of one Spirit" (1 Cor 12:12–13).

It is evident to me and many other observers that the Holy Spirit is powerfully present in the lives and ministries of Protestant and Pentecostal Christians, as much so as in the lives of any Roman Catholic Christians. The notion that Protestant and Pentecostal worship, evangelism, and discipleship is defective in comparison to that of Roman Catholicism is as biblically and theologically dubious as it is empirically implausible. Indeed, the reality is that some of the most vibrant expressions of the faith in the contemporary church are among Pentecostals in countries that have been predominantly (and now nominally) Roman Catholic for centuries.

So in short, I am not a Roman Catholic because the exclusive claims of Rome are constructed on a rickety biblical and historical foundation, one that is also rotten in many places because of recurrent corruption; moreover, it maintains a constricted view of catholicity that is not true to the palpable reality of the larger church and the unique work of the Holy Spirit that makes it truly one.

Appendix

Matthew 16 and the Papacy

IN THIS BRIEF APPENDIX I want to take a look at a popular argument for the papacy based on the "intertextuality" between Matthew 16 and Isaiah 22. Collins and I were critiqued by Joseph Blado for ignoring this argument in our earlier book.[1] Blado's case mainly rests on his interpretation of the controversial text in Matthew 16, buttressed by his interpretation of John 21, and his observation that Peter was present when the Holy Spirit was poured out in Acts 2, 8, and 10. There are, however, serious problems that weaken his argument at each of these points.

In the first place, the papal interpretation of Matthew 16 and John 21 are at odds with the classical patristic interpretation of both these texts. In a historical survey of the Matthew text, Ulrich Luz notes that the papal interpretation, which reads this text as supporting the primacy of Peter and his successors in terms of jurisdiction over the whole church, is a later rereading motivated particularly by Roman Catholic concerns. He goes on to cite the thesis of Karlfried Frohlich that the Roman papal interpretation was rare even in the Middle Ages. That interpretation typically appeared in legal texts whose purpose was to legitimize papal power claims against either Eastern patriarchs or secular Emperors. Luz found Frohlich's thesis supported by his own research.

> My examination of numerous medieval commentaries confirms this. Thomas Aquinas is one of the very few who even mention this interpretation, as one possibility among others. In Catholic exegesis it came to the fore in the sixteenth century, when Catholics had to resist Protestants laying claim to the traditional interpretation. Indirectly, the triumph of the hitherto quite

---

1. Blado, "On the Plausibility of the Papacy."

marginal "papal" interpretation of Matthew 16:18 is a product of the Reformation.[2]

Blado's attempt to strengthen his case by appealing to John 21 is undermined by the same sort of considerations. Eastern Orthodox philosopher David Bradshaw has shown that the consensus of early patristic sources interpreted this text not as bestowing upon Peter some sort of authority over the other apostles and the whole church, but rather, as Peter's restoration to his apostleship after his thrice repeated denial of Christ. Bradshaw cites Cyril of Alexander and Theodore of Mopsuestia in the East, and Ambrose and Augustine in the West as key figures representing this consensus.

Bradshaw goes on to argue that the most direct evidence we have of Peter's understanding of his place in the church is to be found in the two epistles that bear his name. Nothing in those epistles suggests he was given any sort of unique authority by Christ's repeated admonition that Peter should "feed my sheep." To the contrary, in the opening verses of both epistles, Peter identifies himself as "an apostle [or in 2 Peter, a servant and an apostle] of Jesus Christ." More tellingly, he addresses the elders simply as a "fellow elder" and admonishes them, in words reminiscent of John 21 (even using the same word for "feed"), that they should "feed the flock of God which is among you" (1 Pet 5:1–2). Bradshaw comments: "There surely could be no clearer indication that we are not to understand *poimaine* [the Greek word for 'feed'] in John 21 as bestowing a unique right of command, for Peter's usage applies it to the ministry shared by all the elders."[3] This point can be reinforced by observing a similar directive from Paul to the Ephesian elders in Acts 20: "Take heed to yourselves and to all the flock [παντὶ τῷ ποιμνίῳ], in which the Holy Spirit has made you overseers/bishops [ἔθετο ἐπισκόπους], to shepherd [ποιμαίνειν] the church of God which he obtained with the blood of his own Son" (v. 28).

Now here we can ask the sort of question that Blado rightly asks: Is this sort of evidence more to be expected on the Roman papal hypothesis or the denial of the hypothesis? I think it is clear this is more to be expected if the papal hypothesis is false.

But Blado thinks he has an ace in the hole for Roman papal doctrine in his appeal to the intertextuality between Matthew 16 and Isaiah 22, and even suggests that Collins's failure to address this intertextuality is "quite devastating to Collins's interpretation."[4] I would argue, however, that he has

2. Luz, *Studies in Matthew*, 168–69.

3. See David Bradshaw, "Giving Honor to Whom Honor Is Due: A Reply to Michael Root," 24, in Raith, *Gospel of John*, 239–50.

4. Blado, "On the Plausibility of the Papacy," 7.

overplayed his hand here. This is not to deny that there is some degree of "intertextuality" between these two passages. It is no doubt the case that in Matthew 16:19 Jesus alludes to Isaiah 22:19-22, but it is a further question and far from obvious what Jesus intended in doing so. We cannot just assume that he intended to apply everything from the original context in Isaiah to the situation in Matthew 16. The observation that there is an allusion here to Isaiah does not even begin to settle the fundamental question of how Jesus is addressing Peter: as an individual disciple, or as representative of the apostolic circle (and perhaps by extension of the church-as-a-whole), or as the first of a succession of bishops of Rome?

Now if we knew from Jesus' words that he intended us to apply the whole scenario in Isaiah to Peter that would perhaps be more likely on the papal hypothesis than on its denial. But again, that is far from clear. Jesus's words that allude to Isaiah are only these: "I will give you the keys of the kingdom of heaven, and whatever you bind on earth will be bound in heaven, and whatever you loose on earth will be loosed in heaven" (Matt 16:19). Given the Isaiah background, we expect language of opening and closing, as in Isaiah 22:22, but instead we get language about binding and loosing. These lines are metaphorical and the same images are used elsewhere in the New Testament (Matt 18:18; Rev 3:7), as Blado notes. Moreover, this is common rabbinic language, and indeed, "the entire saying is rooted in Jewish thought."[5] In view of all this, it is far from clear from what Jesus says here that he intends to apply to Peter all the things that apply to Eliakim in Isaiah 22. Indeed, if we examine the larger passage in Isaiah 22, it poses problems for the papal interpretation. Consider these further verses from Isaiah.

> I will fasten him like a peg in a secure place and he will become a throne of honor to his ancestral house. And they will hang on him the whole weight of his ancestral house, the offspring and issue, every small vessel, from the cups to all the flagons. On that day says the LORD of hosts, the peg that was fastened in a secure place will give way; it will be cut down and fall, and the load that was on it will perish, for the LORD has spoken. (Isa 22:23-25)

Like the preceding verses, this passage too is rich in imagery and word pictures. But the message it conveys is that Eliakim too will finally fail, like a peg that cannot bear the weight that is placed upon it. So, does this apply to Peter since it is part of the immediately preceding narrative? Does it foreshadow that Peter would ultimately fail in his office as pope? If one wants

---

5. Luz, *Matthew 8-20*, 365.

to rest so much on the intertextuality of these passages as Blado does, that seems like a defensible interpretation of the text.

Here is the important point to keep in mind from this discussion: intertextuality often entails nothing more than borrowing words and phrases, even idioms, without necessarily importing the context from which the material is borrowed. Blado's argument hinges largely on the assumption that Matthew 16 imports the larger context and details of Isaiah 22.

But leaving this problem aside, even if we grant a strong element of intertextuality here, it does not show that Matthew 16 supports Roman Catholic papal theology. It is telling that Blado cites Protestant W. F. Albright as an example of a New Testament scholar who sees significant elements of Isaiah 22 implied in Matthew 16. And yet, Albright was a Protestant who did not see this as a convincing reason to embrace papal theology. Protestants readily agree that Peter was the acknowledged leader of the twelve apostles and had an important leadership role in the early church and can even see this foreshadowed in Isaiah 22. Indeed, Peter was privileged to preach on Pentecost, standing up with the other disciples (Acts 2:14); to be sent (along with John) to the Samaritans, where he lay hands on them and prayed for them to receive the Holy Spirit (Acts 8:14–17); and to be sent to Cornelius to preach the gospel to the gentiles, who also received the Holy Spirit (Acts 10).

But none of this establishes the Roman Catholic claim that Peter was the first bishop of Rome, that he had jurisdiction over the whole church, or that the same authority would accrue to successors. This has been emphasized by Protestant commentators who hold the view that the Greek word *petra* in Matthew 16:18 refers to Petros, Peter. R. T. France, for instance, points out that "there is nothing in this passage about successors to Peter. It is Simon Peter himself, in his historical role, who is the foundation rock. Any link between the personal role of Peter and the subsequent papacy is a matter of later ecclesiology, not of exegesis of this passage."[6]

It is remarkable that Peter drops out of the narrative of Acts after chapter 15, that Paul is the main figure after that, and indeed, that significantly more space is devoted to Paul in Acts overall than to Peter. It is also worth noting in this connection that Paul lays his hands on the Ephesians and prays for the Holy Spirit to come on them, and the Spirit falls on them in the same way described in Acts 2, 8, and 10 (Acts 19:1–7). This at least qualifies the uniqueness of Peter's role in praying for the Holy Spirit to fall onto various groups.

---

6. France, *Gospel of Matthew*, 622.

When all this evidence is taken into account, I think Blado's argument for the papacy is undermined. Indeed, I think the overall evidence actually supports a good inductive argument *against Roman papal theology.*[7]

---

7. More recently, a rather elaborate argument for the papacy based on the intertextuality of Matthew 16 and Isaiah 22 has been developed by Suan Sonna. For critique of Sonna's argument, see various YouTube videos by John Cranman. See Rucker, *Temple Keys*. See too the interview of Rucker by Paul Facey on YouTube.

Bibliography

Abraham, William J. *Canon and Criterion: From the Fathers to Feminism.* Oxford: Clarendon, 1998.
———. *The Divine Inspiration of Holy Scripture.* Oxford: Oxford University Press, 1981.
———. *Divine Revelation and the Limits of Historical Criticism.* Oxford: Oxford University Press, 1982.
———. *Soundings in the Christian Tradition.* Vol. 2 of *Divine Agency and Divine Action.* Oxford: Oxford University Press, 2017.
———. *Systematic Theology.* Vol. 3 of *Divine Agency and Divine Action.* Oxford: Oxford University Press, 2018.
Addison, Brandon. "The Quest for the Historical Church: A Protestant Assessment." *Called to Communion* (blog), March 24, 2014. https://www.calledtocommunion.com/2014/03/the-quest-for-the-historical-church-a-protestant-assessment.
Akin, Jimmy. "Mary and Genesis 3:15." https://jimmyakin.com/mary-and-genesis-315.
Allen, Michael, and Scott R. Swain. *Reformed Catholicity: The Promise of Retrieval for Theology and Biblical Interpretation.* Grand Rapids: Baker Academic, 2015.
Allison, Gregg R. *Roman Catholic Theology and Practice: An Evangelical Assessment.* Wheaton, IL: Crossway, 2014.
Alt, Scott Eric. "We Need to Stop Saying That There Are 33,000 Protestant Denominations." *National Catholic Register* (blog), February 9, 2016. https://www.ncregister.com/blog/we-need-to-stop-saying-that-there-are-33-000-protestant-denominations.
Arbour, Benjamin H. "An Evangelical Protestant's Reflections on Roman Catholic Mariology." *Perichoresis* 18 (2020) 21–38. https://sciendo.com/article/10.2478/perc-2020-0026.
Barrett, Matthew. *The Reformation as Renewal: Retrieving the One, Holy, Catholic and Apostolic Church.* Grand Rapids: Zondervan Academic, 2023.
Behr, John. *Irenaeus of Lyons: Identifying Christianity.* Oxford: Oxford University Press, 2013.
Blado, Joseph E. "On the Plausibility of the Papacy: Scaling the Walls of Contemporary Criticism." *Heythrop Journal* 63 (2022) 531–46. https://onlinelibrary.wiley.com/doi/10.1111/heyj.13326.
Boniface VIII. "*Unam Sanctam*: One God, One Faith, One Spiritual Authority." Promulgated November 18, 1302. https://www.papalencyclicals.net/bono8/b8unam.htm.

Boorstein, Michelle, and Peyton M. Craighill. "Pope Francis Faces Church Divided over Doctrine, Global Poll of Catholics Finds." *Washington Post*, February 9, 2014. https://www.washingtonpost.com/national/pope-francis-faces-church-divided-over-doctrine-global-poll-of-catholics-finds/2014/02/08/e90ecef4-8f89-11e3-b227-12a45d109e03_story.html.

Bray, Gerald. *The Church: A Theological and Historical Account*. Grand Rapids: Baker Academic, 2016.

Brent, Allen. "How Irenaeus Has Misled the Archaeologists." In *Irenaeus: Life, Scripture, Legacy*, edited by Sara Parvis and Paul Foster, 35–52. Minneapolis: Fortress, 2012.

Brown, Raymond E. *Priest and Bishop: Biblical Reflections*. New York: Missionary Society of St. Paul, 1970. Reprint, Eugene, OR: Wipf and Stock, 1999.

Burson, Scott R., and Jerry L. Walls. *C. S. Lewis and Francis Schaeffer: Lessons for a New Century from the Most Influential Apologists of Our Time*. Downers Grove, IL: InterVarsity, 1998.

Carlton, Clark. *The Truth: What Every Roman Catholic Should Know About the Orthodox Church*. Salisbury, MA: Regina, 1999.

Catechism of the Catholic Church. 2nd ed. New York: Doubleday, 1995.

Chirico, Leonardo De. "'Confusion' and 'Failure': Other Roman Catholic Blows Against Pope Francis." *Vatican Files* (blog), March 1, 2019. https://vaticanfiles.org/en/2019/03/vf159.

Collins, Kenneth J., and Jerry L. Walls. *Roman but Not Catholic: What Remains at Stake 500 Years After the Reformation*. Grand Rapids: Baker Academic, 2017.

Cross, Bryan. "The Tu Quoque." *Called to Communion* (blog), May 24, 2010. https://www.calledtocommunion.com/2010/05/the-tu-quoque.

The Documents of Vatican II: Vatican Translation. New York: St Paul's, 2009.

Douthat, Ross. "The New Catholic Truce." *New York Times*, April 10, 2016. http://www.nytimes.com/2016/04/10/opinion/sunday/the-new-catholic-truce.html?mwrsm=Facebook&_r=1.

Duffy, Eamon. *Saints and Sinners: A History of the Popes*. 4th ed. New Haven, CT: Yale University Press, 2014.

———. "Was There a Bishop of Rome in the First Century?" *New Blackfriars* 80 (1999) 301–8. https://onlinelibrary.wiley.com/doi/abs/10.1111/j.1741-2005.1999.tb01680.x.

Eno, Robert B. *The Rise of the Papacy*. Eugene, OR: Wipf and Stock, 2008.

"First Vatican Council." https://www.ewtn.com/catholicism/library/first-vatican-council-1505.

Flint, Thomas. *Divine Providence: The Molinist Account*. Ithaca, NY: Cornell University Press, 1998.

Ford, Paul, ed. *Yours, Jack: Spiritual Direction from C. S. Lewis*. New York: Harper One, 2008.

France, R. T. *The Gospel of Matthew*. New International Commentary on the New Testament. Grand Rapids: Eerdmans, 2007.

Francis. "*Fiducia Supplicans*." December 18, 2023. https://www.vatican.va/roman_curia/congregations/cfaith/documents/rc_ddf_doc_20231218_fiducia-supplicans_en.html.

George, Robert P., and John Keown, eds. *Reason, Morality and Law: The Philosophy of John Finnis*. Oxford: Oxford University Press, 2013.

Goetz, Stewart. *A Philosophical Walking Tour with C. S. Lewis: Why It Did Not Include Rome*. London: Bloomsbury, 2015.
"Grand Jury Report Identifies over 1,000 Victims of Priest Abuse." *CBS News*, August 15, 2018. https://www.cbsnews.com/news/predator-priests-identified-grand-jury-report-pennsylvania-priest-abuse.
Harlan, Chico, and Stefano Pitrelli. "Ex-Pope Benedict Contradicts Pope Francis in Unusual Intervention on Sexual Abuse." *Washington Post*, April 11, 2019. https://www.washingtonpost.com/world/speaking-out-at-this-difficult-hour-a-once-quiet-ex-pope-pens-a-lengthy-letter-on-sexual-abuse/2019/04/11/0ffa162e-5c1a-11e9-a00e-050dc7b82693_story.html.
———. "He Called on the Pope to Resign. Now This Archbishop Is in an Undisclosed Location." *Washington Post*, June 10, 2019. https://www.washingtonpost.com/world/europe/this-archbishop-called-on-the-pope-to-resign-now-hes-in-an-undisclosed-location/2019/06/09/bb69c346-71b5-11e9-9331-30bc5836f48e_story.html.
Hendershott, Anne. "A New Front in the Catholic Campus Culture Wars." *First Things*, August 2012. https://www.firstthings.com/web-exclusives/2012/08/a-new-front-in-the-catholic-campus-culture-wars.
Holmes, Michael W., ed. *The Apostolic Fathers: Greek Texts and English Translations*. 3rd ed. Grand Rapids: Baker Academic, 2007.
Hooper, Walter, ed. *The Collected Letters of C. S. Lewis*. Vol. 2. San Francisco: HarperSanFrancisco, 2004.
"How the Faithful Voted." *Pew Research Center*, November 5, 2008. https://www.pewresearch.org/religion/2008/11/05/how-the-faithful-voted.
Irenaeus. *Against Heresies*. Translated by John Keble. Oxford: James Parker, 1872.
John Paul II. "On Catholic 'Universities.'" Apostolic Constitution given at Saint Peter's, Rome, August 15, 1990. https://www.vatican.va/content/john-paul-ii/en/apost_constitutions/documents/hf_jp-ii_apc_15081990_ex-corde-ecclesiae.html.
Jones, David Albert. "Was There a Bishop of Rome in the First Century?" *New Blackfriars* 80 (1999) 128–43. https://onlinelibrary.wiley.com/doi/abs/10.1111/j.1741-2005.1999.tb01652.x.
Kandra, Greg. "New Gallup Poll Shows More US Catholics Thinking of Leaving the Church." *Deacon's Bench* (blog), March 13, 2019. https://www.patheos.com/blogs/deaconsbench/2019/03/new-gallup-poll-shows-more-u-s-catholics-thinking-of-leaving-the-church.
Kelly, J. N. D., and M. J. Walsh. *A Dictionary of Popes*. 2nd ed. Oxford: Oxford University Press, 2009.
Kreeft, Peter. *Catholics and Protestants: What Can We Learn from Each Other?* San Francisco, Ignatius, 2017.
Kruger, Michael J. *Canon Revisited: Establishing the Origins and Authority of the New Testament Books*. Wheaton, IL: Crossway, 2012.
Küng, Hans. *Truthfulness: The Future of the Church*. New York: Sheed and Ward, 1968.
Lampe, Peter. *From Paul to Valentinus: Christians at Rome in the First Two Centuries*. Minneapolis: Fortress, 2003.
Last, Jonathan V. "The Catholic Church Is Breaking Apart. Here's Why." *Weekly Standard*, September 14, 2018. https://www.bishop-accountability.org/news2018/09_10/2018_09_14_Jonathan_Standard_The_Why.htm.

Leithart, Peter J. *The End of Protestantism: Pursuing Unity in a Fragmented Church*. Grand Rapids: Brazos, 2016.

Levering, Matthew. *Engaging the Doctrine of Revelation: The Mediation of the Gospel through Church and Scripture*. Grand Rapids: Baker Academic, 2014.

Lewis, W. H., ed. *Letters of C. S. Lewis*. New York: Harcourt Brace Jovanovich, 1975.

Licona, Michael R. *The Resurrection of Jesus: A New Historiographical Approach*. Downers Grove, IL: InterVarsity, 2010.

———. *Why Are There Differences in the Gospels? What We Can Learn from Ancient Biography*. New York: Oxford University Press, 2017.

Lightfoot, J. B., and J. R. Harmer. *The Apostolic Fathers*. London: Macmillan, 1981.

Long, D. Stephen. "My Church Loyalties: Why I Am Not Yet a Catholic." *Christian Century*, August 6, 2014. https://www.christiancentury.org/article/2014-07/my-church-loyalties.

Luz, Ulrich. *Matthew 8–20: A Commentary*. Minneapolis: Fortress, 1989.

———. *Studies in Matthew*. Translated by Rosemary Celle. Grand Rapids: Eerdmans, 2005.

Macy, Gary. *The Banquet's Wisdom: A Short History of the Theologies of the Lord's Supper*. Maryville, TN: OSL, 2005.

Madrid, Patrick, ed. *Surprised by Truth: Eleven Converts Give the Biblical and Historical Reasons for Becoming Catholic*. San Diego: Basilica, 1994.

Martel, Frederic. *In the Closet of the Vatican: Power, Homosexuality, Hypocrisy*. London: Bloomsbury Continuum, 2019.

Martin, James. "Does the Holy Spirit Choose the Pope?" *Time*, March 11, 2013. https://ideas.time.com/2013/03/11/does-the-holy-spirit-choose-the-pope.

———. "Pope Francis' Same-Sex Blessings Declaration Is a Major Step Forward for LGBTQ Catholics." *America Magazine*, December 18, 2023. https://www.americamagazine.org/faith/2023/12/18/pope-francis-same-sex-blessings-lgbt-catholic-246755.

McBrien, Richard P. *Catholicism*. New York: HarperOne, 1994.

———. "Why I Shall Not Seek a Mandate." *America Magazine*, February 12, 2000. https://www.americamagazine.org/issue/275/article/why-i-shall-not-seek-mandate.

McInerny, Ralph. "The Liberal Consensus." *Crisis Magazine*, July 1, 1984. https://crisismagazine.com/vault/the-liberal-consensus.

———. "'Quodlibets' on Protesting Too Much." *Crisis Magazine*, May 1, 1987. https://crisismagazine.com/vault/quodlibets-on-protesting-too-much.

McNabb, Tyler Dalton. "Pestilent Popes or a Pestilent Church? Judaism, Catholicism and Skeptical Theism." *Heythrop Journal* 61 (2020) 671–76. https://onlinelibrary.wiley.com/doi/10.1111/heyj.13571.

Metaxas, Eric. *Martin Luther: The Man Who Rediscovered God and Changed the World*. New York: Viking, 2017.

Miller, Nicholas P. *The Religious Roots of the First Amendment: Dissenting Protestants and the Separation of Church and State*. New York: Oxford University Press, 2012.

Mirus, Jeff. "*Ex Corde Ecclesiae* in America." *Catholic Culture*, January 21, 2011. https://www.catholicculture.org/commentary/ex-corde-ecclesiae-in-america.

———. "On the Role of the Holy Spirit in Papal Elections." *Catholic Culture*, March 3, 2017. https://www.catholicculture.org/commentary/on-role-holy-spirit-in-papal-elections.

Molina, Luis De. *On Divine Foreknowledge, Part IV of the Concordia*. Translated by Alfred J. Freddoso. Ithaca, NY: Cornell University Press, 1988.

Murray, Gerald E., and Diane Montagna. "*Fiducia Supplicans* Should Be Revoked: An Interview with Fr. Gerald E. Murray." *First Things*, March 2024. https://www.firstthings.com/web-exclusives/2024/03/fiducia-supplicans-should-be-revoked.

National Council of Catholic Bishops (NCCB). Review of *Catholicism*, by Fr. Richard McBrien. *Catholic Culture*, April 9, 1996. https://www.catholicculture.org/culture/library/view.cfm?recnum=541.

Newman, John Henry. *An Essay on the Development of Christian Doctrine*. South Bend, IN: University of Notre Dame Press, 1989.

Nichols, Aidan. *The Shape of Catholic Theology*. Collegeville, MN: Liturgical, 1991.

Oddie, William. "The German Bishops Have Declared Independence from Rome on Same-Sex Marriage: How Far Will the Rot Spread Now." *Catholic Herald*, August 6, 2015. https://thecatholicherald.com/the-german-bishops-have-declared-independence-from-rome-on-same-sex-marriage-how-far-will-the-rot-spread-now.

O'Loughlin, Michael. "Pew Survey: Percentage of US Catholics Drops and Catholicism Is Losing Members Faster Than Any Denomination." *Crux*, May 12, 2015. https://cruxnow.com/church/2015/05/pew-survey-percentage-of-us-catholics-drops-and-catholicism-is-losing-members-faster-than-any-denomination.

O'Malley, John W. *Vatican I: The Council and the Making of the Ultramontane Church*. Cambridge: Belknap Press of Harvard University Press, 2018.

Ortlund, Gavin. "Why Mary's Assumption Is Indefensible." *Truth Unites*, August 17, 2023. https://www.youtube.com/watch?v=skuBFLns8WA.

"Padre Pio Tops Saints Poll." *Italy Magazine*, November 1, 2006. http://www.italymagazine.com/featured-story/padre-pio-tops-saints-poll.

Pascal, Blaise. *Pensees*. Translated by A. J. Krailsheimer. London: Penguin, 1966.

Paul VI. "*Dei Verbum*." Dogmatic Constitution promulgated November 18, 1965. https://www.vatican.va/archive/hist_councils/ii_vatican_council/documents/vat-ii_const_19651118_dei-verbum_en.html.

Payne, Margaret E. "Letter to the Editor." *Observer*, April 28, 1987, 5.

Peckham, John C. "Sola Scriptura: Reduction Ad Absurdum?" *Trinity Journal* 35 NS (2014) 195–223.

Pelikan, Jeroslav. *Mary Through the Centuries*. New Haven, CT: Yale University Press, 1996.

Peoples, Glenn. "The Protestant Bogeyman of Thousands of Churches." *Right Reason* (blog), September 10, 2007. https://www.rightreason.org/2007/the-protestant-bogeyman-of-thousands-of-churches.

Pink, Thomas. "John Finnis's Alternative History of Trent." Unpublished paper. https://www.academia.edu/37861294/John_Finniss_Alternative_History_of_Trent,%202.

Pius IX. "*Ineffabilis Deus*: The Immaculate Conception." Given at St. Peter's, Rome, December 8, 1854. https://www.papalencyclicals.net/pius09/p9ineff.htm.

———. "The Syllabus of Errors." Given at St. Peter's, Rome, December 8, 1854. https://www.papalencyclicals.net/pius09/p9syll.htm.

Pius XII. "*Munificentissimus Deus*: Defining the Dogma of the Assumption." Apostolic Constitution given at St. Peter's, Rome, November 1, 1950. https://www.vatican.

va/content/pius-xii/en/apost_constitutions/documents/hf_p-xii_apc_19501101_munificentissimus-deus.html.

Plantinga, Alvin. *Knowledge and Christian Belief*. Grand Rapids: Eerdmans, 2015.

———. *Warranted Christian Belief*. New York: Oxford University Press, 2000.

Raith, Charles, ed. *The Gospel of John: Theological-Ecumenical Readings*. Eugene, OR: Wipf and Stock, 2017.

"Religious Landscape Study." *Pew Research Center*, 2014. https://www.pewresearch.org/religious-landscape-study/database.

Reno, R. R. "A Failing Papacy." *First Things*, February 2019. https://www.firstthings.com/article/2019/02/a-failing-papacy.

———. "While We're at It: Bad Bishops, Simon Leys, Etc." *First Things*, August 2014. https://www.firstthings.com/article/2014/08/while-were-at-it.

Rosa, Peter De. *Vicars of Christ: The Dark Side of the Papacy*. Dublin: Poolberg, 2000.

Rose, Devin. *The Protestant's Dilemma: How the Reformation's Shocking Consequences Point to the Truth of Catholicism*. San Diego: Catholic Answers, 2014.

Rucker, Timothy. *The Temple Keys of Isaiah 22:22, Revelation 3:7, and Matthew 16:19*. Tübingen: Mohr Siebeck, 2021.

Ryrie, Alex. *Protestants: The Faith That Made the Modern World*. New York: Viking, 2017.

Sanders, Fred. *The Deep Things of God: How the Trinity Changes Everything*. 2nd ed. Wheaton, IL: Crossway, 2017.

———. "Why the Reformation Should Make You More Catholic." *Gospel Coalition*, October 30, 2017. https://www.thegospelcoalition.org/article/why-the-reformation-should-make-you-more-catholic.

Saward, John. *Sweet & Blessed Country: The Christian Hope for Heaven*. Oxford: Oxford University Press, 2005.

Schillebeeckx, Edward. *Jesus: An Experiment in Christology*. Translated by Hubert Hoskins. New York: Vintage, 1981.

Shatz, Klaus. *Papal Primacy: From Its Origins to the Present*. Translated by John A. Otto and Linda M. Maloney. Collegeville, MN: Liturgical, 1997.

Sonna, Suan. "Roman *and* Catholic: Biblical and Historical Defense of Vatican I Papal Theology in Response to Jerry Walls." *Heythrop Journal* 64 (2023) 120–34. https://onlinelibrary.wiley.com/doi/10.1111/heyj.13979.

Stewart, Kenneth J. *In Search of Ancient Roots: The Christian Past and the Evangelical Identity Crisis*. Downers Grove, IL: InterVarsity, 2017.

Sullivan, Andrew. "The Corruption of the Vatican's Gay Elite Has Been Exposed." *New York Magazine*, February 22, 2019. http://nymag.com/intelligencer/2019/02/andrew-sullivan-the-vaticans-corruption-has-been-exposed.html.

Swinburne, Richard. *The Resurrection of God Incarnate*. Oxford: Clarendon, 2003.

Thompson, James Shotwell, and Louise Ropes Loomis. *The See of Peter*. New York: Columbia University Press, 1991.

Tilley, Terrence W. *Inventing Catholic Tradition*. Maryknoll, NY: Orbis, 2000.

Trueman, Carl. "Pay No Attention to That Man Behind the Curtain! Roman Catholic History and the Emerald City Protocol." *reformation21*, April 2, 2012. https://www.reformation21.org/articles/pay-no-attention-to-that-man-behind-the-curtain-roman-catholic-history-and-the-e.php.

Vallier, Kevin. "The Best Argument Against Catholicism I Know." Unpublished Manuscript.

Vanhoozer, Kevin J. *Biblical Authority After Babel: Retrieving the Solas in the Spirit of Mere Protestant Christianity*. Grand Rapids: Brazos, 2016.
Walls, Jerry L. "Christmas Eve." *Christian Century*, December 12, 2012. https://www.christiancentury.org/artsculture/poems/christmas-eve.
———. *Heaven, Hell and Purgatory: Rethinking the Things that Matter Most*. Grand Rapids: Brazos, 2015.
———. *Heaven: The Logic of Eternal Joy*. New York: Oxford University Press, 2002.
———. *The Problem of Pluralism: Recovering United Methodist Identity*. Wilmore, KY: Good News, 1986.
———. *The Problem of Pluralism: Recovering United Methodist Identity*. Rev. ed. Wilmore, KY: Good News, 1988.
———. *Purgatory: The Logic of Eternal Joy*. New York: Oxford University Press, 2012.
———. "Reformational Theology Found in Catholicism." *Observer*, April 23, 1987, 8.
———. Review of *The Devil All the Time*, by Donald Ray Pollock. *Christianity Today*, July 2011. https://www.booksandculture.com/articles/webexclusives/2011/july/devilalltime.html.
Weinandy, Thomas. "Is Pope Francis a Heretic?" *First Things*, May 2019. https://www.firstthings.com/web-exclusives/2019/05/is-pope-francis-a-heretic.
Wells, David F. *Revolution in Rome*. Downers Grove, IL: InterVarsity, 1973.
Westminster Divines. "The Westminster Confession of Faith." *Ligonier Ministries*, May 12, 2021. https://www.ligonier.org/learn/articles/westminster-confession-faith.
Wilken, Robert Louis. *The First Thousand Years: A Global History of Christianity*. New Haven, CT: Yale University Press, 2012.

GENERAL INDEX

Abraham, William, 28n20, 33n2, 70, 79n23, 178
Accretions, 63, 64, 84
Acts
  Acts 2, 181, 184
  Acts 2:14, 184
  Acts 5:32, 132
  Acts 8, 181, 184
  Acts 8:14–17, 184
  Acts 9:15, 21
  Acts 10, 181, 184
  Acts 15, 21n7, 184
  Acts 17:11, 119
  Acts 19:1–7, 184
  Acts 20:28, 182
  Acts 20:29–30, 41
Agapitus, 33
Agapitus II, 35
Alberic II, 35
Albright, W.F., 184
Alexander V, 37
Alexander VI, 31, 32, 33, 38, 51, 54
Allen, Michael, xviin9, 77, 82, 142n17, 150n34
Ambrose, 182
Amoris Laetitia, 44, 169, 170
Anacletus, 16, 142
Anathema, 6, 9, 19, 20, 24, 105
Anderson, Gary, xii
Anglican, xiii, xvii, 116, 144n20, 147, 151
Anthony of Padua, 149
Anti-Semitism, 41–42
Apocrypha, 75
Apologetics
  Christian, 135, 148
  Protestant, xvi, 97, 136, 148,
  Roman Catholic, xv, xvi, xvii, 12, 16, 17, 55, 59, 87n1, 97, 98, 111, 118, 119, 134, 135, 136, 140, 141, 142, 145, 147, 148, 151, 153, 154, 172, 177
Aquinas, 92, 132n27, 151, 152, 181
Arius, 23, 78, 79
Arminian, xvii, 122, 129
Athanasius, 75n12, 151
Augustine, 75n12, 151, 182
Authority
  Authority, Nature of, 111, 112, 114, 120, 121, 140
  Canonical Authority, 70, 71, 72
  Christological & Divine Authority, 2, 23, 25, 57, 70, 72, 74, 76, 91, 113, 114, 115, 120, 121, 127, 128, 130, 131
  Conciliar Authority, 65, 107
  Confessional Authority, 77, 111, 112, 113, 114, 119, 120, 124, 129
  Creedal Authority, 57, 59, 68, 69, 76, 77, 95, 96, 99, 111, 112, 123, 147
  Ecclesial Authority, 56, 57, 73, 74, 76, 92, 115, 129, 137, 139, 167
  Ecumenical Authority, 77, 123
  Episcopal Authority, 4, 12, 14, 15, 22, 39, 49, 55, 57, 58, 162, 163
  Magisterial Authority, 28n20, 57, 58, 59, 68, 69, 72, 76, 94, 95, 96, 97, 99, 109, 110, 112, 114, 124, 144, 163

Moral Authority, 136, 175
Papal Authority, 1, 4,5, 7, 9, 14, 21, 22, 23, 24, 26, 29, 33, 37, 30, 46, 49, 55, 57, 58, 59, 162, 163, 164, 168, 174, 176
Pastoral Authority, 77
Petrine Authority, 4, 21, 22, 23, 24, 39, 49, 55, 57, 147, 174, 182, 184
Protestant Authority
Problematic Authority, 56, 112, 113, 114, 115, 116, 118, 119, 120, 121,129, 130, 133
Tu Quo-Que & Authority, 111, 112, 128, 130, 132, 133
Roman Authority, 1, 4, 5, 12, 14, 15, 17, 21, 22, 24, 25, 26,29, 39, 46, 49, 55, 57, 58, 59, 60, 68, 69, 72, 76, 83, 93, 94, 95, 96, 97, 99, 106, 107, 108, 110, 113, 114, 116, 124, 129, 130, 139, 144, 147, 155, 164, 168, 173, 176, 184
Scriptural Authority, xviii, 4, 56, 57, 59, 68, 69, 71, 72, 73, 74, 76, 77, 79, 80, 82, 92, 94, 95, 99, 113, 115, 118, 121, 132, 137, 139, 141, 147

Backus, Irena, 143
Bad Popes, 31–38, 43–50, 53–55
Bainton, Roland, 143
Baptism, xi, 22, 65, 81, 102, 103, 104, 105, 106, 110, 127, 179
Baptist, xvii, 118
Benedict XVI, 44, 47, 49
Bergoglio, Jorge, 46
Bernard of Clairvaux, 42
Birth Control, 155, 162, 163, 164
Blado, Joseph, ix, 181, 182, 183, 184, 185
Boniface VIII, 36, 176, 177n4
Borgia, Cesare, 38
Borgia, Roderigo, 31, 38, 48, 54
Botterill, Steven, 91
Bottum, Jody, xii
Bradshaw, David, 23, 182
Bray, Gerald, 143, 171
Brown, Raymond, 26, 27, 116

Calvinism, 67, 122, 129, 146, 151
Calvin, John, 132n27, 136, 137, 138, 146
Canon: 20n4, 56, 69, 71, 72, 73, 74, 75, 76, 85, 136, 137, 138, 139, 140, 145, 147
Carmichael, Amy, 152
Carmy, Shalom, xii
Catechism of the Catholic Church, 4n3, 4n4, 49n40, 57, 58n4, 58n5, 59n6, 77, 85, 94, 102n3, 103, 104n5, 113n5, 115n13, 169n29, 169n31
Catherine of Genoa, 152
Chadwick, Henry, 143
Chadwick, Owen, 143
Chalcedon, 22, 24, 25, 33
Chambers, Oswald, 152
Christology, 22, 23, 33, 123
Clarity of Scripture, 79, 80, 84, 85, 118, 121, 126, 130, 132
Clement, 13, 15, 16, 18, 19, 142
Clement VII, 37
Coercion, 101, 104, 105, 106, 107, 108, 109, 110, 129, 130, 176
College
  Cardinals, 35, 38
  Bishops, 50, 162
Collins, Kenneth, ix, xvii, 15n30, 17n35, 22n7, 26n12, 38n17, 40n19, 76n15, 92n12, 100n25, 104n7, 173n1, 178n4, 181, 182
Colson, Chuck, xii
Communion
  Holy, xiv, 153, 154, 161, 169, 170, 171, 178
  In Protestantism, 103–4, 171
  With Rome, xiv, xviiin11, 4, 7, 57, 58, 113, 178
  Reunited, 177
Compatibilist Freedom, 51
Conclave, 43
Conspicuous Corruption, 31, 32, 54, 55, 174
Conspicuous Sanctity, 32
Constance, Council of, 37
Constantinople, 24, 33, 178
Contraception, 161, 163, 164

Conversion
    Experience, xi, 25, 26
    To Protestantism, 110, 128, 129, 130, 150
    To Roman Catholicism, xiii, xiv, xv, xvi, 1, 46, 57, 80, 98, 100, 101, 113, 114, 117, 119, 124, 127, 128, 129, 134, 143, 146, 147, 148, 150, 153, 154, 171, 172, 178
Corinthians, Epistles
    1 Corinthians 12:12-13 127, 179
    1 Corinthians 15, 3
    1 Corinthians 15:1-7, 120
    1 Corinthians 15:3, 8
    1 Corinthians 15:3-8, 8
    1 Corinthians 15:14, 3
    1 Corinthians 15:15, 3
    1 Corinthians 15:17, 3, 29, 99
    1 Corinthians 15:19, 3
    2 Corinthians 4:6, 131
Council of Trent, 75, 76, 91, 105, 107, 108, 109
Craig, William Lane, 136
Creeds, 2, 8, 22, 23, 28, 57, 59, 60, 66, 69, 76, 77, 78, 79, 80, 85, 95, 96, 97, 98, 99, 112, 120, 122, 123, 127, 131, 150, 155, 158, 176
Cross, Bryan, 111-13, 114, 115, 116, 117-18, 119, 120, 121, 124, 125, 126, 127, 128, 129, 130, 131, 132, 133
Cyprian, 22, 151
Cyril of Alexander, 182

Dante, 36, 148, 152, 176
Day, Dorothy, 152
De Chirico, Leonardo, 46
Denys the Carthusian, 92
De Sales, Francis, 151
Descartes, 145, 146
Dignitatis Humanae, 107, 108
Divorce, 44, 45, 153, 161, 169, 170, 171
Doctrinal Development, xv, 20, 22, 23, 59-65, 67, 78, 80, 81, 82, 83, 84, 85, 87, 92, 108, 143, 154
Dominicans, 122, 123
Douthat, Ross, 169, 170, 171

Duffy, Eamon, 11, 13, 14n27, 15, 16, 19, 33, 34, 35, 36, 37n13, 37n14, 38n15, 38n16, 43
Dulles, Avery, xii
Dulles Colloquium, xii, xiii, xiv
Duns Scotus, 92

Eastern Orthodox, xiii, 4, 5, 11, 13n25, 23, 24, 25, 29, 52, 68, 77, 116, 117, 122, 142, 143, 145n25, 147, 150, 161, 176, 178, 181, 182
Ecumenical, xii, xiii, xiv, xv, xvi, xviii, 23, 68, 76, 77, 80, 85, 93, 122, 127, 139, 150, 176
Edwards, Jonathan, 136
Eleutherius, 12
Eliakim, 183
Eno, Robert, 13, 14, 15n29, 18, 22, 23, 24
Ephesians, Epistle of
    Ephesians 3:7-9, 21
Epiphanius, 92
Episcopacy
    Monarchical Episcopacy, 12, 13n23, 20, 142, 174
    Monoepiscopacy, 19
Epistemology
    Certainty
    Cartesian Certainty, 75, 145-146
    Infallible Certainty, 61, 147
    Rational Certainty, 96-97
    Justified, 23, 24, 58, 71, 72, 75, 124
    Rational, xiv, 4, 10, 26, 27, 28n20, 56, 57, 59, 60, 64, 66, 71, 74, 97, 98, 136, 137, 144, 147, 175
    Rationalism, 82
    Warrant, 23, 24, 26, 27-29, 70, 71, 72, 73, 74, 80, 81, 84, 88, 116, 123, 125, 132, 147, 176
Erasmus, 105, 108
Eucharist, 65, 105, 150, 178
Ex Cathedra, 5, 50, 51, 52, 95, 96, 123
Excommunication, 37, 161n18, 169
Ex Corde Ecclesiae, 166, 167

Farnese, Giulia, 31
Fiducia Supplicans, 45, 46, 170

Finnis, John, 105n8, 105n9, 105n10, 108, 109, 110
Firmilian, 22
First Things, xiii, 44, 46, 49
Fitzmyer, Joseph, 152
Flanagan, Bryan, 49
Flint, Thomas, 50–53
France, R.T., 184
Francis, 43, 44, 45, 46, 49, 170, 171, 176
Franciscan, 28n20
Frazier, T.L., 141, 144
Freddoso, Alfred, 122
Freddoso, Fred, xii
Frederick, 36
Frohlich, Karlfried, 181

Galatians, Epistle of
   Galatians 1:11–12, 70
   Galatians 1:15–17, 21
   Galatians 2:6–10, 21
   Galatians 2:8, 21
   Galatians 2:9, 21
   Galatians 2:11–14, 21
   Galatians 4:4, 89n5
Genesis
   Genesis 3:15, 86, 87n2
   George, Robert, xii
Gonzalez, Justo L., 143
Gregory VII, 36
Gregory XI, 37
Gregory the Great, 32
Griffiths, Paul, xii
Grodi, Marcus, 144, 146, 147

Hahn, Scott, 134
Hart, David, xiii
Hauerwas, Stanley, xiii
Hebrews, Epistle of
   Hebrews 1:3, 131
   Hebrews 2:11, 90
   Hebrews 2:17, 90
   Hebrews 4:16, 90
Hendershott, Anne, 167
Hermas, 13, 15, 18
Hill, Charles, 143
Holmes, Michael W., 143

Homosexuality, 44, 45, 159, 160, 167, 175
Honorius IV, 36
Hormisdas, 34
Humanae Vitae, 163
Hume, David, 149

Ignatius, 13, 14, 15, 18, 144
Incarnation, 2, 3, 4, 20, 23, 26, 64, 66, 67, 68, 78, 88, 91, 99, 100, 141
Index of Prohibited Books, 149
Indulgences, 65, 66, 117
Infallibility:
   Authority, 65, 97
   Biblical, 56, 97, 123, 124
   Conciliar, 107, 122
   Creedal, 122
   Dogmatic, 4n2, 5, 20, 52, 91, 92, 96, 97, 99, 100, 107, 123, 173, 176
   Ecclesial, 56, 73, 106, 139
   Nature of: 57
   Papal: 1, 4, 5, 7, 28n20, 38, 50, 51, 52, 53, 91, 95, 96, 99, 123, 155, 173
   Roman & Magisterial: 95, 96, 97, 99, 107, 122, 123, 124, 139, 140, 144, 145
Innocent III, 36
Innocent IV, 36
Innocent VIII, 31, 38
Invincible Ignorance, 103, 104
Invisible Church, 126, 127
Irenaeus, 12, 13
Isaiah, Book of
   Isaiah 6:1–7, 72
   Isaiah 22, 181, 182, 184, 185n7
   Isaiah 22:19–22, 183
   Isaiah 22:22, 183
   Isaiah 22:23–25, 183

James, 21
Jensen, Robert, xiii
Joan of Arc, 115, 132
John VIII, 34
John X, 34
John XI, 35
John XII, 35, 53
John XIX, 35

John XXIII, 163
John, Apostle, 21, 184
John, Epistles of, 89n5
John, Gospel of
   John 1:18, 126
   John 8:46, 126
   John 10:27, 74
   John 14:16, 25, 144
   John 14:26, 70
   John 15:26, 70
   John 15:26–27, 132
   John 16:12–14, 70
   John 16:12–15, 131–32
   John 16:13, 79, 144
   John 19:25, 89
   John 21 22n9, 181, 182
   John 21:15–17, 20
John Paul II, 32, 166
Jones, David Albert, 13n25, 16n34, 19
Justification, 65, 88, 103, 123, 151, 158, 173

Kempis, Thomas a, 152
Kenny, Anthony, 149
Keys of the Kingdom, 6, 8, 9, 20, 183, 185n7
Kreeft, Peter, 56, 73, 87, 88, 90
Kruger, Michael J., 71–76, 137, 138n6, 140
Küng, Hans, 156

Lampe, Peter, 11, 12, 17
Latourette, Kenneth Scott, 143
Leibniz, 136
Leithart, Peter, xviin9, 177, 178
Leo V, 34
Leo VI, 34
Leo X, 38
Levering, Matthew, 80, 81 83
Lewis, C.S., xv, 100, 131, 136, 152, 177
Libertarian Freedom, 52, 53, 122
Licona, Michael, 11, 89n4
Lightfoot, J.B., 143, 144n23
Lindbeck, George, xiii
Linus, 12, 16, 142
Long, Steve, 150
Lord's Supper, xviii, 154
Lord's Table, xiv

Ludlow, Morwenna, 143
Luke, Gospel of, 87
   Luke 1:48, 89
   Luke 2:36, 89
   Luke 11:27–28, 90
   Luke 22:32, 50, 89
   Luke 23:37, 89
   Luke 24:25–49, 70
Lumen Gentium, 7, 49n40, 85n29, 162
Lutherans, xvii, 95n19, 151
Luther, Martin, 31, 42, 54, 90, 95n19, 141
Luz, Ulrich, 181, 183n5

Machiavelli, 38
Macy, Gary, 151
Magnificat, 89
Malloy, Edward, 167
Mark, Gospel of
   Mark 3:20–21, 89
   Mark 3:33–5, 89
   Mark 15:40–41, 47, 89n4
   Mark 16:1, 89n4
Marozia, 34, 35
Marsden, George, 143
Marshall, Bruce, xiii
Martin IV, 36
Martin, James, 45–46
Mary
   Bodily Assumption of Mary, 1, 5, 52, 92, 93, 95, 96, 97, 99, 100
   Immaculate Conception, 1, 5, 52, 91, 92, 93, 95n19, 101, 155
   Marian Dogmas, 1, 5, 84, 87, 91, 92, 93, 95, 98, 99, 100, 101, 123, 155, 176
   Marian Piety, 87, 88, 90, 91, 92, 100
   Marian Maximalism, 91–2
   Redeemer, 87, 88, 89, 90
Marx, Cardinal Reinhard, 168
Mass, xiv, 43, 64, 66
Matthew, Gospel of
   Matthew 16, 22, 28, 181, 182, 183, 184, 185n7
   Matthew 16:15, 79
   Matthew 16:18–19, 144
   Matthew 16:18, 182, 184
   Matthew 16:19, 183

(Gospel of Matthew continued)
   Matthew 18:18, 144, 183
   Matthew 27:56, 61, 89
   Matthew 28:20, 144
   Matthew 28:21, 89
McBrien, Richard P., xviiin11, 165–66
McGrath, Alister, 143
McInerny, Ralph, 156, 157, 165

McNabb, Tyler, 41, 42
Meilaender, Gilbert, xiii
Metaxas, Eric, 31, 90
Methodist Church, xiii, xvin7, 67, 124, 157, 158, 159
Middle Knowledge, 50, 51, 52, 53
Mirus, Jeff, 46, 47, 167n27
Molina, Luis de, 50, 51, 122
Molinism, 50, 51, 52, 53, 122, 123
Monan, Donald, 167
Morris, Tom, xii
Murray, Gerald E., 46
Murray, John Courtney, 107, 108

National Council of Catholic Bishops Committee on Doctrine, 165–66
Neuhaus, Richard John, xii, xiii
Newman, John Henry, xv, 59–68, 77, 78, 80, 81, 82, 83, 84, 143, 147, 152, 156
Nicaea, 22, 80
Nicene
   Creed, 23, 57, 60, 66, 76, 77, 78, 79, 80, 85, 95, 96, 97, 123
   Christianity, 147
   Fathers, 78, 79, 80
Nichols, Aiden, 123, 124
Noll, Mark, 143
Novak, David, xiii
Novak, Michael, xiii, 156, 165
Nuechterlein, James, xiii

Oberman, Heiko, 143
O'Connor, Flannery, 152
Octavian, 35, 53
Oddie, William, 168
Oden, Tom, xiii, 143
O'Malley, John W., 16, 173n2
Order of Being, 2,3, 99n23

Order of Knowing, 2, 98, 99n23

Padre Pio, 149
Pannenberg, Wolfhart, 136
Pascal, 10, 17, 18
Pastor Aeternus, 16
Paul V, 122
Paul VI, 4n3, 7, 57n3, 94n18, 149, 162, 163, 164
Paul, the Apostle, 2, 3, 8, 13, 21, 22, 41, 57, 70, 73, 89n5, 116, 118, 119, 120, 131, 182, 184
Peckham, John, 141, 142n17
Pelikan, Jaroslav, 92, 93
Penance, 65, 117, 169,
Pentecostal, xvi, xvii, xviii, 67, 104, 129, 177, 178, 179
Perspicuity, 79, 82
Peter, the Apostle, 1, 4, 5, 6, 7, 8, 9 11, 12, 13, 16, 18, 19, 20, 21, 22, 23, 24, 25, 26, 28, 39, 41, 43, 49, 50, 55, 57, 58, 118, 120, 125, 142, 147, 174, 178, 181–84
Peter, Epistles of
   1 Peter, 90n5
   1 Peter 1:1, 21
   1 Peter 5:1, 21
   1 Peter 5:1–2, 182
   2 Peter, 90n5, 182
   2 Peter 1:1, 21
   2 Peter 3:16, 118
Philip of France, 36
Philippians, Epistle to
   Philippians 2:8, 88
Pink, Thomas, 105n8, 105n9, 105n10, 109
Pisa, Council, 37
Pius IX, 5, 93, 101, 102, 105, 154, 173
Pius XI, 163
Pius XII, 5, 93, 163
Plantinga, Alvin, xii, 27, 28, 29, 71, 72n7, 132, 136, 152
Pluralism, 154, 157, 158, 159, 165, 166, 167, 171
Predestination, 118, 122, 146, 151
Protestant's Dilemma, 134–35
Providence, 47–54, 73, 74, 78, 175
Psalms, Book of

GENERAL INDEX

Psalm 19:7–8, 72n5
Psalm 27:4, 72
Psalm 50:2, 72
Psalm 96:6, 72
Psalm 119:103, 72n5
Psalm 129, 72n5
Purgatory, xii, xiii, xiv, 65, 117

Rahner, Karl, 156
Ratzinger, 47, 48, 49, 53
Reconciliation, Sacrament of, 169
Reformation, xvii, xviii, 30, 54, 82, 91, 117, 123, 132, 141, 145, 151, 177, 182
Reformed Catholicity & Christianity, xi, xvii, xviii, 57, 77, 81, 82, 85, 95, 99, 111, 112, 143, 177, 178
Reformed Theology, xvii 137, 146, 158
Reformers, xvii, 77, 137, 141, 150, 177
Reforming Catholic Confession, xvii, xviii, 171
Reid, Thomas, 136, 152
Religious Freedom, 102, 105–6, 107, 108, 110n18
Remarriage, 45, 153, 161, 169, 170, 171
Reno, Rusty, xiii, xiv, 44, 45, 46
Resurrection, 2, 3, 4, 6, 8, 9, 10, 11, 17, 19, 25, 26, 30, 36, 65, 70, 89, 97, 98, 99, 100, 132, 140, 174
Revelation
   Revelation 1:12–17, 72
   Revelation 3:7, 183
   Revelation 4:3, 72
Robinson, Marilynne, 152
Romans
   Romans 1:4, 2
   Romans 10:9–10, 9
   Romans 11:13–14, 21
   Romans 15:15–16, 21
   Romans 16, 23n7
Rose, Devin, 16, 135, 136, 137, 138, 141, 142, 151, 152
Ryrie, Alex, 110n18, 143

Sacraments, xiv, xviii, 45, 64, 65, 105, 109, 118, 153, 161n18, 169, 171, 173, 174, 177

Salvation Outside the Church, 102–4
Same-Sex Relationships, 45, 46, 160, 161, 167, 170
Schaff, Philip, 143
Schillebeeckx, Edward, 25, 26, 30
Schism, 36–37, 93, 113, 125, 149, 168,
Schism of 1054, 123, 139
Separated Brethren, 4, 103–4, 110, 178
Sergius III, 34
Sexual Abuse, 44, 49, 126n23, 175
Sforza, Asconio, 31
Shatz, Klaus, 13
Silverius, 34
Sixtus IV, 38
Sola Scriptura, xvii, xviii, 77, 82, 84, 118, 140, 141, 142, 147
Stephen VI, 34
Stephen VII, 34
Stephen, Bishop, 22
Succession
   Apostolic, 111, 112, 114, 115, 116, 123, 124,125, 126, 128, 154, 178
   Petrine, 4, 6, 7, 8, 9n13, 12, 13, 18, 20, 21, 23, 24, 28, 39, 40, 41, 43, 49, 55, 57, 58, 174, 181, 183, 184
Sullivan, Andrew, 175
Sungenis, Bob, 139, 140
Surprised by Truth, 134
Swain, Scott R., xviin9, 77, 82, 143n17, 151n34
Swenson, Julie, 143
Swinburne, Richard, 11, 152
Syllabus of Errors, 102, 107, 108, 154

Theodicy, 48, 53, 54
Theodore of Mopsuestia, 182
Theophylacts, 34
Tilley, Terrence, 108
Timothy, Epistles to
   1 Timothy 3:1–7, 32
   1 Timothy 3:8–13, 39
Titus, Epistle to
   Titus 1:5–9, 32
Toledo, Francisco de, 105
Tolkien, J.R.R., 152
Transubstantiation, 99, 117, 123, 173,

Trinity, 2, 3, 4, 20, 23, 26, 79n23, 92, 99, 130, 140
Trueman, Carl, 149

Unam Sanctam, 36, 176, 177n4
Unitarianism, 67
Urban VI, 37

Vallier, Kevin, 106
Vanhoozer, Kevin, xvii, xviii
Vatican I, 4, 5, 6, 7, 8, 16, 21, 22, 24, 25, 38, 39, 54, 87, 173
Vatican II, xi, 7, 87, 102, 103, 107, 108, 117, 123, 124, 130, 154, 162, 163, 164, 171, 178
Vigano, 44, 49
Vigilius, 33, 34
Virgin Birth, 5, 155

Visible Church, 115, 125, 126, 127

Webb, Steve, xiii
Weigel, George, xiii
Wells, David, 87n1, 164
Wesleyan, xvii, 67, 129, 158,
Wesley, John, 67, 136, 152, 158
Westminster Confession, 118, 124, 129
Wilberforce, William, 152
Wilken, Robert, xiii, 26n15
Willard, Dallas, 152
Wood, Steve, 153, 154, 171
Wright, N.T., 136, 152

Xavier, Francis, 152

Young Earth Creationism, 16, 97

www.ingramcontent.com/pod-product-compliance
Lightning Source LLC
Chambersburg PA
CBHW031813220426
43662CB00007B/623